TRAEGER GRILL & SMOKER COOKBOOK

The Perfect Guide to Mastering the Wood Pellet Grill with 300 Tasty Recipes, Essential Techniques & Tips

Rachel Dash

© Copyright 2021 by - All rights reserved.

This document is geared towards providing exact and reliable information regarding the topic and issue covered. The publication is sold with the idea that the publisher is not required to render accounting, officially permitted, or otherwise qualified services. If advice is necessary, legal or professional, a practiced individual in the profession should be ordered.

From a Declaration of Principles which was accepted and approved equally by a Committee of the American Bar Association and a Committee of Publishers and Associations.

In no way is it legal to reproduce, duplicate, or transmit any part of this document in either electronic means or in printed format. Recording of this publication is strictly prohibited and any storage of this document is not allowed unless with written permission from the publisher. All rights reserved.

The information provided herein is stated to be truthful and consistent, in that any liability, in terms of inattention or otherwise, by any usage or abuse of any policies, processes, or Instructions contained within is the solitary and utter responsibility of the recipient reader. Under no circumstances will any legal responsibility or blame be held against the publisher for any reparation, damages, or monetary loss due to the information herein, either directly or indirectly.

Respective authors own all copyrights not held by the publisher.

The information herein is offered for informational purposes solely and is universal as so. The presentation of the information is without a contract or any type of guarantee assurance.

The trademarks that are used are without any consent, and the publication of the trademark is without permission or backing by the trademark owner. All trademarks and brands within this book are for clarifying purposes only and are the owned by the owners themselves s, not affiliated with this document.

TABLE OF CONTENTS

INTRODUCTION 1

CHAPTER 1: WHAT IS TRAEGER WOOD PELLET GRILL?..3
   1.1 COMPONENTS OF TRAEGER WOOD PELLET GRILL..4
   1.2 TRAEGER WOOD PELLET GRILL COMPARISON...5
   1.3 TRAEGER VS. OTHER WOOD PELLET GRILLS 6
   1.4 CLEANING THE TRAEGER GRILL 7

CHAPTER 2: GETTING STARTED WITH TRAGER WOOD PELLET GRILL 9
   2.1 STEP 1- UNBOXING AND ASSEMBLE 9
   2.2 STEP 2 – CALIBRATING AND SEASONING 10
   2.3 ESSENTIAL TIPS AND TRICKS 10
   2.4 TOP TIPS FOR SUCCESSFUL GRILLING 12
   2.5 SHOPPING GUIDE FOR TRAEGER WOOD PELLET GRILL 13

CHAPTER 3: MAINTENANCE AND FREQUENTLY ASKED QUESTIONS..............................15
   3.1 CREOSOTE AND GREASE FORMATION 15
   3.2 FLUE (SMOKE STACK) CLEANING 15
   3.3 GREASE CLEANING 15
   3.4 EXTERIOR SURFACE CLEANING 16
   3.5 KEEP THE GRILL SAFE OUTSIDE 16
   3.6 PORCELAIN GRILL CLEANING..16
   3.7 FAQS (FREQUENTLY ASKED QUESTIONS) 16

CHAPTER 4: TRAEGER GRILL APPETIZERS, SIDES AND SNACKS 19
   4.1 TRAEGER GRILLED BRUSSELS SPROUTS..19
   4.2 TRAEGER GRILLED CARROTS 19
   4.3 TRAEGER FUNERAL POTATOES 19
   4.4 CHEESY TRAEGER BROCCOLI AU GRATIN 19
   4.5 GRILLED DINNER ROLLS 19
   4.6 GRILLED ONIONS..19
   4.7 TRAEGER GRILLED SPINACH 20
   4.8 TRAEGER GRILLED HOMEMADE CROUTONS 20
   4.9 TRAEGER SMOKED MAC AND CHEESE 20
   4.10 BAKED POTATO SKINS WITH PULLED PORK 20
   4.11 TRAEGER SMOKED SMASHED POTATOES 20
   4.12 SMOKED GARLIC BUTTER 20
   4.13 TRAEGER GRILLED CHEDDAR BAY BISCUITS 21
   4.14 TRAEGER CORN ON THE COB 21
   4.15 TRAEGER GRILLED PROSCIUTTO ASPARAGUS 21
   4.16 TRAEGER GRILLED SPAGHETTI SQUASHE 21
   4.17 TRAEGER GRILLED BUTTERNUT SQUASH 21
   4.18 LOADED SMOKED MASHED POTATOES 22
   4.19 SMOKED BACON RANCH ROTINI AND CHEESE 22
   4.20 GRILLED CAESAR PASTA SALAD 22
   4.21 TRAEGER GRILLED ZUCCHINI AND YELLOW SQUASH 22

4.22 Grilled Mexican Street Corn 22
4.23 Traeger Smoked Baked Potato 22
4.24 Grilled Garlic Rosemary Smashed Potatoes 23
4.25 Traeger Bacon-Wrapped Scallops 23
4.26 Roasted Elk Jalapeno Poppers 23
4.27 Smoked Salmon Dip 23
4.28 Lemon Garlic Grilled Asparagus in Foil 23
4.29 Grilled Sweet Potatoes 23
4.30 Smoked Eggs 24
4.31 Hot & Seasoned Grilled Corn 24
4.32 Cheese Trinity with Grilled Potatoes and Chives 24

CHAPTER 5: TRAEGER GRILL PORK RECIPES 26

5.1 Pulled Pork Enchiladas with Smoke-Roasted Red Sauce 26
5.2 Exquisite Ribs 26
5.3 Pork Tenderloin Wrapped in Fresh Rosemary 26
5.4 Slow Smoked Pulled Pork 26
5.5 Citrus Brined Pork Roast with Fig Mustard 27
5.6 Crispy Pork Belly 27
5.7 BBQ Pulled Pork with Paleo Vinegar Sauce 27
5.8 Smoked Pork Loin Tacos 27
5.9 Cuban Pork Sandwich 27
5.10 Cider Brined Pork Chops with Apple-Pear Compote 28
5.11 Smoked Ribs 28
5.12 Pork Butt Burnt Ends 28
5.13 Smoked Spiral Ham with Honey Glaze 28
5.14 Easy Smoked Pork Butt 28
5.15 Cider Brined Pulled Pork 29
5.16 Easy Smoked Pork Loin 29
5.17 Smoked Pork Chops with Ale-Balsamic Glaze 29
55.18 Grilled Pork Chops with Pineapple-Mango Salsa 29
5.19 BBQ Pulled Pork Cubano Sandwich 29
5.20 Smoked Pulled Pork Enchiladas 29
5.21 Pineapple-Glazed Smoked Ham 30
5.22 Pork Shoulder 30
5.23 Sausage Stuffed Mushrooms 30
5.24 Cherry Coke Ribs 30
5.25 Smoked Pork Tenderloin 30
5.26 Sticky Teriyaki BBQ Pork and Pineapple Skewers 30
5.27 Smoked Moink Burger 30
5.28 Braised Pork Chile Verde 31
5.29 BBQ Spare Ribs with Spicy Mandarin Glaze 31
5.30 Smoked Bacon Wrapped Meatballs 31
5.31 Smoked Spicy Asian Pork Ribs 31
5.32 Grilled Bacon-Wrapped Pork Chops with Rosemary 31
5.33 Traeger Pork Tenderloin with Mustard Sauce 31
5.34 Garlic Herb Grilled Pork Chops 32
5.35 Pigs in Blanket 32
5.36 Traeger Smoked Stuffed Pork Tenderloin 32
5.37 Traeger Blackened Pork Chops 32
5.38 Shake and Bake Pork Chops 32

CHAPTER 6: TRAEGER GRILL BEEF RECIPES...34

6.1 SMOKED TRI-TIP 34
6.2 T-BONE GRILLED STEAK..34
6.3 SMOKED TERIYAKI BEEF JERKY 34
6.4 MEATBALL STUFFED SHELLS 34
6.5 REVERSE-SEARED FLAT IRON STEAK 34
6.6 TEQUILA LIME BEEF TACOS 35
6.7 SMOKED AND SEARED STRIP STEAK...35
6.8 SLOW SMOKED BEEF BRISKET 35
6.9 CHIPOTLE RUBBED TRI-TIP 35
6.10 THE PERFECT CHEESEBURGER..35
6.11 PELLET GRILL PICANHA 35
6.12 BEEF BIRRIA TACOS 36
6.13 SMOKED PRIME RIB 36
6.14 PHILLY CHEESE STEAK SANDWICH 36
6.15 MINI SMOKED MEATLOAF 36
6.16 TRAEGER POT ROAST 36
6.17 MARINATED SMOKED FLANK STEAK 36
6.18 MEXICAN CARNE ASADA 37
6.19 BAKED CORNED BEEF AU GRATIN 37
6.20 TRAEGER SMOKED MEATLOAF 37
6.21 GRILLED STEAK FAJITAS 37
6.22 GRILLED MEXICAN STYLE SURF AND TURF 37
6.23 TRAEGER GRILLED TOMAHAWK 37
6.24 PRIME RIB SANDWICH PINWHEEL 37
6.25 GRILLED BEEF BULGOGI 38
6.26 CARNE ASADA..38
6.27 GRILLED NEW YORK STRIP 38
6.28 SMOKED BEEF RIBS 38
6.29 GRILLED BEEF SHORT RIB LOLLIPOP 38
6.30 BRISKET CHILI 38
6.31 SMOKED BRISKET 38
6.32 GRILLED FILET MIGNON 38
6.33 TRAEGER SMOKED MISSISSIPPI POT ROAST 39
6.34 GRILLED CURRIED FLANK STEAK 39
6.35 BEEF SIRLOIN AND TOMATO VINAIGRETTE 39
6.36 SPICY TENDERLOIN STEAKS 39

CHAPTER 7: TRAEGER GRILL POULTRY RECIPES...41

7.1 TRAEGER SMOKED TURKEY...41
7.2 BRINED SMOKED TURKEY..41
7.3 SMOKED CHICKEN BREASTS 41
7.4 SMOKED WHOLE CHICKEN 41
7.5 ALABAMA CHICKEN LEG QUARTERS 41
7.6 CHICKEN LOLLIPOPS 42
7.7 SMOKED CHICKEN THIGHS 42
7.8 TRAEGER CHICKEN TERIYAKI 42
7.9 SMOKEY WINGS 42
7.10 CHICKEN SAUSAGE ROLLS 42
7.11 TRAEGER GRILLED CHICKEN BREAST 42
7.12 GRILLED BBQ ORANGE CHICKEN 42

7.13 Chicken Wings 43
7.14 Whole BBQ Chicken 43
7.15 Citrus Turkey 43
7.16 Herb Buttered Chicken 43
7.17 Smoked Hassel Back Pesto Chicken 43
7.18 Smoked Herb Butter Turkey 43
7.19 Grilled Chicken Salad 44
7.20 Honey Balsamic Chicken Legs 44
7.21 Mayo & Herb Roasted Turkey 44
7.22 Honey Lime Chicken Adobo Skewers 44
7.23 Baked Chicken Pot Pie 44
7.24 Braised Brunswick Stew 44
7.25 Skillet-Roasted Bird 45
7.26 Pretzel Mustard Chicken 45
7.27 Grilled Sweet Cajun Wings 45
7.28 Smoked and Braised Duck Legs 45
7.29 Roast Chicken and Pimento Potatoes 45
7.30 Grilled Nashville Hot Chicken Mac & Cheese 45
7.31 Traeger Grilled Nashville Hot Chicken 45
7.32 Sweet Chili Chicken Leg Quarters 46
7.33 Traeger Smoked Turkey Legs 46
7.34 Traeger Smoked Cornish Hens 46
7.35 Sweet Tea BBQ Chicken Thighs 46
7.36 Savory Grilled Chicken 46
7.37 Greek Chicken Marinade 46
7.38 Easy Grilled Curry Chicken 46
7.39 Gold BBQ Grilled Chicken 46
7.40 Smoked Buttermilk Fried Chicken 47
7.41 Pellet Grill Jerk Chicken Thighs 47
7.42 Beer Can Chicken 47
7.43 Traeger Chicken Wings with Spicy Miso 47
7.44 Traeger Turkey Breast 47
7.45 Grilled Marinated Chicken 47

CHAPTER 8: TRAEGER GRILL SEAFOOD RECIPES 49

8.1 Traeger Halibut with Parmesan 49
8.2 Traeger Cioppino 49
8.3 Blackened Catfish Tacos 49
8.4 Traeger Honey Garlic Salmon 49
8.5 Traeger Lobster Rolls 49
8.6 Traeger Tuna Melt Flatbread 50
8.7 Traeger Chimichurri Shrimp 50
8.8 Traeger Spicy Fried Shrimp 50
8.9 Smoked Lobster Tails 50
8.10 Traeger Grilled Crab Legs 50
8.11 Foil Packet Salmon 50
8.12 Easy Shrimp Diablo 50
8.13 Salmon Miso Poke Bowl 51
8.14 Salmon Orzo Pasta Salad 51
8.15 Grilled Salmon Sandwich 51
8.16 Traeger Grilled Shrimp Scampi 51
8.17 Red Snapper Recipe 51

8.18 BBQ Salmon with Bourbon Glaze 51
8.19 Smoked Trout 51
8.20 Lemon Ginger Grilled Shrimp 52
8.21 Sesame Crusted Halibut with Tahini Mayonnaise 52
8.22 Grilled Teriyaki Salmon 52
8.23 Lemon Pepper Traeger Grilled Salmon 52
8.24 Traeger Grilled Lemon Dill Salmon 52
8.25 Traeger Grilled Salmon with Togarashi 52
8.26 Traeger Smoked Salmon 52
8.27 Sriracha Salmon Stuffed Mushrooms 53
8.28 Smoked Salmon Dip 53
8.29 Traeger Grilled Rockfish 53
8.30 Grilled Lingcod 53
8.31 Pan Seared Lingcod 53
8.32 Molasses Glazed Salmon 53
8.33 Traeger Teriyaki Smoked Shrimp 53
8.34 Grilled Crab Cakes 53
8.35 Crab-Stuffed Lingcod 54
8.36 Smoked Scalloped Potatoes 54
8.37 Shrimp Ceviche 54
8.38 Smoked Salmon Eggs Benedict 54
8.39 Garlic Dill Smoked Salmon 54
8.40 Smoked Salmon Chowder 55
8.41 Grilled Salmon in Onion Sauce 55
8.42 Grilled Shrimp in Chives 55
8.43 Grilled Curried Sardines 55

CHAPTER 9: TRAEGER GRILL LAMB RECIPES 57

9.1 Ground Meat Kebabs 57
9.2 Braised Lamb Shank 57
9.3 Lamb Wraps BBQ Style 57
9.4 Leg of Lamb Gyros 57
9.5 Grilled Lamb Burger 58
9.6 Grilled Lamb Lollipops with Mango Chutney 58
9.7 Lamb Burgers with Pickled Onions 58
9.8 Slow Roasted BBQ Lamb Shoulder 58
9.9 Braised Irish Lamb Stew 59
9.10 Grilled Butterflied Leg of Lamb 59
9.11 Roasted Rack of Lamb 59
9.12 Lamb Stew 59
9.13 Grilled Lamb Chops with Rosemary Sauce 59
9.14 Greek Style Roast Leg of Lamb 59
9.15 Lamb Sausage Smoked 60
9.16 Pistachio Crusted Roasted Lamb 60
9.17 Rosemary Lamb 60
9.18 Chipotle Lamb 60
9.19 Rosemary Citrus Grilled Lamb Chops 60
9.20 Grilled Rack of Lamb 60
9.21 Easy Lamb Chops 60

CHAPTER 10: TRAEGER GRILL VEGETABLES RECIPES 62

10.1 Roasted Broccoli Cheese Soup 62
10.2 Traeger Grilled Vegetables 62
10.3 Roasted Carrots with Pistachio and Pomegranate Relish 62
10.4 Smoked Pumpkin Soup 62
10.5 Mashed Red Potatoes 62
10.6 Baked Breakfast Mini Quiches 62
10.7 Roasted Butternut Squash Soup 63
10.8 Grilled Veggie Burgers with Lentils and Walnuts 63
10.9 Smoked Hummus with Roasted Vegetables 63
10.10 Baked Creamed Spinach 63
10.11 Butter Braised Green Beans 63
10.12 Traeger Stuffed Peppers 63
10.13 Traeger Lasagna 63
10.14 Twice Baked Potatoes 64
10.15 Smoked Bean Salad 64
10.16 Pasta Salad 64
10.17 Green Bean Casserole with Shallots 64
10.18 Herbs Infused Creamy Mashed Potatoes 64
10.19 Squash Au Gratin 64
10.20 Baked Sweet Potato Hash 65
10.21 Roasted Onion Bacon Salad 65
10.22 Veggie Sandwich 65
10.23 Baked Corn Pudding 65
10.24 Peach Salsa 65

CHAPTER 11: TRAEGER GRILL BONUS RECIPE 67

11.1 Traeger Banana Bread 67
11.2 Smoked Baked Potato Soup 67
11.3 Traeger Eggnog Cheesecake 67
11.4 Smoked Crumb Apple Pie 67
11.5 Smoked Strawberry Crisp 67
11.6 Smoke S'mores Nachos 68
11.7 Hot Dog Burnt Ends 68
11.8 Baked Blueberry Brioche French Toast 68
11.9 Apple Cake 68
11.10 Bacon Cinnamon Rolls 68
11.11 Baked Deep Dish Supreme Pizza 68
11.12 Smoked Apple Pie 69
11.13 Cast Iron Pizza Lasagna 69
11.14 Traeger Grilled French Toast 69
11.15 Greek Chicken Pizza 69
11.16 Grilled Sweet Potatoes 69
11.17 Grilled King Crab Legs 69
11.18 Smoked Salmon Scrambled Eggs 70
11.19 Grilled Peaches with Yogurt and Granola 70
11.20 Smoked Buffalo Shrimp 70
11.21 Traeger Mini Meatloaf Burgers 70
11.22 The Best Grilled Pizza 70
11.23 BBQ Smoked Sausage Bites 70
11.24 Spinach Dip Rollups 70

11.25 Pellet Grill Pasties 70
11.26 Broccoli Chicken Divan 71
11.27 Grill Carnitas 71
11.28 Traeger Bean Tostadas 71
11.29 Spot Prawn Skewers 71
11.30 Bacon Sweet Potato Pie 71
11.31 Grilled Apple Crisp 71
11.32 Smoked Maple Cupcakes 71
11.33 Chocolate Pecan Bacon Pie 72
11.34 Pear Cobbler 72
11.35 Baked Deep Dish Apple Pie 72
11.36 Maple Bacon Pull-Apart 72
11.37 Cast Iron Berry Cobbler 72
11.38 Smoked Cocktail 73
11.40 Garden Gimlet Cocktail 73
11.41 Gin & Tonic 73

CHAPTER 12: DRESSINGS AND SAUCES 75

12.1 Traeger Smoked Salsa Verde 75
12.2 Traeger Thanksgiving Dressing 75
12.3 Smoked Caramelized Onion Dip 75
12.4 Sherri Mushroom Sauce 75
12.5 Savory Vegetable Dip 75
12.6 Hot Pepper Sauce 75
12.7 Nut Butter Hummus 75
12.8 Honey Peachy Spread 76
12.9 Orange Basil Vinaigrette 76
12.10 Citrus Vinaigrette 76
12.11 Cilantro Lime Dressing 76
12.12 Italian Salad Dressing 76
12.13 Special Vinaigrette 76
12.14 Grilled Mango Chutney 76
12.15 Lemon-Garlic Dressing 76
12.16 Sweet Potato Caramel 76
12.17 Creamy Avocado Lime Dressing 77
12.18 Ranch Coconut Milk Dressing 77
12.19 Shallot Lemon Dressing 77
12.20 Mango Guacamole 77
12.21 Blueberry Salsa 77
12.22 Texas Barbeque Rub 77
12.23 Varied Grilled Vegetables 77

CONCLUSION 78

RECIPE INDEX 79

INDEX BY INGREDIENTS 87

Introduction

For as long as we can recall, grilling is something we've grown up seeing others do. As children, watching those big hot dogs plump up and break open, got everyone mesmerized. Think of the scent of meat from those thick fatty burgers, all the fat dripping on coal with a hiss, a burst of fire and smoke twirling along the sizzling sides into the glistening red coals.

Grilling is quick cooking over high heat, whereas barbecue is slow cooking with indirect, low heat over several hours. With each cooking process, one will usually need separate equipment (although confusingly, you can smoke on grills and grill on certain smokers). However, Traeger has made it simpler with its various settings and smoke fire grill that tastes exquisitely different from charcoal.

Fire introduces the food's real taste to the forefront. Cooking with 100% organic hardwood pellets helps the flavor to be much stronger with your favorite recipes. Like a real outdoor boss, one can BBQ, grill, braise, smoke, roast, and bake with Trager's 6-in-1 functionality. Each function always produces effective flavors with assorted firewood pellets, and smoke yields consistent results every time you cook. Cook it all with simplicity, ease, from low and slow to high and fast. Setting up the grill is as simple as setting up the Traeger oven.

The automated controls ensure that the cook maintains stable temperatures. It comes fitted with WiFIRE® powered controls in the latest Pro, Timberland, and Ironwood range-allowing the user the ability to change temperatures for purely precision cooking in five-degree increments. Fruit flavored organic wood pellets, such as apple and cherry, offer a sweeter taste and best suit for cooking meat, baked goods, and pork. For savory pork, beef, and vegetables, bolder staples like mesquite, oak, and hickory are custom-fit. Any time you press ignite, a Traeger wood pellet grill offers superior flavor, ease of use, repeatable, reliable performance.

Nothing corresponds to the taste of pure hardwood. Thanks to their precise temperature management, the advanced controls can help carry the culinary skills to the next stage. A quick start-up would allow one to grill faster, while the method of convection heating excludes the need to watch the grill at all times. Now you don't have to go out for a flavored smoky barbecue dinner; you have to go with your friends and family to the backyard as Traeger believes in bringing people together.

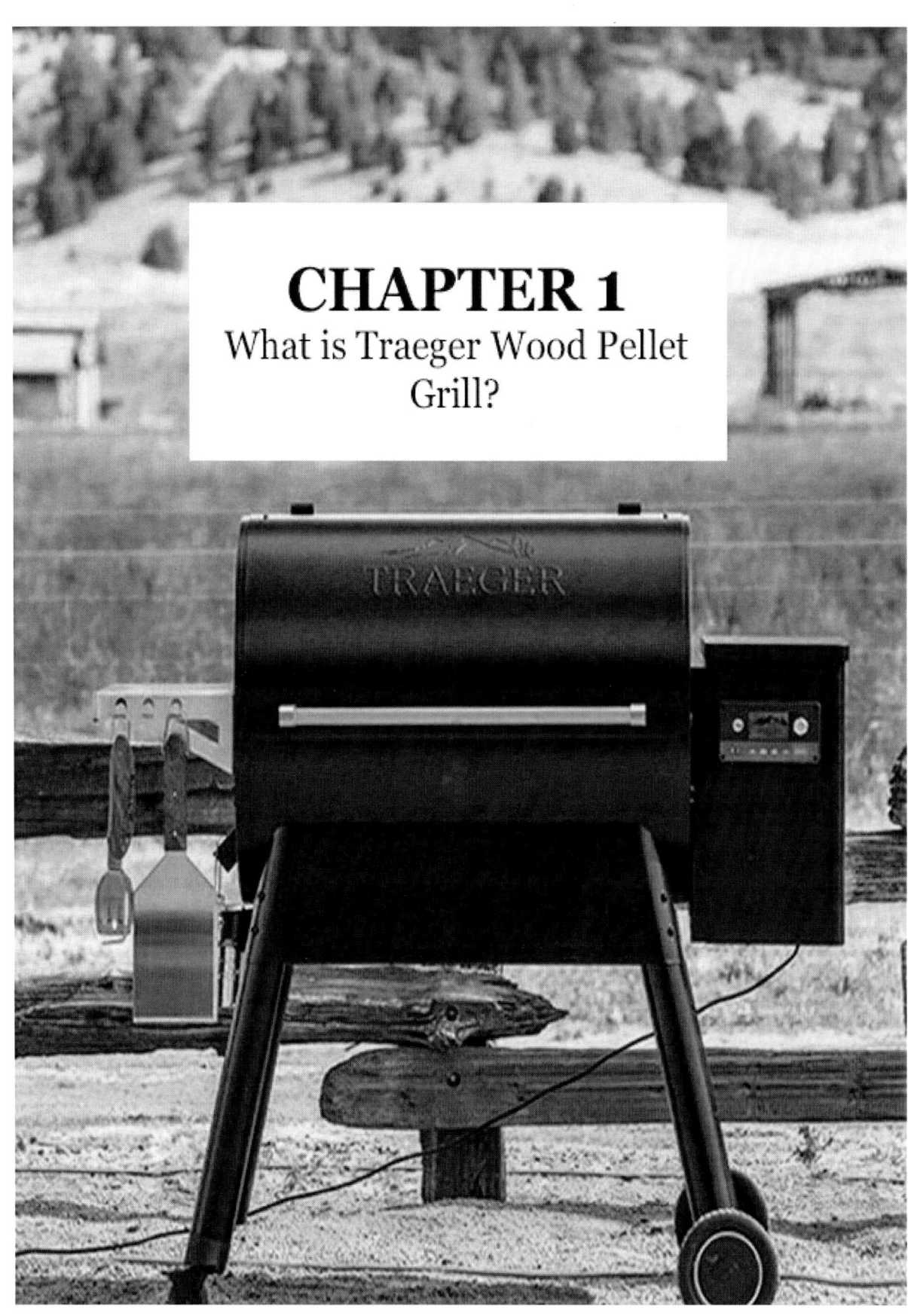

CHAPTER 1
What is Traeger Wood Pellet Grill?

Chapter 1: What is Traeger Wood Pellet Grill?

Grilling is simple, but there's still a need for perfection, as it's made better with a wood pellet Traeger grill. You need three items if you're going to have a barbecue: meat, smoke, and grill. Nothing brings more taste than wood fire and smoke to meat. It is as easy as that. These factors will blend to cook up food that is ridiculously tasty and irresistible. It needs a lot of experience and practice to do so regularly. That said, one device that makes the process even smoother is known to us, and that's an outdoor grill called the Traeger wood pellet grill.

The Traeger, an electronic grill that burns wood pellets for fuel, brings phenomenal flavor to all it cooks, let it be it poultry, burgers, seafood, ribs, or immense beef and pork slabs. On this grill, one can prepare anything from savory to smoky dessert in only a matter of time, and every recipe is taken to new levels. Specifically, when it comes to the outcome, words can't give this grill justice. Usually, pellet grills cost more than gas grills, but flavors are brought to another degree by Traeger. Yeah, it is almost comically pricey. Similar wood pellet smokers may be purchased for a fraction of the amount. Alternatives are available, but they do not produce the same results when it comes to flavor.

In addition to that, most wood-fired grills, Traeger grills, are built to burn exclusive wood pellets, so one needs to consider you will have to buy them exclusively. At huge stores such as Home Depot, one can get 20-pound bags for around $19. Cooking with pellets is a common option on many grills. For a modest amount, they deliver 40-pound bags of their right combination wood pellet blend. No matter the grilling or barbecue, Traeger cooks them to perfection. Meats that are fatty and tough need a slow cooking, lengthy phase to cook the collagen and other tissues to render the meat tender and juicy. That's why Traeger is the ultimate choice. On the other side, tender or lean meat, seafood, and chicken need to be rapidly cooked over high heat to get the inner temperature to a comfortable level without letting them dry. Its integrated controls are one explanation for the high price of the Traeger. The grill will connect to the Wi-Fi network at your house. It also provides a temperature probe that helps one monitor food during a cookout, paired with the Traeger app. There is a vast library of recipes on the app. These recipes will serve as cooking systems that the grill can automatically operate, rather than simple reference content. The pellet wood grill cooks everything to perfection.

The highlighted points of the Traeger grill are:

- Versatility: You activate the ability to barbecue, smoke, bake, braise, and roast; as one fires up Traeger, you become master of all trades.
- Convenience: The ease of use and easy controls of Traeger enables one to concentrate on what Consistency: Constant temperature gets you consistent outcomes, ensuring that instead of tending to the fire, you can focus on food as well as other things around you.
- Community: Every day is a new day with new recipes. Traeger provides VIP client support to help give ideas, tricks, and tools. Traeger is a network of sharing and motivation in the wood-fired movement.
- Makes a difference: the food, your friends, and your family.

1.1 Components of Traeger Wood Pellet Grill

Traeger is the number one selling wood pellet grill, mastered by decades of learning the wood-fired cooking art. Traeger grill delivers reliable performance, any single time. With Traeger, feed your appetite for wood-fired taste.

The Wood Pellet Traeger Grill has three major components:
- Ignite the fire
- Set it and forget it
- Enjoy food together

An auger carries organic hardwood pellets from the hopper to the fire pot, where the Hot Rod ignites them to fuel the fires and give a tasty wood-fired taste to the meal. For even continuous cooking, a fan disperses heat and smoke. A drip tray holds fire off the food and avoids flare-ups. It's all controlled by a system that retains the exact temperature so that one can spend more time enjoying the grill with family and friends that matter more than babysitting the grill.

It's as simple to set the temperature on the Traeger grill as to turn the oven on. The automated controls ensure that the food receives accurate, stable heat throughout the process. And if that is not enough, all the Pro, Timberland, and Ironwood series come fitted with WiFIRE® powered controls, allowing you the option to use the App of Traeger or the smart home computer to monitor grill from everywhere. Wood pellets take the food's real taste to the surface. Cooking with organic and specifically made hardwood pellets helps the flavor much more with your favorite recipes. With Trager's six-in-one flexibility, you can grill, braise, smoke, broil, and bake, as mentioned above. Consistently reliable smoke and fire, every time, deliver accurate results and properly cooked food. Cook anything you want, from tough meats to sweetened baked goods.

The number one wood-fired grill needs the market's best pellets. It's produced from all-natural organic hardwood, creating great smoke; true flavor doesn't just appear. It begins with pellets of hardwood developed in an American mill. The pellets are optimized for optimum quality and are specially built to fit with Traeger grills, so you get flavorful results each time. The pellets are also available in several varieties to accommodate any food style. Fruit pellets such as apple and cherry share a sweeter, subtler taste that better suits beef, pork, baked goods, and seafood. For savory meat, vegetables, and wild game, wood pellets like mesquite, oak, and hickory are tailor-made.

Various flavorings are available with the Trager wood pellet grill since they were specially designed for the grill to make the culinary experience more unique and enjoyable. Do not make the error of sticking regular wood pellets in the Trager pellet grill manufactured to operate with different wood.

1.2 Traeger Wood Pellet Grill Comparison

Traeger and any other wood pellet grill are a good place to begin if you're searching for the deep, smoky taste that pellet grills will add to the outdoor cooking adventure; we should include the other pellet grill. We can match some of the companies' best-selling items to see which a perfect fit is for you. Wood-pellet grills offer the food a special taste that one doesn't get from conventional gas or charcoal grills. Pellet grills allow a low-temp and slow cooking an easy task.

If you want to change the backyard barbecue with a modern grilling system, Traeger, and any other grill that uses wood pellets, are two of the main grills for wood-pellet smokers to think. We brought together a reference to compare the similarities between Traeger and other pellet grills after reviewing features and reading user feedback. For consideration, we have listed some of the top-selling items from the labels.

1.3 Traeger vs. Other Wood Pellet Grills

The taste of food grilled over hardwood pellets allows effective temperature regulation. Pellet grills are highly flexible; most Traeger grills provide many functions in one place, as compared to any other pellet grill providing 500 °F and a "low-and-slow" mode. For a specific temperature setting, these grills come fitted with digital controls.

With numerous varieties of wood pellets, pellet grills also help one to subtly flavor the meat. With their blend of wood types, both Traeger and another grill offer their line of pellets. Other grills have a stronger reputation for turning into unusable sawdust, which can be an issue for some. Still, some people don't have a problem with them because they are cheaper than Traeger pellets but slightly different.

The first thing to remember is to compare and contrast when determining which pellet grill to buy. Traeger and any other grills both sell in several sizes, but Traeger has a larger variety of cooking area available if you're searching for small or big grills.

You will surely acknowledge the grill's mobility. Do you want to pack it or carry it for fishing or a tailgating gathering? All manufacturers produce compact grills, but Trager's lineup offers smaller, compact, easier-to-move options than other grills. Traeger is the oldest pellet grill company, and the new technology appears to upgrade its grills. The pellet grills from Traeger are less costly and come with a five-year guarantee. Like every other smoker, though, one may enjoy some features more than others as part of grilling enjoyment.

Traeger developed the hardwood pellet grill barbecue more than 29 years ago. It is now one of the best-selling brands famous for pellet grills. This is so even though the patent expires and creativity in that field tends to be at the core of it. In 2017, Traeger launched one of its grills with a Wi-Fi remote, enabling consumers to monitor the temperature from a distance. This model is expanding, with 3 of its product lines fitted with WiFIRE technology by last year.

Where are Traeger model grills made? Initially, Traeger grills were produced in the USA, but the brand has shifted production to China.

The Traeger Pro 575 is made for anyone, whether you're searching for a backyard barbecue for a big family or a little group, it has a cooking area of 575 square-inches and carries 17.98 pounds of pellets in the hopper. You will cook sufficiently steaks or hamburgers using this grill to serve 8-12 people at once easily. In five-degree increments, one can adjust the temperature, exercising specific control with the cooking experience. You can change the temperature scale as large as 500 °F with the D2 Pro Drivetrain.

You can monitor the settings from a distance on the mobile with Trager's WiFIRE® Technology. This ensures one doesn't actively tend to the grill for all-day cooking like brisket, though it smokes steadily over many cooking hours.

If you choose to serve a crowd or smoke huge quantities of beef, the Timberline Traeger 1300 has a total cooking area of 1,300 square inches and contains 23.80 pounds of pellets in its hopper. For better insulation, it also has a complete double-wall, an interior of stainless steel, and the same Pro D2 Drivetrain, allowing for consistency in the grilling experience.

The Traeger Timberline Pellet Grill comes fitted with several other functions, such as the Traeger pellet tracker, which warns you when the pellets run low, and a magnetic cutting bamboo board, WiFIRE® technology, which allows you to monitor the grill from your smartphone's settings. Traeger says this ensures that a 20-pound bag offers (at low or high heat) from 6-20 hours of cooking time.

1.4 Cleaning the Traeger Grill

With other grills, there's no distinction between ashes or looking after the coals. It is not something we can term enjoyable to clean a gasoline grill, but it is far simpler to clean a wood pellet grill, specifically Traeger wood pellet, than the Timberline wood smoker. Having to deal with food grease is only the beginning with pellet grills. All the burning wood smoke circulating inside its central cavity contains a sticky creosote residue, a mixture of other organic compounds, and wood tars that give its distinctive smoking taste to food. Cleaning creosote becomes a messy task. As the Trager model focuses on cleaning differently, you need to scrub with soft bristle brushes to clean the grill for proper ventilation so that the grill and people around it will not be placed at risk.

Put a wide enough container below the hopper cleanout situated on the hopper's back to accommodate the discharged pellets. Disassemble the fastener mounted on the hopper's cleaning door and raise the door to open so that the pellets drop into the bucket below. To force out the last few pellets through the handle, you may need to use a spoon or a spatula. Then shut the door, put back the fastener into the hopper, and reload the Traeger Wood Pellets with another flavor. Connect the grill back in and follow the initialization guidelines for a smoky round of cooking.

CHAPTER 2
Getting Started with Traeger Wood Pellet Grill

Chapter 2: Getting Started with Trager Wood Pellet Grill

You have to start here before enjoying some of the recipes with family and friends.

Get yourself a drink and a friend because, with frosty ones and buddies, Traegering is even more pleasant. It is also because two persons are required to assemble the Traeger. You can learn how to set up, season the grill, and make the most of the grill here.

2.1 Step 1- Unboxing and Assemble

First thing, let's bring this Traeger grill together. Ask for assistance from a buddy, and get started. You can watch videos on how the grill should be installed, download the Traeger app, and link to WiFire, since this grill is clever. Last but not least, one should learn to mount the pellet sensor and calibrate it to know when and how to empty the hopper. Failure to ensure the required clearances (air regions) for combustible materials is a significant cause of fires. It is of great importance that the grill assembly should be according to the guideline. You must check with full directions from the owner's guide.

These are general assembly rules; full directions can vary as they come uniquely to the grill you are using:

- Mount the legs
- Attach the handle of the chrome door
- Attach the chimney cap and flue pipe assembly
- Position the heat baffle
- Position the grease drain pan
- Position the porcelain grill
- Hang the dripping bucket

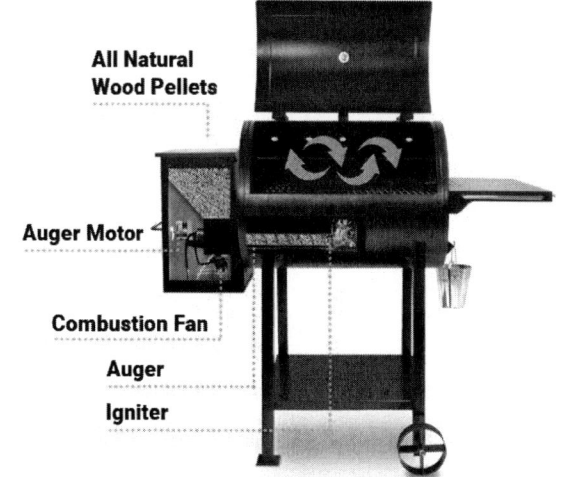

2.2 Step 2 – Calibrating and Seasoning

Without preparing seasoning first, you wouldn't roast a delicious cut of beef or cook any fresh vegetables, and the Trager's grill is the same. To launch down the road to wood-fired taste, you should learn how to do the initial burn. This one-time cooking period guarantees maximal taste and calibrates the optimal efficiency of the Traeger.

- Prime the auger tube with pellets.
- Plug in the grill to an electrical outlet and press Turn On.
- Add flavored hardwood pellets to the hopper.
- Turn the main power switch On.
- Switch the dial to "Select Auger" and then select "Prime Auger."
- As pellets begin to drop into the firepot, select "Done" to turn off the Auger.
- Turn clockwise the selection dial to 350 °F or 177 °C and press the dial.
- Select "Ignite," then close the lid; when the temperature reaches 350 °F, let it run for 20 minutes.
- Switch temperature to 450 °F or 232 °C.
- When the temperature has reached 450 °F, let it run for 1/2 an hour.
- Shut down the grill by pressing on the Selection dial for more than three seconds on a Grill of Pro Series. For a Timberline or Ironwood, press the Standby button for more than three seconds to start the shutdown cycle.
- As the shutdown cycle complete, seasoning of the grill is also complete.

Get ready to make delicious brisket, fall of the bone, tender ribs, and flavorful pulled pork now that you've done seasoning the grill.

2.3 Essential Tips and Tricks

When working on the grill in chilly weather, enclose the lid to keep the food hot: for children and adults, the Traeger fire pit is a pleasant warming station to gather around and chat while the wood pellet Traeger does all the hard work. Everybody is glad to get an appetizer as a tasty treat.

To maintain the grill temperature high, keep the cover closed: you can use a pre-heated cast-iron skillet from the kitchen after the steaks have been grilled to a medium to medium-rare to transport the beef from the Traeger grill to the kitchen table.

Make sure it is well illuminated in the grilling area: you can set the Traeger grill to smoke mode to warm up the grill to add more heat and then load it with marinated thick steaks. Put a few sticks around the Traeger fire pit, lighting it up, and let the little one's grill marshmallows as the meat cooks and the smoke wafts through the back yard.

Always wrap the grill with cover when not using, it would keep the sun damage away and the paint protected: at temperatures below 35 °F, solid wood pellet burns faster. A blanket that provides insulation prevents the heat and keeps the metal hot, not letting the hardwood heat escaping.

To help save fuel, keep the grill closed as much as possible: keeping the grill closed will make it simple to cook meat, particularly in winter weather.

To keep it cozy, never place the smoker's barbecue in an enclosed patio or garage: scarcely open the grill and move the meat to the hot spot on the grill. Before shutting the barbecue, rapidly place a remote probe thermometer. The grill can take time to heat up in the cold weather, and never put the grill in the garage or closed space.

Removable drip bucket liners: tired of getting the gooey mess clean up? Or Bump the bucket off unintentionally as you bring the cover on or take it off and become a messy spill? Get the disposable bucket liners, and make it easier for yourself to clean up.

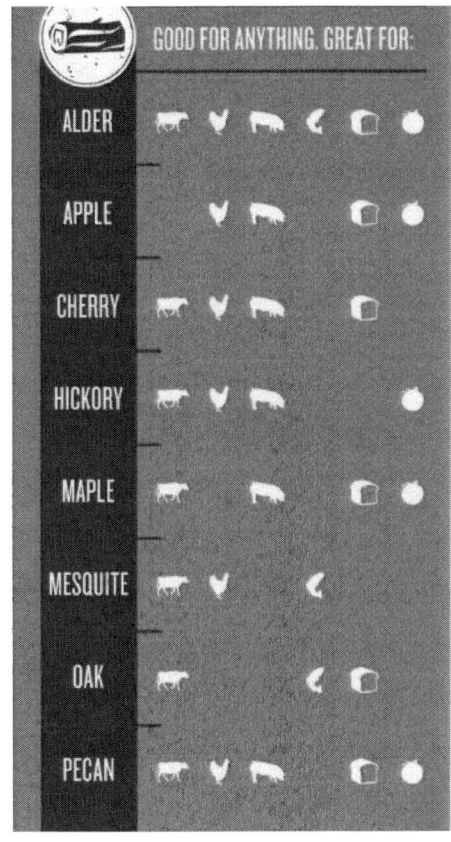

Drip tray liners: do not use aluminum foil; stop playing around, and get real—no smaller sheets of foil tearing or oily aluminum blackening and wadding. Again, cleaning up better is the hack here, so use drip tray liners.

Smoking meat and temperature magnets for meat: frantically searching the web for meat temperature is old now. Put these magnets into a pellet hopper. Find out fast what internal temp you're looking for, so you have the meat cook perfectly done all the way every time.

Bucket Head Vacuum: sometimes you will need to swap pellets from hickory to apple. But what if the hopper is filled with 3/4 of its capacity? Grab a bucket head, vacuum out the pellets, and you will get storage ready! Traeger also makes a standard bucket stand storage lid set with filters.

Here's a quick guide to wood pellets for different kinds of meats. For a delicious and unique taste, you may use a combination of wood pellets. Or follow this guide.

2.4 Top Tips for Successful Grilling

- Start grilling with a clean and preheated grill.
- Do not move too much of the food around.
- When grilling, close the lid.
- Do not press or flatten the meat.
- Use more grass-fed meat.
- Have a bottle spray, ready to flare-up.
- Define numerous "zones" for different grilling.
- Use a thermometer for meat.
- Grill them low and slow.
- Do not put cold food directly on the grill.
- Undercook meats, only marginally enough that they manage to cook when resting.
- In the end, baste with sauce.
- Season the meat beforehand with a dry rub.
- Don't over char the meat to properly cook.
- Marinate the food before grilling.
- Keep things simple when serving the crowd.

GRILLING THE PERFECT STEAK

TRAEGER	INTERNAL TEMPERATURE	GRILL TIME AT 400°F	CENTER COLOR
RARE	120-130°F	2:30 MIN. PER SIDE	RED
MEDIUM RARE	130-135°F	3:30 MIN. PER SIDE	PINK WITH THIN BROWN STRIPES ON TOP & BOTTOM.
MEDIUM	135-145°F	4:30 MIN. PER SIDE	SOME PINK
WELL	145-155°F	5:30 MIN. PER SIDE	SLIVER OF LIGHT PINK
WELL DONE	155-165°F	6:30 MIN. PER SIDE	MOSTLY BROWN
WHAT HAVE YOU DONE??	165°F+	8-10 MIN. PER SIDE	BROWN THROUGHOUT

2.5 Shopping Guide for Traeger Wood Pellet Grill

You should have all the required equipment to experience the best of grilling. These are hand-picked items, the ones we feel are important for any grill owner.

- **Premium wood pellets** specifically made for the Traeger grill
- **Burger press**
- Spices mix and different rubs
- **Stainless steel flexible skewers**
- **Meat shredding stainless steel claws**
- **Large sharp slicing knife**
- **Pink butcher paper**
- **Spray bottles**
- **Magnetic clamp grill light**
- Meat flipper
- **Non-stick rib rack**

- **High-temperature gloves**
- **Vacuum sealer**
- **Meat injector kit**
- BBQ tongs
- Silicone basting brush
- **Cutlery sets** and **gourmet knife**
- **Grill cover**
- All-natural grill cleaner
- **For Searing**; the **Grill Grates**
- Cutting board
- **Smoker shelf stainless steel**
- **Wireless thermometers**

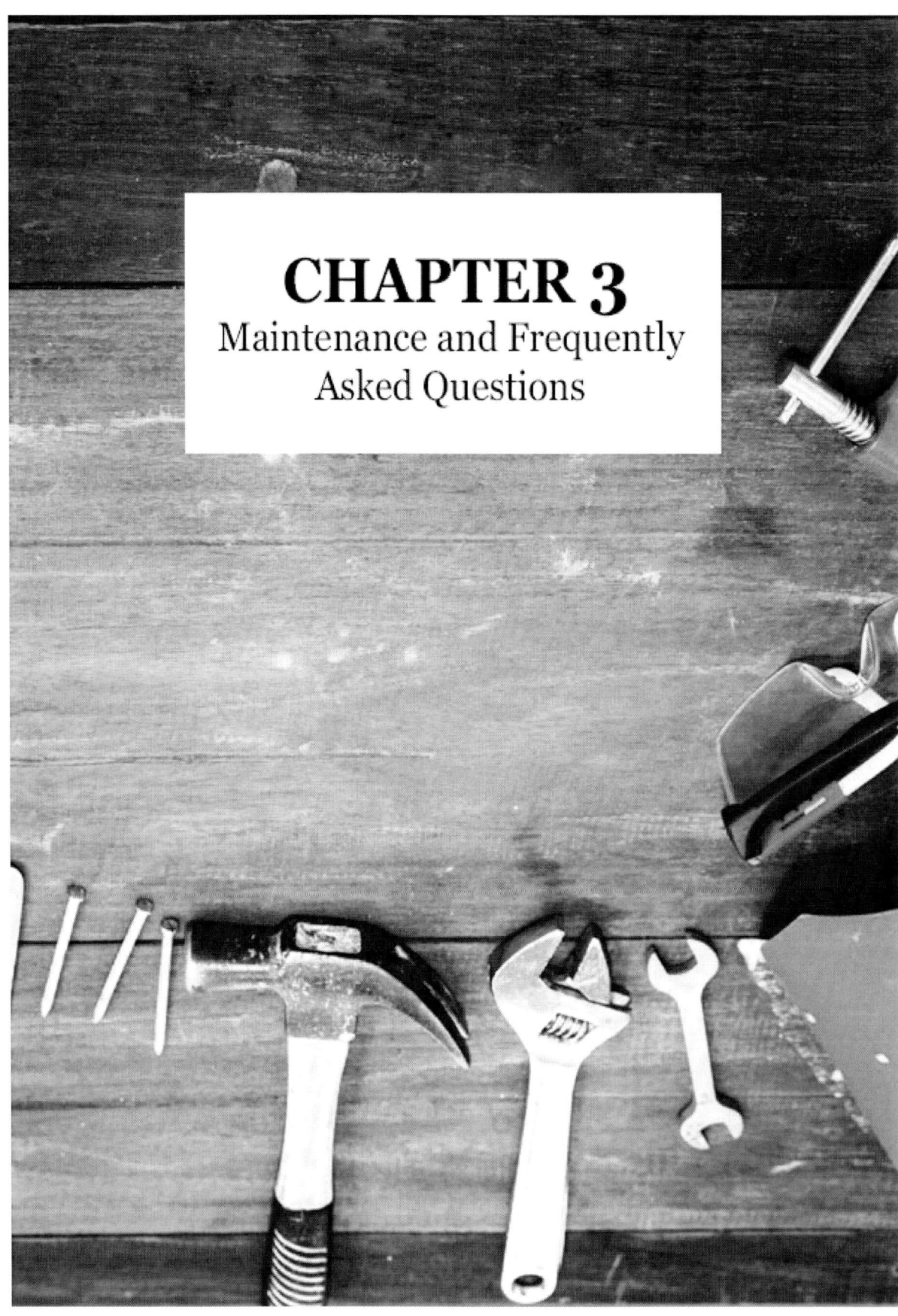

CHAPTER 3
Maintenance and Frequently Asked Questions

Chapter 3: Maintenance and Frequently Asked Questions

Here are few tips to help you maintain the Traeger grill and smoker for longer.

3.1 Creosote and Grease Formation

As wood pellets are burned gradually, organic vapors, tar, and other fumes are formed to create creosote as they mix with outside moisture. The creosote vapors encapsulate in a slow-burning fire's cool exhaust flue. Consequently, creosote builds up on the lining of the duct. Creosote creates a great fire when sparked. Airborne grease particles may migrate into the cooking chamber, and, just like creosote, some of this airborne grease may collect on the flue casing, which can lead to a spark.

The flue exhaust should be checked at least twice a year to assess whether grease or creosote buildup has developed. Oily particles from the food would still spill through the grease drain pan and channel into the grease drain, and eventually swept up in the bucket from the grease drain hose. Grease can collect in both of these areas. The grease sink, the grease drain tube, and the container should be checked for evidence of grease accumulation at least twice a year. It should be discarded after creosote has formed to reduce the possibility of burning.

3.2 Flue (Smoke Stack) Cleaning

Disconnect the electricity before wiping the flue pipe; please ensure that the grill is cooled down. From the head of the flue pipe, detach the chimney cap assembly. It can be cleaned with biodegradable grease remover or warm soapy water. Use a wooden, rigid, non-metallic device to remove the creosote and grease buildup from within the flue tubing's horizontal and vertical portions. It may be cleaned with paper towels or disposable towels until the grease and creosote have been softened from the flue pipe covering. Do not coat the interior of the grill with water or some other liquid cleaner. Attach the chimney cap assembly after the flue pipe has been wiped.

3.3 Grease Cleaning

Disconnect the electricity. Accumulated grease is simpler to wipe off when the grill is already warm, not smoking, be careful not to have yourself burnt. You should wear gloves. Clean the grease from the V-shaped grease drain and the drain tube regularly. A grease fire could occur because too much grease has built up in the V-shape grease drain.

3.4 Exterior Surface Cleaning

Disconnect the electricity. To clean the oil off the grill's exterior, use a disposable towel lessened with warm soapy water. The outdoor grill surfaces should not be cleaned by oven cleaners, abrasive cleaners, or abrasive cleaning papers.

3.5 Keep the Grill Safe Outside

During the heavy rain, if the grill is placed outside, you should take proper care of it to ensure that water will not get into the hopper. If wet, wood pellets grow massively and jam the auger.

3.6 Porcelain Grill Cleaning

Cleaning the porcelain grill serves well when it is still warm. Be careful not to have yourself burnt. Use a long-handled brush for cleaning. Rapidly brush the porcelain grill after removing the meal. It will just take a minute and will be prepped for the next.

Before removing the ash, ensure the grill has cool down. Ash management can only be performed following the advice of the guidebook. Large amounts of ash in the firepot, particularly in the "Smoke" mode, can cause the fire to go out. To eliminate the ash deposition, the firepot must be examined, and ash removed periodically.

3.7 FAQs (Frequently Asked Questions)

Too Much Smoke?

It is common for a grill to have thicker smoke at the start. When the grill is closer to the temperature of the smoke, the smoke should thin out. For the smoke to thin out, allow the grill some time.

What to Do If the Smoke Stays Heavy?

The fire is unable to reach the correct temperature as well as the pellets are just scorching. Look at the following signs if this is the case:

- Pellets are the most common concern. They're not going to burn as hot while they carry moisture.
- Whether pellets are light in color, dull, break quickly, dusty, or whether the pellets' bag has wood shavings, pellets can be compromised.
- And if you think the pellets are not all right, test a new sample, so to be sure. Pellets will also take on moisture without our knowing.
- Ensure that the induction fan operates correctly.
- You should be able to sense the air in the firepot blowing. When measuring this, be careful not to hit the hotrod.
- No noisy sounds should be made by the fan, such as scratching or squealing.

Digital Setting for Starting the Grill?

For the grill's smart controls, the auto-start process is the same. Switch the "Light-on" and turn the dial to "Smoke" mode as the door opens. You should see whitish-gray smoke emerging from the grill when the pellets burn in around two minutes. After ensuring that the pellets have sparked, shut the door, and adjust the dial/temperature to the preferred cooking mode.

Digital Setting for Smoke, High and Medium?

Remember that factors like outside weather, rainfall, wind, and altitude influence the grill's temperature. When considering how long it would take for food to cook on the grill, please keep this in mind.

Digital thermostat recommended settings smoke is 150–180°F. For Medium 225–275°F. For High 350–500°F. These are 3-Speed smoker regulation settings.

How Should I Protect the Finished Paint?

To patch any marks, do touch-up paint, also use a protective cover on the grill. A Traeger Grill Cover is strongly recommended to shield the grill. The Traeger Dealer has coverings, and touch-up paint is available, use good-quality car wax on the grill's exterior surfaces after 90 days. Put wax on a cold grill.

Where Will I Get a New Part for the Grill?

Check with the local dealer at Traeger. They should have the part in stock, or they might be willing to order the part for you. Or you can notify the Traeger Parts Department to put an order. Make sure to provide details.

Start-Up Procedure

Closed Lid: Adjust the Traeger grill straight to the correct temperature when cooking and let it preheat for almost 15 minutes with the lid closed.

Open Lid: Adjust the Traeger grill to the smoke setting when cooking with the lid open. Wait to set up the fire for almost 4 to 5 minutes. Close the lid.

Raise the temperature and let it preheat for about 10 to 15 minutes to the required temperature.

CHAPTER 4
Traeger Grill Appetizers, Sides and Snacks

Chapter 4: Traeger Grill Appetizers, Sides and Snacks

4.1 Traeger Grilled Brussels Sprouts

(**Ready in about**: 35 minutes | **Serving**: 4| **Difficulty**: Easy)
Nutrition per serving: Kcal: 153| **Fat**: 10 g | **Net Carbs**: 5g | **Protein**: 011 g

Ingredients
- 1/2 teaspoon of salt
- 1 cup of bacon, reserve the fat
- 1/2 teaspoon pepper
- 2 cups Brussels sprouts

Instructions
1. Cook the bacon crispy on the stovetop, and reserve the fat.
2. Crumble the bacon into pieces.
3. Clean and trim the Brussel sprout and cut in half.
4. In a safe grill pan, add ¼ cup of fat (bacon) on medium flame.
5. When bacon fat is hot, add Brussel sprouts 1/2 side down and sprinkle salt and pepper; let it brown for 3 to 4 minutes.
6. Let the grill to preheat 350-375°F. Place the pan on the grill and cook for 18-20 minutes.
7. Serve hot.

4.2 Traeger Grilled Carrots

(**Ready in about**: 25 minutes | **Serving**: 6| **Difficulty**: Easy)
Nutrition per serving: Kcal: 250| **Fat** 25 g| **Net Carbs**: 6g **Protein**: 1 g

Ingredients
- 1/2 teaspoon of black pepper
- 1/2 teaspoon of salt
- 1 tablespoon of olive oil
- Fresh thyme
- 1/4 cup of butter
- 2 cups of large carrots

Instructions
1. Wash and pat dry the carrots and do not peel.
2. Drizzle with olive oil. Sprinkle salt to the carrots.
3. Let the grill preheat to 350°F.
4. Put carrots directly on the grill. Close the lid.
5. Cook for 20 minutes.
6. Meanwhile, in a pan, melt butter on medium flame. Do not burn the butter.
7. Slightly brown the butter.
8. Take carrots on a serving plate, drizzle black pepper, and browned butter. Top with fresh thyme.

4.3 Traeger Funeral Potatoes

(**Ready in about**: 70 minutes | **Serving**: 8| **Difficulty**: Easy)
Nutrition per serving: Kcal: 403| **Fat**: 37 g| **Net Carbs**: 14 g | **Protein**: 4 g

Ingredients
- 1/2 cup of grated cheddar cheese
- 1 can of cream chicken soup
- 1/4 cup of melted butter
- 3 cups of corn flakes (crush slightly)
- 1 cup of sour cream
- 1 32-ounce package of hash browns, frozen
- 1 cup of mayonnaise

Instructions
1. Let the grill preheat to 350 °F, take a 13 by 9" baking pan, and spray oil on it.
2. In a bowl, combine all ingredients except for butter and corn flakes.
3. Add this mixture into the prepared baking pan.
4. Mix the melted butter with corn flakes.
5. Add corn flakes mix on top of the hash brown mix.
6. Grill for 1 and 1/2 an hour at 350 °F until hash brown is soft.
7. Cover with foil if the top browns too much.
8. Serve hot.

4.4 Cheesy Traeger Broccoli Au Gratin

(**Ready in about**: 45 minutes | **Serving**: 12| **Difficulty**: Easy)
Nutrition per serving: Kcal: 480| **Fat**: 35 g| **Net Carbs**: 84 g | **Protein**: 20 g

Ingredients:
- 3/4 cup of salted butter
- 1/2 cup of flour
- 1/2 teaspoon of dry mustard
- 2 tablespoons of olive oil
- 6 cups of fresh broccoli florets
- 1/4 cup of diced onion
- 6 cups of whole milk
- 1/2 teaspoon of salt
- 6 cups of cheddar blend cheese, shredded
- 1/4 teaspoon of garlic powder

Instructions
1. Let the grill preheat to 375°F. Add broccoli to a baking sheet and drizzle with olive oil.
2. Roast for 4-5 minutes.
3. In a pan, melt the butter. Sauté onions for 4-5 minutes at low flame.
4. Add in flour, keep mixing—Cook for 5 minutes.
5. Add garlic powder, milk, salt, and dry mustard. Mix well.
6. Cook until the mixture is thickened. Turn off the heat.
7. Add broccoli in a well-oiled grill-safe pan. Add sauce on top, mix in 3/4 of cheese. Add the rest of the cheese on top.
8. Grill until cheese starts to brown until sauce is bubbly or for 20 - 25 minutes.

4.5 Grilled Dinner Rolls

(**Ready in about**: 3 hours and 5 minutes | **Serving**: 24| **Difficulty**: Easy)
Nutrition per serving: Kcal: 350| **Fat**: 13 g| **Net Carbs**: 50 g | **Protein**: 8 g

Ingredients:
- 3/4 cup of sugar
- 4 cups of milk
- 4 teaspoons of yeast
- 10 cups of flour
- 1 and 1/2 tablespoons of salt
- 1 and 1/4 cup of oil
- 1/2 cup of buttermilk powder

Instructions
1. In a microwave, heat the milk until lukewarm. Add yeast, sugar, salt, and oil to milk and mix with a dough hook until yeast is combined with the mixture.
2. In a bowl, mix flour with buttermilk powder. Add this to the milk mixture while the mixer is running until dough forms.
3. The dough should be stretchy and soft.
4. Let the dough rise for about 1-2 hours in an oiled bowl, covered with a towel, or let it rise overnight in the refrigerator.
5. Form rolls from this dough. Place on well-oiled parchment paper.
6. Let them rise for 1-2 hours.
7. Let the grill preheat to 350°F. Bake the rolls at 350 °F or until golden brown.
8. Drizzle butter on top of rolls, serve warm.

4.6 Grilled Onions

(**Ready in about**: 20 minutes | **Serving**: Varies| **Difficulty**: Easy)
Nutrition per serving: Kcal: 89| **Fat**: 2 g| Net Carbs: 3 g | **Protein**: 2 g

Ingredients:
- 1 tablespoon of olive oil
- 2 sweet onions
- Salt and fresh ground pepper

Instructions
1. From 3/4 of an inch of onion root, add in wooden skewers through the center of sweet onion.
2. Place the skewer so that the skewer is going through the center of the side of the onion.
3. Cut the skewers so there's no excess skewer remain.
4. Brush with oil, season with pepper and salt.
5. Grill at 350 °F until onions become tender.
6. Serve hot.

4.7 Traeger Grilled Spinach

(**Ready in about**: 20 minutes | **Serving**: 6| **Difficulty**: Easy)
Nutrition per serving: Kcal: 33| **Fat**: 1 g| **Net Carbs**: 4 g| **Protein**: 3 g
Ingredients
- 2 bunches of fresh spinach, washed and dried
- 1/2 teaspoon of salt
- 1 teaspoon of avocado oil

Instructions
1. Let the grill preheat to 400-425°F.
2. Add salt, pepper, and avocado oil over spinach. Coat well.
3. Place spinach on the grill and cook for 4 to 5 minutes or until spinach is vibrant in color.
4. Serve hot.

4.8 Traeger Grilled Homemade Croutons

(**Ready in about**: 40 minutes | **Serving**: 8| **Difficulty**: Easy)
Nutrition per serving: Kcal: 188| **Fat**: 0 g| **Net Carbs**: 20 g | **Protein**: 4 g
Ingredients
- 2 tablespoons of Mediterranean blend seasoning
- 6 cups of cubed bread
- 1/4 cup of olive oil

Instructions
1. Let the grill preheat to 250°F.
2. In a bowl, mix seasoning and oil and coat the bread cubes well.
3. On a baking sheet, place coated bread cubes.
4. Bake for 1/2 an hour or until golden brown, and stir every 5 minutes.
5. Serve warm.

4.9 Traeger Smoked Mac and Cheese

(**Ready in about**: 1 hour and 5 minutes | **Serving**: 8| **Difficulty**: Easy)
Nutrition per serving: Kcal: 528| **Fat**: 40 g| **Net Carbs**: 26 g | **Protein**: 5g
Ingredients
- 2 and 1/2 cups of small pasta shells, cooked
- 1/3 cup of flour
- 6 cups of whole milk
- 1/2 teaspoon of salt
- 2 cups of cheddar jack cheese
- 1/2 teaspoon of dry mustard
- 1/2 cup of salted butter
- A dash of Worcestershire sauce
- 2 cups of smoked white cheddar
- 1 cup of crushed Ritz

Instructions
1. Let the grill preheat for 5-10 minutes; on "Smoke," keep the lid open until a fire is established. Turn the grill to 325 °F and now close the lid.
2. Melt butter on medium flame, add in flour. Keep whisking and cook for 5 to 6 minutes until color changes to light tan.
3. Add in Worcestershire sauce, milk, dry mustard, and salt. Mix until the sauce thickens.
4. Add in the pasta shells and 1 cup of cheese mix well.
5. Put this mix in a 10 by 13 oiled baking dish and top with cheese and the crushed Ritz.
6. Let the Traeger preheat to 325°F. Bake for 1/2 an hour or until cheese is melted and bubbly. Serve right away.

4.10 Baked Potato Skins with Pulled Pork

(**Ready in about**: 1 hour and 15 minutes | **Serving**: 6| **Difficulty**: Easy)
Nutrition per serving: Kcal: 345| **Fat**: 23 g| **Net Carbs**: 27 g | **Protein**: 6 g
Ingredients:
- Vegetable oil, as needed
- Salt, to taste
- 4 russet potatoes
- 4 whole baker style potatoes
- 1 cup of Mozzarella cheese
- 2 tablespoon melted butter
- 3 cups of pulled pork
- 1 cup of cheddar cheese
- 4 tablespoons of BBQ sauce (Sweet & Heat)
- Chopped green onion, sour cream, bacon, for serving

Instructions
1. Let the Traeger preheat to 450 °F for 15 minutes, keep the lid closed.
2. Coat the potatoes well with oil and season with salt.
3. Add potatoes directly to the grill, cook for 45 minutes, or until tender check with a fork.
4. Take potatoes of the Traeger and slice in half, and hollow out. Leave ¼ of potato skin.
5. Drizzle melted butter inside the potato and cook on the grill at 450 °F until golden brown for 5-6 minutes.
6. In a bowl, mix cheeses, pork, and BBQ sauce.
7. Stuff the potato skins with this pork mix.
8. Place back on the grill, keep the lid closed, cook until cheese melts.
9. Top with bacon, sour cream, and green onions.
10. Serve right away.

4.11 Traeger Smoked Smashed Potatoes

(**Ready in about**: 40 minutes | **Serving**: 6| **Difficulty**: Easy)
Nutrition per serving: Kcal: 345| **Fat**: 23 g| **Net Carbs**: 27 g | **Protein**: 6 g
Ingredients:
- 3 tablespoons of avocado oil
- 1/2 cup of salted butter
- 1-2 pounds of baby potatoes
- 1-2 tablespoons of Kosher salt

Instructions
1. Let the Traeger preheat to 375°F.
2. Coat the potatoes with avocado oil, and put them in the microwave.
3. Microwave for 3 minutes, or until tender.
4. Put potatoes in 10 by 13 pan, and smash with a fork.
5. Drizzle with oil, season with pepper and salt.
6. Grill for 1/2 an hour.
7. Serve right away.

4.12 Smoked Garlic Butter

(**Ready in about:** 30 minutes | **Serving**: 6| **Difficulty**: Easy)
Nutrition per serving: Kcal: 272| **Fat**: 31 g| **Net Carbs**: 2 g| **Protein**: 0 g
Ingredients:
- 2 sticks of salted butter
- Fresh parsley and basil
- 3 cloves of garlic, cut into sliced

Instructions
1. In a small pan, add all ingredients.
2. Let the pellet grill preheat to 180°F, and put the pan inside.
3. Cook for 20-25 minutes, or till garlic is tender and butter is melted.
4. Take out from the grill, let it cool for 10 minutes.

4.13 Traeger Grilled Cheddar Bay Biscuits

(**Ready in about**: 33 minutes | **Serving**: 12| **Difficulty**: Easy)
Nutrition per serving: Kcal: 107| **Fat** 19.4 g| **Net Carbs**: 15.3 g | **Protein**: 4 g

Ingredients:
For Biscuits:
- 1/2 teaspoon of garlic powder
- 1 tablespoon baking powder
- 2 and 1/2 cups of bread flour
- 1/2 teaspoon of cream of tartar
- 1/2 teaspoon of salt
- 1/8 teaspoon of cayenne pepper
- 1 stick of softened salted butter
- 1 and 1/2 teaspoons of sugar
- 1/2 cup of sour cream
- 1 and 1/4 cup of milk
- 1 and 1/2 cups of sharp shredded cheddar cheese, smoked preferably

For Topping:
- 1 stick of salted butter
- 1/4 teaspoon of salt
- 1 teaspoon of garlic powder
- 1 teaspoon of parsley

Instructions

1. Let the Traeger preheat to 400 to 450 °F degrees for 15-20 minutes.
2. In a bowl, add cream of tartar, cayenne pepper, flour, salt, sugar, garlic powder, and baking powder. Mix until combined.
3. Add softened butter into the flour mixture and mix with a fork. Let it be lumpy.
4. Add in milk, sour cream, and cheddar cheese.
5. Mix until moistened. Do not over mix.
6. In a pan, add parsley, 1 stick of butter, salt, and 1 teaspoon of garlic powder. Add parchment paper to a baking sheet.
7. Place dough mixes on a prepared baking sheet. Top with half-melted butter.
8. Put in Traeger away from the hottest part, and bake until tops are light brown or 20-25 minutes.
9. Drizzle with the rest of the butter serves hot.

4.14 Traeger Corn on the Cob

(**Ready in about**: 30 minutes | **Serving**: 10 | **Difficulty**: Easy)
Nutrition per serving: Kcal: 60| **Fat**: 3 g| **Net Carbs**: 2 g | **Protein**: 4.4 g

Ingredients
- 1/4 cup of Traeger vegetable rub
- 1/4 cup of avocado oil
- 10 ears of sweet fresh corn

Instructions
1. Peel and trim corn rub with oil and vegetable rub.
2. Grill for 20 minutes at 350 °F on Trager grill.
3. Serve hot.

4.15 Traeger Grilled Prosciutto Asparagus

(**Ready in about**: 20 minutes | **Serving**: 5| **Difficulty**: Easy)
Nutrition per serving: Kcal: 83| **Fat** 4 g| Net Carbs: 3 g| **Protein**: 4 g

Ingredients
- 1 tablespoon of Traeger vegetable rub
- 1 tablespoon of oil
- 1/4 cup of prosciutto, cut into wide slices
- 2 cups of asparagus, trimmed

Instructions
1. Let the grill preheat to 375°F.
2. Coat the asparagus in oil and vegetable rub.
3. Wrap the prosciutto around the asparagus. Place these on the tray.
4. Place on grill and cook for 10 minutes. Turn halfway through. Serve hot.

4.16 Traeger Grilled Spaghetti Squashe

(**Ready in about**: 30-45 minutes | **Serving**: 8| **Difficulty**: Easy)
Nutrition per serving: Kcal: 195| **Fat**: 18 g| **Net Carbs**: 10 g| **Protein**: 1 g

Ingredients
- 6 tablespoons of butter, divided
- 1/2 teaspoon of salt
- 1 spaghetti squash
- 1/2 cup of butter
- 1 teaspoon of fresh parsley, roughly chopped
- 2 tablespoons of brown sugar

Instructions
1. Let the grill preheat to 350°F.
2. Halves the squash lengthwise and take out the seeds.
3. Sprinkle brown sugar and salt on each 1/2 of the squash, and place 3 tablespoons of butter in each 1/2 of the squash.
4. Place on grill and cook for 30-45 minutes, or until fork-tender.
5. Meanwhile, take 3 tablespoons of butter. Brown the butter on medium flame, until golden brown. Do not burn the butter.
6. Take out the squash and make strands with a fork. Add browned butter on top, sprinkle the salt.
7. Enjoy hot.

4.17 Traeger Grilled Butternut Squash

(**Ready in about**: 55 minutes | **Serving**: 8| **Difficulty**: Easy)
Nutrition per serving: Kcal: 155| **Fat**: 12 g| **Net Carbs**: 14 g| **Protein**: 1 g

Ingredients:
- 1/2 cup of brown sugar
- 1 butternut squash
- 1 teaspoon of salt
- 1/2 cup of butter

Instructions
1. Clean the butternut squash and slice in half.
2. Take out the seeds and sprinkle salt and rub butter all over. Then sprinkle brown sugar all over.
3. 3. Pierce the squash with a fork. So, butter and brown sugar will penetrate deep.
4. Put on preheated grill at 350 °F till fork tender, or for 45 minutes.
5. 5. Serve it as it is, or mash the squash serve the way you like.

4.18 Loaded Smoked Mashed Potatoes

(**Ready in about**: 1 hour and 55 minutes | **Serving**: 6| **Difficulty**: Easy)
Nutrition per serving: Kcal: 612| **Fat**: 46 g| **Net Carbs**: 38 g| **Protein**: 15 g
Ingredients:
- Water, enough to boil potatoes
- 2 tablespoons of salt
- 1/2 cup of softened cream cheese
- 3 pounds of russet potatoes, cut into cubes
- 1/2 cup of heavy cream
- 1/2 cup of sour cream
- 1 teaspoon of salt
- 1 cup of softened butter
- 1 tablespoon of Ranch dressing mix, dry
- 1/2 teaspoon of pepper
- 1/2 cup of cheddar cheese
Toppings:
- 1/4 cup of chopped green onion
- 1/2 cup of cooked bacon, chopped
- 1/2 cup of cheddar cheese

Instructions
1. In a pan, add water and 2 tablespoons of salt and boil the peeled, cubed potatoes for 15-20 minutes.
2. Drain the potatoes and mash the potatoes; add heavy cream, butter, and cream cheese.
3. Mash to your liking.
4. Spray oil in a grill-safe dish and add mashed potatoes to the dish
5. Let the grill preheat to 350 °F, place the dish on the grill, and bake for 45 minutes.
6. Cover the foil if the top starts to brown.
7. Take out from grill and add cheese, bacon on top, and green onion.

4.19 Smoked Bacon Ranch Rotini and Cheese

(**Ready in about**: 1 hour and 5 minutes | **Serving**: 8| **Difficulty**: Easy)
Nutrition per serving: Kcal: 605| **Fat**: 41 g| **Net Carbs**: 30 g| **Protein**: 9 g
Ingredients:
- 1/2 cup of salted butter
- 1/3 cup of flour
- 2 cups of bacon, cooked and crumbled
- 6 cups of 2% milk
- 1 packet of ranch dressing mix
- A dash of Worcestershire sauce
- 2 cups of smoked white cheddar
- 1 cup of crushed Ritz
- 2 cups of rotini pasta, cooked
- 2 cups of cheddar Jack cheese

Instructions
1. Preheat the Traeger to 325°F.
2. Melt butter over medium flame, add in flour. Keep whisking for 5-6 minutes.
3. Add in the Worcestershire, ranch powder, and milk, then turn the heat down low. Mix until the sauce becomes thick.
4. Add in rotini pasta, bacon, 1 cup of cheese and put in 10 by 13 oiled baking dish.
5. Top with cheese and Ritz.
6. Place on grill and cook for 1/2 an hour at 325°F.
7. Serve hot.

4.20 Grilled Caesar Pasta Salad

(**Ready in about**: 2 hour and 20 minutes | **Serving**: 12| **Difficulty**: Easy)
Nutrition per serving: Kcal: 112| **Fat**: 3 g| **Net Carbs**: 16 g| **Protein**: 6 g
Ingredients:
- 1 cup of shaved, parmesan cheese
- 2 cups of dressing
- 2 heads of grilled romaine, roughly chopped
- 1 pound of pasta
- 2 cups of croutons
- Two halves of chicken breast
- Traeger poultry rub, enough to coat the chicken
- Olive oil, as needed

Instructions
1. Cook the pasta as per instructions. Drain and rinse with cold water.
2. Rub the chicken breast with poultry rub and let it rest for 30-40 minutes.
3. Let the Traeger preheat to 350 F.
4. Drizzle the chicken breast with olive oil, put directly on Traeger, and grill for 20 minutes or until internal temperature reaches 165-170 F.
5. Take chicken off the grill, let it sit for ten minutes, cut into cubes.
6. In a bowl, add grilled chicken, pasta, chopped romaine, parmesan, and dressing. Toss well.
7. Keep in the fridge for 1-2 hours or serve right away.
8. Add croutons on top and serve.

4.21 Traeger Grilled Zucchini and Yellow Squash

(**Ready in about**: 15 minutes | **Serving**: 8| **Difficulty**: Easy)
Nutrition per serving: Kcal: 48| **Fat**: 2 g| **Net Carbs**: 7 g| **Protein**: 2 g
Ingredients:
- 2 teaspoons of avocado oil
- 2 zucchinis
- 1 tablespoon of Greek freak seasoning
- 2 yellow squashes

Instructions
1. Let the grill preheat to 375°F.
2. Cut the squash into quarters, coat with oil, and sprinkle with seasoning.
3. Place on Traeger and cook for 10-15 minutes. After 3-4 minutes, turn the squash.
4. Serve hot.

4.22 Grilled Mexican Street Corn

(**Ready in about**: 25 minutes | **Serving**: 4| **Difficulty**: Easy)
Nutrition per serving: Kcal: 262| **Fat** 20 g| **Net Carbs**: 21 g| **Protein**: 5 g g
Ingredients:
- 4 corns on the cobb
- 4 tablespoons of mayonnaise
- 2 tablespoons of butter
- 1/4 cup of crumbled Cotija cheese
- 1 teaspoon of salt
- 1/4 cup of chopped cilantro
- Two limes
- 1/2 teaspoon of chili powder

Instructions
1. Coat the cobbs with 1 tablespoon of butter and 1/4 teaspoon of salt.
2. Wrap the coated cobbs with aluminum foil and place them on the grill.
3. Let grill for 20 minutes and turn every 5 minutes. Do not burn the corns.
4. Remove the foil, and spread mayonnaise on cobbs.
5. Add the chili powder, crumbled Cotija cheese, and cilantro.
6. Serve with lime.

4.23 Traeger Smoked Baked Potato

Ready in about: 3 hours and 10 minutes | **Serving**: 6| **Difficulty**: Easy)
Nutrition per serving: Kcal: 370| **Fat**: 8 g| **Net Carbs**: 64 g **Protein**: 8 g
Ingredients:
- 1 tablespoon of Kosher salt
- 6 russet potatoes
- 1/4 cup of avocado oil
For Toppings:
- Butter
- Sour Cream
- Chives
- Bacon
- Cheddar Cheese

Instructions
1. Let the pellet grill preheat to 200-220°F.
2. Clean the potatoes and pierce with a fork all over.
3. Put potatoes on the grill at 200 °F for 2 hours.
4. Take the potatoes out and raise the temperature to 400°F.
5. Coat potatoes with oil and salt.
6. Put the potatoes back on the grill for 1 hour until fork tender.
7. Serve with toppings.

4.24 Grilled Garlic Rosemary Smashed Potatoes

(**Ready in about**: 1 hour | **Serving**: 8| **Difficulty**: Easy)
Nutrition per serving: Kcal: 287| **Fat**: 12 g| **Net Carbs**: 23 g| **Protein**: 7.8 g

Ingredients:
- 2 tablespoons of olive oil
- 6 cups of small red potatoes
- 3/4 teaspoon of salt
- For grilling:
- 1 tablespoon of chopped, fresh rosemary
- 2 cloves of minced garlic
- 3 tablespoons of olive oil
- 1/4 teaspoon of garlic salt
- Grated Parmesan cheese, as needed
- 1/4 teaspoon of black pepper

Instructions
1. Let the grill preheat to 375°F. Prepare a baking dish with parchment paper.
2. Pat dry the potatoes. Coat the potatoes with 2 tablespoons of oil, and sprinkle salt. Place on a baking sheet.
3. Bake until fork-tender or for 40-50 minutes. Cool them completely.
4. In a bowl, add black pepper, chopped fresh rosemary, olive oil, salt, and garlic salt.
5. Smash the potatoes of ¾ inch thickness.
6. Brush the potatoes with oil. Sprinkle with seasoning and grill for 10 minutes.
7. Top with cheese and serve.

4.25 Traeger Bacon-Wrapped Scallops

(**Ready in about**: 5-10 minutes | **Serving**: 8| **Difficulty**: Easy)
Nutrition per serving: Kcal: 261| **Fat**: 14 g| **Net Carbs**: 5 g| **Protein**: 28 g

Ingredients:
- 1/2 pound of bacon
- Sea salt, to taste
- 1 pound of large sea scallops

Instructions
1. Let the Traeger preheat to 350-375°F.
2. Pat dry the scallops well.
3. Wrap in bacon pieces secure with a toothpick.
4. Place wrapped scallops on the grill, keep the lid closed for 5-7 minutes. Turn the pieces to cook properly.
5. Serve hot.

4.26 Roasted Elk Jalapeno Poppers

(**Ready in about**: 10-15 minutes | **Serving**: 10| **Difficulty**: Easy)
Nutrition per serving: Kcal: 153| **Fat**: 8.9 g| **Net Carbs**: 7.9 g| **Protein**: 12 g

Ingredients
- 1 and 1/2 cups of garlic and herb-flavored cream cheese
- 1 cup of Worcestershire sauce
- 1 cup of lime juice
- 10 pieces of bacon
- 1 cup of light soy sauce
- 4 steaks of elk
- 20 jalapeno peppers
- Honey, to taste

Instructions
1. In a bowl, mix soy sauce, lime juice, and Worcestershire sauce. Add sliced steaks to cover it, and keep in the fridge for 4-6 hours or overnight.
2. Let the grill preheat to 350 °F, keep the lid closed.
3. Cut the jalapenos lengthwise, take out the seeds.
4. Slice the bacon in half.
5. Add cream cheese into jalapenos halves.
6. Attach 1 slice of elk with jalapeno, wrap with 1 piece of bacon. Secure with toothpick
7. Grill at 350 °F, for 10-15 minutes, until jalapenos are charred and soft.
8. Take off from grill and top with honey and serve.

4.27 Smoked Salmon Dip

(**Ready in about**: 40-60 minutes | **Serving**: 2| **Difficulty**: Easy)
Nutrition per serving: Kcal: 113| **Fat**: 9 g| **Net Carbs**: 2 g| **Protein**: 5 g

Ingredients
- 3 cups of sour cream
- 1/2 cup of softened cream cheese
- 1/4 teaspoon of garlic powder
- 2 salmon fillets
- 1 tablespoon of lemon juice
- 1/4 teaspoon of cayenne pepper
- 1 teaspoon of fresh dill
- 2 teaspoons of prepared horseradish

Instructions
1. In a bowl, add all ingredients except the cheese. Combine well.
2. Preheat your smoker to 200°F, adding your pellets.
3. Add the salmon to the mix and grill for 40 minutes or until salmon reaches your desired doneness.
4. Retire salmon from grill and add the cheese while hot.

4.28 Lemon Garlic Grilled Asparagus in Foil

(**Ready in about**: 25 minutes | **Serving**: 4| **Difficulty**: Easy)
Nutrition per serving: Kcal: 59| **Fat**: 4 g| **Net Carbs**: 6 g| **Protein**: 2 g

Ingredients:
- 2 cups of asparagus, cleaned and trimmed
- 1 tablespoon of olive oil
- Salt and black pepper, to taste
- 3 cloves of minced garlic
- Lemon zest: One teaspoon
- 2 tablespoons of lemon juice

Instructions
1. Let the grill preheat to medium (325 °F) heat.
2. In a bowl, add asparagus and lemon juice, garlic, olive oil—coat well and season with salt and pepper.
3. Place asparagus into two different foil sheets, 1/2 in 1 and 1/2 in another. Wrap tightly.
4. Place foil packets on the grill and cook for 10-20 minutes, or until tender.

4.29 Grilled Sweet Potatoes

(**Ready in about**: 20-30 minutes | **Serving**: 6| **Difficulty**: Easy)
Nutrition per serving: Kcal: 117| **Fat**: 8 g| **Net Carbs**: 11 g| **Protein**: 1 g

Ingredients:
- 2 tablespoons of olive oil
- 1/2 teaspoon of Kosher salt
- 2 medium sweet potatoes, unpeeled
- 1/2 teaspoon of ground pepper

Instructions
1. Boil the potatoes for 20 minutes. Drain and set aside.
2. Let the grill preheat to high (450 °F). Slice the potatoes into 1/4-inch-thick rounds. Drizzle olive oil and add salt and pepper.
3. Grill the potatoes for two and a half minutes on each side until browned marks appear.
4. Serve hot.

4.30 Smoked Eggs

(**Ready in about**: 2 hours and 10 minutes | **Serving**: 12| **Difficulty**: Easy)
Nutrition per serving: Kcal: 189| **Fat**: 7 g| **Net Carbs**: 2 g| **Protein**: 16 g

Ingredients:
- 12 eggs

Topping:
- BBQ sauce

Instructions
1. Preheat the Traeger to 325°F.
2. Put eggs directly on the grill and cook for 1/2 an hour, with the lid closed.
3. Take eggs out and place them in ice water.
4. Lower the grill's temperature to 175°F.
5. Peel eggs and put again on the grill and cook for 1/2 an hour to 1 hour.
6. Baste eggs with BBQ sauce and serve.

4.31 Hot & Seasoned Grilled Corn

(**Ready in about**: 20-25 minutes | **Serving**: 4| **Difficulty**: Easy)
Nutrition per serving: Kcal: 270| **Fat**: 18 g| **Net Carbs**: 28 g| **Protein**: 5 gg

Ingredients:
- 4 corn, on the cobs
- 1 tablespoon of onion powder
- 1 tablespoon of garlic powder
- 1/2 tablespoon of ground black pepper
- 1/4 tablespoon of chili pepper
- 1/4 tablespoon of dried thyme
- 1 tsp dried oregano
- 2 tablespoons of butter
- 1/2 tablespoon of salt

Instructions
1. Peel and clean corn cobs.
2. Melt the butter and apply over corn.
3. Preheat pellet grill to 400°F.
4. Mix oregano, garlic powder, onion powder, salt, pepper, thyme, and chili.
5. Apply the mixture over each corn cob.
6. Grill for about 15-20 minutes, always turning.
7. Remove from grill and let it cool

4.32 Cheese Trinity with Grilled Potatoes and Chives

(**Ready in about**: 1 hour and 15 minutes | **Serving**: 8| **Difficulty**: Easy)
Nutrition per serving: Kcal 335| **Fat** 15 g| **Net Carbs** 30 g| **Protein** 12 g

Ingredients:
- 1 small chopped onion
- 1/3 cup of parmesan cheese, grated
- 1/2 cup of shredded cheddar cheese
- 4 russet potatoes, cut into 1/4 inch thick
- 1/2 cup of shredded mozzarella cheese
- 1/2 teaspoon of black pepper
- 1 and 1/2 cups of cream
- 2 tablespoons of softened butter
- 2 cloves of minced garlic
- 2 teaspoons of seasoned salt
- 1 tablespoon of chives
- 1/2 teaspoon of salt
- 2 tablespoons of all-purpose flour

Instructions
1. Let the grill preheat to 375°F.
2. Oil the 10-inch skillet with cooking spray.
3. In a bowl, add garlic, flour, and 1/2 of cream. Mix well.
4. Add onion and potatoes into the skillet, sprinkle with 1/2 seasoning.
5. Add 1/2 of the sauce over potatoes, add another layer of onion and potato on top. Add 1/2 of the seasoning and sauce over.
6. Bake for 45-50 minutes on a pellet grill. Turn the pan halfway.
7. Mix cheeses in a bowl and add over top of potatoes and bake for 10-15 minutes until cheese is melted and bubbly.
8. Sprinkle the chives and serve

CHAPTER 5
Traeger Grill Pork Recipes

Chapter 5: Traeger Grill Pork Recipes

5.1 Pulled Pork Enchiladas with Smoke-Roasted Red Sauce

(**Ready in about**: 60 minutes | **Serving**: 8| **Difficulty**: Medium)
Nutrition per serving: Kcal: 345| **Fat**: 32 g| **Net Carbs**: 16 g| **Protein**: 20 g

Ingredients:
- 1 head bulb of garlic
- 3 cups of pulled pork
- 3 cups of fresh tomatoes
- 1 onion
- 2 tablespoons of chili powder
- Hot pepper sauce, to taste
- 1 cup of Monterey Jack cheese, shredded
- 1/4 cup of enchilada sauce
- 8 tortillas, whole flour
- 2 teaspoons of cumin

Instructions
1. Set the Traeger to high (450 °F) and close the lid for 15 minutes.
2. Cut the top of the garlic bulb and wrap it in foil. Add tomatoes, onion sliced in 1/2 wrapped garlic on the grill.
3. Let it cook until the garlic has softened, or for 10 to 15 minutes. Raise the temperature to 375 °F and close the lid.
4. Unwrap the garlic, add tomatoes, onion, and garlic to the blender.
5. Add hot sauce, chili powder, salt, and cumin to the blender.
6. Pulse on high until creamy. If the sauce is thick, add a few tablespoons of water.
7. In a baking dish (9 by 13), spread a thin layer of prepared sauce.
8. In a bowl, add pulled pork and mix with ¼ cup of sauce. Mix to combine.
9. In each tortilla, add 1/3 cup of pulled pork and some cheese.
10. Wrap the tortillas and place them in a baking dish.
11. Cover with cheese and the rest of the sauce.
12. Place the baking dish on the grill grate and bake for 25 minutes, or until cheese is melted and sauce is bubbly.
13. Serve hot.

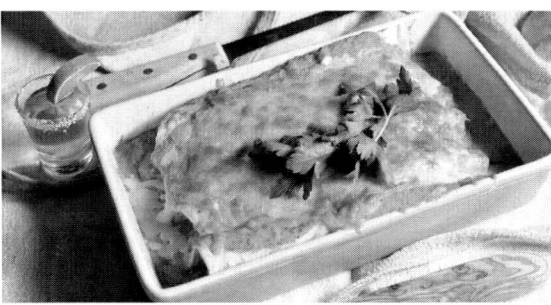

5.2 Exquisite Ribs

(**Ready in about**: 6 hours and 20 minutes |**Serving**: 5-6| **Difficulty**: Medium)
Nutrition per serving: Kcal: 234| **Fat**: 24 g| **Net Carbs**: 12 g| **Protein**: 26 g

Ingredients:
- 2 racks of ribs
- 1 tablespoon of granulated onion
- 1/4 cup of kosher salt
- 1 teaspoon of chipotle powder
- 4 tablespoons of mild chili powder
- 1 tablespoon of ground cumin
- 1 tablespoon of granulated garlic
- 1 tablespoon of coarse black pepper
- 1/2 cup of brown sugar
- 1 tablespoon of ground coriander
- 3 cups of apple juice

Instructions
1. In a bowl, add all ingredients, mix well.
2. Rub this mixture on both sides of the ribs. Marinate overnight.
3. Let the Traeger preheat to 200°F.
4. Make a pan of foil, place over grill add apple juice to it.
5. Place ribs on the grill, and cook for 5 hours.
6. If you want moist ribs after every 15 minutes, brush the apple juice over the ribs. Or skip this step if you want dry ribs.
7. Close the lid and cook for 1 more hour.
8. Serve hot.

5.3 Pork Tenderloin Wrapped in Fresh Rosemary

(**Ready in about**: 60 minutes | **Serving**: 8-9| **Difficulty**: Medium)
Nutrition per serving: Kcal: 244| **Fat**: 16 g| **Net Carbs**: 13 g| **Protein**: 25.5 g

Ingredients:
- 1-1.5 pounds of pork tenderloin
- 1 tablespoon of Dijon mustard
- 1 tablespoon of olive oil
- 4 cloves of minced garlic
- 3 or 4 sprigs of fresh rosemary
- 1/4 teaspoon of black pepper

Instructions
1. Let the grill preheat to 375°F.
2. In a bowl, mix black pepper, olive oil, crushed garlic, and Dijon mustard to make a paste.
3. Spread this mixture all over the tenderloin.
4. Cut food string into 10 inches pieces.
5. Place string two inches apart. Place 3-4 sprigs of herb across strings.
6. Place coated tenderloin over herbs and strings. Tie the strings and place the rest of the springs.
7. Trim the strings if in excess.
8. Place the tied tenderloin in the middle rack and close the lid.
9. Cook for 10-15 minutes. Turn the tenderloin over and grill for another 10-15 minutes. Cook until the internal temperature (as read by a meat thermometer) reaches 145°F.
10. Let it rest for 5 minutes, then remove the herbs and string.
11. Slice and serve.

5.4 Slow Smoked Pulled Pork

(**Ready in about**: 8-10 hours and 15 minutes | **Serving**: 8-9| **Difficulty**: Hard)
Nutrition per serving: Kcal: 312| **Fat**: 17 g| **Net Carbs**: 10.1 g| **Protein**: 16.5 g

Ingredients:
- 1 pork shoulder of 7-8 pounds, rinsed and trimmed
- 1 tablespoon of kosher salt
- 2 tablespoons of Dijon mustard
- 1 teaspoon of chipotle powder
- 1 tablespoon of garlic granules
- 1 teaspoon of thyme
- 1 teaspoon of chili powder
- Mustard based BBQ sauce
- 1 teaspoon of black pepper

Instructions
1. Do not cut the fat cap of pork.
2. Coat the pork shoulder with Dijon mustard.
3. In a bowl, add chipotle powder, chili powder, garlic granules, thyme, black pepper, and salt mix well.
4. Rub this spice mix all over pork shoulder. Place on grill and fat cap side up.
5. Smoke until internal temperature reaches from 160-225°F.
6. Take out from grill and immediately wrap in aluminum foil.
7. Put it back on the grill until the internal temperature reaches 240 °F, slow smoke until the internal temperature (as read by a meat thermometer) reaches from 195-240 °F for 8-10 hours.
8. Remove from the grill and let it rest.
9. Unwrap and enjoy.

5.5 Citrus Brined Pork Roast with Fig Mustard
(**Ready in about**: 30-40 minutes | **Serving**: 6| **Difficulty**: Medium)
Nutrition per serving: Kcal: 332| **Fat**: 16.8 g| **Net Carbs**: 11.1 g| **Protein**: 21 g

Ingredients:
- 1/2 cup of salt
- 2 tablespoons of extra-virgin olive oil
- 1/4 cup of brown sugar
- 3 cloves of garlic
- 6 peppercorns
- 1 lemon, cut into half
- 1/2 teaspoon of dried fennel seed
- 2 bay leaves, dried
- 1/2 teaspoon of red pepper flakes
- 1/2 cup of apple juice
- Icy water
- 5 pounds of pork loin
- Salt and black pepper, to taste
- 1/2 cup of orange juice
- 2 tablespoons of butter
- 1 cup of sugar
- 1 shallot, thinly sliced
- 1/2 teaspoon of minced garlic
- 1 and 1/4 cup of black figs, trimmed and quartered
- 1 cup of Cognac
- 1/2 teaspoon of Dijon mustard

Instructions
1. To make the brine, in a pot, add 1/2 a cup of salt, red pepper flakes, lemon, brown sugar, bay leaves, orange juice, garlic cloves, apple, black peppercorns, and fennel seeds.
2. Let it simmer until sugar and salt have dissolved.
3. Add this mixture over ice and keep in the fridge until cooled completely.
4. Submerge the pork in cool brine and hold the pork down with some weight if necessary. Keep in the fridge overnight.
5. Take out from brine and pat dry. Coat with oil and season with black pepper and salt.
6. Set the Traeger to high and close the lid for 15 minutes.
7. Put the pork on grill grates and cook for 20-25 minutes, at 450 °F, until internal temperature reaches (as read by a meat thermometer) 140 °F in the thickest part of pork.
8. Let it rest for 10 minutes.
9. To make Fig Mustard, in a pan on medium flame, add butter and melt.
10. Sauté shallots for 2 minutes until softened. Add garlic and cook for 30 seconds. Add sugar and cognac, let it simmer.
11. Add in figs cook until liquid is reduced to a syrupy consistency, for 20 minutes.
12. Season with black pepper and salt.
13. Pour this sauce over sliced pork and serve.

5.6 Crispy Pork Belly
(**Ready in about**: 4 hours and 15 minutes | **Serving**: 6| **Difficulty**: Medium)
Nutrition per serving: Kcal: 324| **Fat**: 18.1 g| **Net Carbs**: 9.8 g| **Protein**: 19.8 g

Ingredients:
- 1 and 1/2 cups of chicken stock
- Dry bacon rub, as needed
- 3 pounds of pork belly
- 1 Onion, sliced thin

Instructions
1. Let the Traeger preheat to 225°F.
2. Place an iron pot over grill grates and place a rack over it. Put pork belly on a wire rack and smoke for 2 hours.
3. Raise the temperature to 325°F. Put the pork belly inside the pot and cover it; cook for 2 hours until internal temperature reaches 185°F.
4. Place the meat on the griddle, put the fat side down, and cook for 1 minute.
5. Let it rest for 15 minutes, slice, and serve.

5.7 BBQ Pulled Pork with Paleo Vinegar Sauce
(**Ready in about**: 10 hours | **Serving**: 6| **Difficulty**: Medium)
Nutrition per serving: Kcal: 324| **Fat**: 18.1 g| **Net Carbs**: 9.8 g| **Protein**: 19.8 g

Ingredients:
- 1 tablespoon of red-hot sauce
- 1 teaspoon of red pepper flakes
- 1 teaspoon of kosher salt
- 2 cups of apple cider vinegar
- 1/2 cup of unsweetened apple juice
- 6-10 pounds of pork butt
- 1 teaspoon of mustard powder
- 4 tablespoons of honey
- 1 teaspoon of cinnamon
- 1 teaspoon of garlic powder
- 6 tablespoons of paprika
- 1 teaspoon of ground sage
- 1/2 teaspoon of coarse ground black pepper

Instructions
1. Preheat the Traeger to 225 °F, close the lid.
2. In a bowl, add 4 tablespoons of honey, 1 teaspoon of red pepper flakes, 1 teaspoon of kosher salt, apple cider vinegar, red hot sauce, and 1/2 a teaspoon of coarse black pepper. Mix well and set it in the fridge.
3. In a bowl, add 6 tablespoons of paprika, 1 teaspoon of mustard powder, 2 teaspoons of kosher salt, 1 teaspoon of garlic powder, 2 teaspoons of pepper, 1 teaspoon of cinnamon, 1 teaspoon of ground sage, and 1/2 a teaspoon of black pepper. Mix well.
4. Trim the fat off the pork, and season with spice rub. Let it marinate for 20 minutes.
5. Place pork directly on grill grates, at 225 °F, and cook for 4 and a half hours or until internal temperature (as read by a meat thermometer) reaches 155-165°F.
6. Wrap the pork in a double layer of aluminum foil. Add the apple juice inside and put on the grill.
7. Raise the temperature to 250 °F cook for 3 hours until the internal temperature reaches 204-to 206°F, as read by a meat thermometer.
8. Cooking time should be 8-10 hours.
9. Serve and enjoy.

5.8 Smoked Pork Loin Tacos
(**Ready in about**: 4 hours and 10 minutes | **Serving**: 12| **Difficulty**: Medium)
Nutrition per serving: Kcal: 303| **Fat**: 13 g| **Net Carbs**: 2 g| **Protein**: 38 g

Ingredients:
- 4-pound of pork loin
- 1 cup of Mexican beer
- 1/4 cup of chili-lime seasoning
- 1 can of 8-ounces of El Pato yellow
- 2 tablespoons of Pepper
- 2 tablespoons of salt
- 2 tablespoons of garlic
- 1 can of 8-ounces of El Pato green

Instructions
1. Let the grill preheat to 200-225°F.
2. Rub the pork with salt, garlic, chili-lime, and pepper.
3. Place the pork in Traeger and smoke for 2 hours.
4. Take the meat off the grill and place in tin foil, makeshift pan, or in grill safe pan.
5. Pour the beer with roast and El Pato cans. Cover it tightly and cook at 325 °F, for 1-2 hours until the internal temperature (as read by a meat thermometer) reaches 195-200°F.
6. If there is still liquid present, flip the meat to the other side.
7. Serve on tortillas.

5.9 Cuban Pork Sandwich
(**Ready in about**: 5 hours| **Serving**: 4| **Difficulty**: Medium)
Nutrition per serving: Kcal: 303| **Fat**: 13 g| **Net Carbs**: 2 g| **Protein**: 38 g

Ingredients:
- 3 cups of chicken stock
- 4 dill pickle, cut into slices
- 1 tablespoon of butter
- 1 pound of prosciutto
- 1 onion, cut into slices
- 1 cup of Swiss cheese, sliced
- 1/4 cup of mayonnaise
- Pork rub, enough to coat the meat
- 3 and 1/2 pounds of pork shoulder
- 1/4 cup of Dijon mustard
- 4 bread rolls, slice in halved
- 1 tablespoon of vegetable oil

Instructions
1. Let the grill preheat to 250°F.
2. Rub the pork rub on pork, place on grill grates—smoke for 1 hour, and flip and grill on the other side for another hour.
3. In a pot, add chicken stock and onion. Add pork to the pot. Cover with foil and braise for 2 hours.
4. Raise temperature to 300 °F, let it braise for another hour.
5. Toss the meat in reduced sauce.
6. Take off from grill.
7. Place a pan over the grill and add butter and coat the rolls, press with hands.
8. Mix mayonnaise, mustard, and drizzle over the rolls.
9. Make the sandwich by combining pork and the rest of the ingredients.
10. Serve right away.

5.10 Cider Brined Pork Chops with Apple-Pear Compote

(**Ready in about**: 80 minutes | **Serving**: 4| **Difficulty**: Medium)
Nutrition per serving: Kcal: 303| **Fat**: 13 g| **Net Carbs**: 2 g| **Protein**: 38 g

Ingredients:
- 1/4 cup of kosher salt
- 3 pods of star anise
- 2 cinnamon sticks
- 6 6-8 ounces of bone-in pork chops; single-cut
- 12 black peppercorns
- 6 cloves
- 1-inch of fresh ginger, crushed
- 1/4 cup of apple cider
- 3 tablespoons of butter, divided
- 3 tablespoons of minced onion
- 1/2 teaspoon of cinnamon
- 1/4 teaspoon of ground nutmeg
- 1/2 cup of apple cider
- 1/4 teaspoon of cloves
- 2 tablespoons of olive oil
- 3 cups of diced pears and apples
- 1/2 cup of chicken stock
- 2 teaspoons of fresh thyme leaves
- 2 tablespoons of Dijon mustard
- 24 cups of water

Instructions
1. To make the brine, in a pan, add water and salt. Heat until salt dissolves.
2. Turn off the heat and add ginger, 1/4 cup of apple cider, 2 cinnamon sticks, 12 black peppercorns, star anise pods, 6 cloves, 1/4 cup kosher salt. Mix well and let it steep; cool it with ice until it reaches room temperature.
3. Make it to 24 cups of water by adding cool water. Keep in the fridge.
4. Add pork chops in a big sealable bag or a glass dish with a lid. Add enough brine until they are submerged.
5. Keep it submerged for 4 hours or overnight.
6. 1 hour before cooking, take the pork chops out.
7. Wash with water and pat dry. Let the pork chops rest at room temperature for 1 hour.
8. In a large pan, make the compote. Heat 2 tablespoons of butter. Add a pinch of salt and chopped shallot, sauté for 2-3 minutes, add pears and apple—Cook for 3-5 minutes.
9. Add 1/4 teaspoon of cloves, 1/2 teaspoon of cinnamon, 2 teaspoons of fresh thyme leave, and 1/4 teaspoon of ground nutmeg. Mix well.
10. Raise the heat, add apple vinegar, chicken stock. Let it simmer. Turn the heat to low, and cook for 5 minutes.
11. Turn off the heat and add in 1 tablespoon of butter, mustard, and salt if required.
12. Preheat the Traeger to 500 °F, keep the lid closed for 15 minutes.
13. Rub olive oil over pork chops.
14. Place directly on the grill and cook for 7 minutes with a closed lid.
15. Flip the meat and cook for 5-12 minutes, until internal temperature reaches 150°F.
16. Let it rest for 10 minutes.
17. Serve with pear apple compote.

5.11 Smoked Ribs

(**Ready in about**: 6 hours and 20 minutes | **Serving**: 8| **Difficulty**: Medium)
Nutrition per serving: Kcal: 212| **Fat**: 12 g| **Net Carbs**: 14 g| **Protein**: 17 g

Ingredients:
- 1/2 cup of BBQ sauce, divided
- 2 racks of ribs
- 4 tablespoons of yellow mustard
- 1 cup of apple juice, divided
- Dry rub, as needed

Finishing Sauce:
- 3 tablespoons of honey
- 2 cup of BBQ sauce
- 3 tablespoons of brown sugar

Instructions
1. Clean the ribs and remove the membrane, tear it off.
2. Add the dry rub to a dish.
3. Spread the mustard all over the ribs. Coat in dry rub completely.
4. Cover with plastic wrap. Keep in the fridge for two hours or overnight.
5. Preheat the Traeger to smoker 225°F keep the bone side down and let it smoke for 3 hours.
6. In a spray bottle, mix 1/2 a cup of water and equal volume apple juice and spray on ribs every 30 minutes.
7. After 3 hours, take out the ribs.
8. Wrap the ribs in aluminum foil. Mix 1/2 cup of apple juice and equal volume BBQ sauce. Pour over ribs and seal well.
9. Again, smoke ribs for 2 hours at 225°F.
10. In a bowl, for finishing sauce, mix brown sugar, BBQ sauce, and honey. Take out ribs from smoker and coat ribs with finishing sauce and serve.

5.12 Pork Butt Burnt Ends

(**Ready in about**: 4 hours and 20 minutes | **Serving**: 15| **Difficulty**: Medium)
Nutrition per serving: Kcal: 257| **Fat**: 9 g| **Net Carbs**: 14 g| **Protein**: 21 g

Ingredients:
- 1 cup of Sweet & Smokey rub
- 2 cups of BBQ sauce
- 3 tablespoons of honey
- 10-pounds of pork butt, bone-in
- 5 tablespoons. of butter, cut into cubes
- 3 tablespoons. of brown sugar

Instructions
1. Let the smoker preheat to 250°F.
2. Chop pork into 1 by 1 piece.
3. In a bowl, add pieces and coat with rub well.
4. Place all pieces on an aluminum foil or grill safe oiled baking sheet. Smoke for 2-3 hours until they develop a nice color.
5. Take out from grill and place in new baking sheets. In another bowl, add brown sugar, BBQ sauce, and honey. Cover the pieces well and cover with aluminum foil.
6. Again, smoke them for 1 and a half hours, stirring after every 30 minutes, cook until the internal temperature reaches 190°F, as read by a meat thermometer.
7. Serve right away.

5.13 Smoked Spiral Ham with Honey Glaze

(**Ready in about**: 3 hours and 20 minutes | **Serving**: 12| **Difficulty**: Medium)
Nutrition per serving: Kcal: 321| **Fat**: 19 g| **Net Carbs**: 13 g| **Protein**: 21 g

Ingredients:
- 8-10 pounds of smoked spiral ham Honey Glaze:
- 1 cup of packed brown sugar
- 3 tablespoons of honey
- 2 and 1/4 cups of ginger ale
- 1 and 1/2 teaspoons of Dijon mustard
- 4 and 1/2 teaspoons of apple cider vinegar
- 2 cloves of minced garlic

Instructions
1. In a pan, mix brown sugar, apple cider vinegar, ginger ale, and honey. Let it boil and reduce it by half, cook for almost 15 minutes. Add in the rest of the ingredients. Except for pork. Cook for 5 minutes. Turn off the heat.
2. Clean and trim the ham, pour honey glaze between the pieces. Do not completely detach the pieces and brush with the remaining glaze.
3. Let the Traeger smoker preheat to 230-240°F.
4. Place the glazed ham in a tray and put the tray in Traeger, and close the lid. Keep basting the ham after every 20 minutes.
5. It will take 3 hours. Serve right away.

5.14 Easy Smoked Pork Butt

(**Ready in about**: 17 hours and 15 minutes | **Serving**: 16| **Difficulty**: Medium)
Nutrition per serving: Kcal: 217| **Fat**: 10 g| **Net Carbs**: 4g| **Protein**: 27 g

Ingredients:
- 8-10 pounds of pork shoulder, bone-in roast
- 3 tablespoons of yellow mustard
- 1/2 cup of sweet & smoky rub

Instructions
1. Let the Traeger grill preheat to 225°F.
2. Safe 1 tablespoon of sweet & smoky rub for later use.
3. Cover the cleaned pork shoulder with yellow mustard. Cover in sweet & smoky rub; make sure it is covered well.
4. Place the coated pork on grill grates. Close the lid.
5. Smoke until internal temperature reaches (as read by a meat thermometer) 195 °F or 201°F. Total time will be 15-20 hours.
6. Let it rest for 1 hour. Sprinkle the reserved rub all over and serve.

5.15 Cider Brined Pulled Pork

(**Ready in about**: 9 hours and 15 minutes | **Serving**: 24| **Difficulty**: Medium)
Nutrition per serving: Kcal: 243| Fat: 8 g| Net Carbs: 14g| **Protein**: 23 g

Ingredients:
- 8 pounds of pork butt
- 8 cups of apple cider
- Rub Ingredients:
- 5 tablespoons of brown sugar
- 2 tablespoons of smoked paprika
- 1 tablespoon of garlic powder
- 2 tablespoons of kosher salt
- 5 tablespoons of sugar
- 1 tablespoon of black pepper
- 1 tablespoon of onion powder

Instructions
1. In a bowl, add all the rub ingredients. Mix until sugar and salt are dissolved.
2. In a large pot, add apple cider. Add in 1/2 of the rub ingredients. Mix well. Add in the pork butt keep it submerged.
3. Keep in the fridge for 8 hours and less than 12 hours —It is important.
4. Keep safe the rest of the rub ingredients.
5. Let the smoker preheat to 225°F. Keep the lid closed. Keep safe the brine and pat dry the pork. With the reserved rub, massage the pork.
6. Place meat on grill grates directly, keep the fatty side up—Cook for 3 hours. After every hour, brush the pork with marinade.
7. Add 4-6 cups of brine to a pot and let it boil.
8. Raise the temperature of the smoker to 250 °F after 3 hours.
9. Place the roast in aluminum foil, add 2 cups of boiled brine in, and cook for 6-8 hours or until the thickest part's internal temperature (as read by a meat thermometer) reaches 200°F.
10. Cover the meat with aluminum foil if it is browning too much.
11. Let it rest for 20 minutes. Slice and serve.

5.16 Easy Smoked Pork Loin

(**Ready in about**: 3 hours and 20 minutes | **Serving**: 24| **Difficulty**: Medium)
Nutrition per serving: Kcal: 231| Fat: 7 g| Net Carbs: 11 g| **Protein**: 28 g

Ingredients:
- Pork Loin Dry rub, as needed
- 10-11 pounds of pork loin

Instructions
1. Let the grill preheat to 220°F. May use combination pellets for this recipe.
2. Clean and trim the pork loin.
3. Rub the dry rub on pork. Let it rest at room temperature for 30 minutes.
4. Place meat directly on grill grates fat side up, cook for 2-3 hours at 220 °F until internal temperature (as read by a meat thermometer) reaches 145°F.
5. Let it rest for 10 minutes. Slice and serve.

5.17 Smoked Pork Chops with Ale-Balsamic Glaze
(Ready in about: 1 hour and 20 minutes | **Serving**: 4| **Difficulty**: Medium)
Nutrition per serving: Kcal: 211| **Fat**: 8 g| **Net Carbs**: 10.7 g| **Protein**: 23.7 g

Ingredients:
- 4 8-ounce chops bone-in pork
- 1/2 cup of balsamic vinegar
- 3/4 cup of ginger ale
- 1/4 cup of brown sugar
- Traeger Pork & Poultry rub
- 2 sprigs of rosemary, chopped

Instructions
1. Let the Traeger preheat to 165 °F, keep the lid closed for 15 minutes, and use super smoke if possible.
2. Coat the pork well in Pork & Poultry rub.
3. Place the ribs on grill grates and smoke for 1/2 an hour.
4. Additionally, add balsamic vinegar, ginger ale, rosemary leaves, and brown sugar in a pan on medium flame until it becomes a slightly thick cook for 15-20 minutes.
5. Take out the ribs, let the smoker's temperature rise to 500 °F, and preheat with the lid closed for 15 minutes.
6. Drizzle olive oil on ribs and cook for 5 minutes at 500°F.
7. Flip the ribs and baste with glaze. Cook until the internal temperature reaches 145 °F or until 5 minutes.
8. Let it rest 10 minutes before slicing.

55.18 Grilled Pork Chops with Pineapple-Mango Salsa

((**Ready in about**: 50 minutes | **Serving**: 4| **Difficulty**: Medium)
Nutrition per serving: Kcal: 199| Fat: 7 g| Net Carbs: 8.9 g| **Protein**: 12.4 g

Ingredients:
- 2 tablespoons of Traeger Pork & Poultry rub
- 2 tablespoons of cilantro
- 3 16-ounce of thick-cut bone-in pork chops
- 1/2 of a pineapple, cut into cubes
- 1 diced red bell pepper
- 1 clove of minced garlic
- 1 mango, cut into cubes
- 1 diced and seeded jalapeno
- 1/2 chopped red onion
- 1/4 cup of Traeger BBQ apricot sauce
- Juice of a lime
- Salt and pepper, to taste

Instructions
1. Rub the Pork & Poultry mix on pork chops well. Keep in the fridge for 1/2 an hour.
2. To make mango pineapple salsa, mix mange cubes, red bell pepper, pineapple cubes, onion, cilantro and jalapeno, garlic, salt, pepper, and lime juice. Mix well set it aside.
3. Let the Traeger preheat to 500°F. Keep the lid closed for 15 minutes.
4. Cook the pork chops for 7-10 minutes on each side on the grill. Flip and brush with BBQ apricot sauce and cook until internal temperature (as read by a meat thermometer) reaches 145°F.
5. Serve on the side of the sauce.

5.19 BBQ Pulled Pork Cubano Sandwich

(**Ready in about**: 10-20 minutes | **Serving**: 4| **Difficulty**: Medium)
Nutrition per serving: Kcal: 178| Fat: 9 g| Net Carbs: 10.4 g| **Protein**: 13 g

Ingredients:
- Juice from 4 oranges
- Salt and pepper: to taste
- Juice from 4 limes
- 4 tablespoons of chili powder
- 1 loaf of crusty bread
- 8 ounces of leftover pulled pork
- 3 tablespoons of brown sugar
- Melted butter, as needed
- 4 Swiss cheese slices
- Yellow mustard, as needed

Instructions
1. In a pan, on medium flame, add lime juice, pepper, salt, orange juice, chili powder, brown sugar mix until it turns syrupy.
2. Mix with leftover pulled pork.
3. Let the Traeger preheat to 500 °F preheat with lid closed.
4. Place 2 cast iron pans on the grill, let them heat up by closing the lid.
5. Slice the bread, spread butter on one side and the other side mustard. Add cheese slices, sliced ham, and pulled pork, and pickles if you want.
6. Place sandwiches in a pan put the other pan on top to smash the sandwich. Close the lid and cook for 4-5 minutes, until cheese is melted.

5.20 Smoked Pulled Pork Enchiladas

(**Ready in about**: 1 hour and 5 minutes | **Serving**: 12| **Difficulty**: Easy)
Nutrition per serving: Kcal: 634| Fat: 18 g| Net Carbs: 18 g| **Protein**: 21 g

Ingredients:
- 4 cups of shredded smoked pulled pork
- 1 28-ounce can of enchilada sauce
- 2 tablespoons of chili lime seasoning blend
- 4 cups of Mexican-blend cheese, shredded
- 12-15 tortillas

Instructions
1. Let the smoker preheat to 325°F.
2. Pour enchilada sauce and spread thinly in an oiled baking pan.
3. Mix 2 cups of cheese, chili lime seasoning with pulled pork.
4. Coat both sides of shells in sauce and stuff with pork filling 1/3 of a cup.
1. Wrap tortilla tightly and place in prepared baking pan.
2. Pour the enchilada sauce over the tortilla in a baking pan. Sprinkle cheese over.
3. Bake until everything is heated through or for 30-40 minutes.
4. Serve right away.

5.21 Pineapple-Glazed Smoked Ham

(**Ready in about**: 3 hour and 20 minutes | **Serving**: 12| **Difficulty**: Medium)
Nutrition per serving: Kcal: 188| **Fat**: 8 g| **Net Carbs**: 17 g| **Protein**: 2 g

Ingredients:
- 1 spiral smoked ham
  Glaze:
- 1 cup of brown sugar
- 2 tablespoons of cornstarch
- 1 20-ounce can of pineapple chunks
- 1/3 cup of orange juice
- 1 stick of butter
- 2 tablespoons of cold water
- 1 and a half-ounce of triple sec liquor

Instructions
1. Preheat the Traeger to 325°F.
2. Slice the ham's top in a crisscross, put in a baking pan with aluminum foil underneath.
3. Place in preheat the grill and cook for 60 minutes.
4. Meanwhile, in a pan, add orange juice, pineapple, brown sugar, and butter. Let it boil.
5. As it's boiling, add triple sec. in a mug, mix corn starch with water and add in boiling mixture.
6. Let the sauce thicken slightly. Take off the heat.
7. Use 1/2 of the glaze and brush the ham.
8. Cook for 1/2 an hour, brush again with glaze. Cook for 15-20 minutes until the meat's internal temperature reaches 135°F.
9. Switch grill to smoke mode and smoked ham for 20-25 minutes.
10. Let it rest for 10 minutes.
11. Slice and serve with glaze.

5.22 Pork Shoulder

(**Ready in about**: 7 hours | **Serving**: 12| **Difficulty**: Medium)
Nutrition per serving: Kcal: 134| **Fat**: 9 g| **Net Carbs**: 8 g| **Protein**: 12 g

Ingredients:
  Vinegar Sauce
- 6 pounds of pork shoulders
- 1 cup of paprika
- 1 cup of brown sugar
- 1 and 1/4 cup of white sugar
- 3 tablespoons of black pepper
- 1 gallon of apple cider vinegar
- 1 32-ounce package of xanthan gum
- 1/3 cup of salt
- 3 tablespoons of cayenne
- 1 cup of water
  For Injection:
- 3 cups of vinegar sauce
- 2 cans of peach nectar

Instructions
1. In a pan, add ingredients of vinegar sauce and let it boil.
2. Clean and score the meat. Mix the injection ingredients.
3. Inject the pork before smoking during 6 hours.
4. Let it smoke until the internal temperature reaches (as read by a meat thermometer) 195-225 °F
5. Serve hot.

5.23 Sausage Stuffed Mushrooms

(**Ready in about**: 1 hours | **Serving**: 4| **Difficulty**: Easy)
Nutrition per serving: Kcal: 134| **Fat**: 9 g| **Net Carbs**: 8 g| **Protein**: 12 g

Ingredients:
- 2 cups of Italian ground sausage
- 4 cups of large mushrooms
- 1/2 cup of seasoned bread crumbs
- 1 teaspoon of garlic
- 1/2 cup of Parmesan cheese
- 2 tablespoons of finely chopped onions
- 1 cup of chopped spinach

Instructions
1. Let the grill preheat to 400°F. Place cleaned and trimmed mushroom on a buttered pan.
2. In a bowl, mix cheese, onions, spinach, garlic, bread crumbs, cheese, and sausage mix well.
3. Stuff the mushroom cap with a stuffing mix.
4. Smoke for 1/2 an hour at 400°F.
5. Serve right away.

5.24 Cherry Coke Ribs

(**Ready in about**: 7 hours | **Serving**: 12| **Difficulty**: Medium)
Nutrition per serving: Kcal: 406|**Fat**: 21 g| **Net Carbs**: 26 g| **Protein**: 22 g

Ingredients:
- 1/2 cup of barbecue rub
- 2 racks of baby back ribs

  Sauce:
- 1/4 of a cup of Bourbon brown sugar
- 1 cup of cherry cola
- 1 cup of BBQ sauce

Instructions
1. Let the grill preheat to 180-200°F. Coat the ribs with dry BBQ rub.
2. Put on grill and smoke for 4-5 hours.
3. Raise the temperature to 275-300°F.
4. Put the ribs in a tin pan.
5. Mix the sauce ingredients, and pour over ribs.
6. Cover the ribs and cook for 3-4 hours. Uncover and baste after every hour cook to your desired wellness.
7. Serve hot.

5.25 Smoked Pork Tenderloin

(**Ready in about**: 3 hours and 30 minutes| **Serving**: 4| **Difficulty**: Medium)
Nutrition per serving: Kcal: 231|**Fat**: 14 g| **Net Carbs**: 6 g| **Protein**: 19 g

Ingredients:
- 2 1-1/2-pound of pork tenderloins silver skin trimmed
- 1/2 cup of apple juice
- 1/4 cup of brown sugar
- 3 tablespoons of honey
- 2 tablespoons thyme leaves
- 1/2 tablespoon of black pepper
- 3 tablespoons of Traeger Pork & Poultry rub

Instructions
1. In a bowl, add Traeger Pork & Poultry rub, black pepper, apple juice, thyme leaves, warmed honey, and brown sugar. Mix well.
2. Coat the pork well with spice rub mix and place in a bowl cover with plastic wrap.
3. Keep in the fridge for 2-3 hours.
4. Preheat the Traeger to 225 °F, use super smoke.
5. Place meat directly on grill and smoke for 2-3 hours until internal temperature reaches 145°F.
6. Let it rest and serve.

5.26 Sticky Teriyaki BBQ Pork and Pineapple Skewers

(**Ready in about**: 3 hours and 10 minutes| **Serving**: 2| **Difficulty**: Medium)
Nutrition per serving: Kcal: 188|**Fat**: 9 g| **Net Carbs**: 8 g| **Protein**: 17 g

Ingredients:
- 18 Pieces of fresh pineapple
- 6 scallions
- 1 pound of pork sirloin
- 1 cup of marinade roast meat
- 6 skewers

Instructions
1. Thread pork, pineapple pieces, scallion pieces on a skewer.
2. Repeat until all ingredients are threaded.
3. Place skewers on a plate, pour marinade over them, coat well, cover, and refrigerate for 1-3 hours.
4. Let the Traeger preheat at 225°F.
5. Place skewers directly on the grill and cook for 10 minutes, turn once or more.

5.27 Smoked Moink Burger

(**Ready in about**: 1 hour and 10 minutes| **Serving**: 4| **Difficulty**: Medium)
Nutrition per serving: Kcal: 161|**Fat**: 7 g| **Net Carbs**: 12 g| **Protein**: 13 g

Ingredients:
- 1/4 cup of Worcestershire sauce
- 1 pound of ground sirloin
- Salt and black pepper, to taste
- 1 teaspoon of minced garlic
- 1/2 pound of ground pork

Instructions
1. In a bowl, mix all ingredients. Make into 6 patties.
2. Preheat the Traeger to 350 °F, keep the lid closed for 15 minutes.
3. Cook for almost an hour, until internal temperature reaches 160 °F
4. Enjoy with burger buns.

5.28 Braised Pork Chile Verde

(**Ready in about**: 2 hours and 20 minutes| **Serving**: 6| **Difficulty**: Medium)
Nutrition per serving: Kcal: 181|**Fat**: 10.2 g| **Net Carbs**: 9 g| **Protein**: 12 g

Ingredients:
- 2-3 pounds of pork shoulder, sliced into 1 and a half-inch cube
- 4 tablespoons of olive oil
- Salt and black pepper, to taste
- 1 pound of tomatillos, washed
- 1 tablespoon of all-purpose flour
- 2 cups of chicken stock
- 4 cloves of garlic
- 2 cans of green chili
- 1 onion, slice into one-inch chunks
- 1/4 cup of cilantro, chopped
- 1 tablespoon of cumin
- Juice of 1/2 lime
- 2 jalapenos
- 1 tablespoon of dried oregano

Instructions
1. Coat pork in all-purpose flour. Season with black pepper and salt.
2. Preheat the grill to 500 °F for 15 minutes.
3. Put an iron skillet on the bottom rack and let it heat for 20 minutes.
4. Add onion, tomatillos, garlic, and jalapeños, to a parchment paper baking tray.
5. Drizzle 2 tablespoons of olive oil, black pepper, and salt on vegetables, coat well.
6. Add 2 tablespoons of olive oil in a preheated iron pan and add the pork shoulder. Do not overcrowd the meat.
7. Place the baking tray of vegetables on the top rack and close the lid.
8. Cook for 20 minutes. Vegetables and pork will develop a nice brown color.
9. Take the vegetables out after 20 minutes, blend until pureed.
10. Add puree, chicken stock, pork, cumin, oregano, and chili in a pan.
11. Keep the pan on the grill and cook for 325 °F. Cook for 1 hour to 90 minutes.
12. When the pork is tender, you may add chicken stock and cook more if all the liquid is gone.
13. Serve right away with tacos or sandwiches.

5.29 BBQ Spare Ribs with Spicy Mandarin Glaze

(**Ready in about**: 5 hours and 15 minutes| **Serving**: 6| **Difficulty**: Medium)
Nutrition per serving: Kcal: 213|**Fat**: 13 g| **Net Carbs**: 14 g| **Protein**: 16 g

Ingredients:
- 1 cup of honey
- 3 spare ribs, remove the membrane
- 1 and 1/2 cups of brown sugar
- 1 teaspoon of soy sauce
- 3 tablespoons of yellow mustard
- Traeger Pork & Poultry rub
- 1 teaspoon of sesame oil
- 1 tablespoon of Worcestershire sauce
- 1 teaspoon of garlic powder
- 1 and 1/2 cups of Traeger Mandarin glaze

Instructions
1. Preheat the Traeger to 225 °F keep the lid closed for 15 minutes.
2. Mix Worcestershire sauce and mustard and rub on meat well.
3. Place on the grill and smoke for 3 hours.
4. Put ribs in a foil pan. Spread honey on the ribs and sprinkle Pork & Poultry rub and brown sugar and pour Dr. Pepper over.
5. Cover the ribs with aluminum foil and cook for 2 hours at 275°F.
6. Take the ribs out and switch the grill to high. Combine garlic powder, Mandarin glaze, soy sauce, and sesame oil.
7. Brush the ribs with glaze mix and cook on Traeger for 8-10 minutes more.

5.30 Smoked Bacon Wrapped Meatballs

(**Ready in about**: 2 hours and 10 minutes| **Serving**: 8| **Difficulty**: Medium)
Nutrition per serving: Kcal: 243|**Fat**: 17 g| **Net Carbs**: 13 g| **Protein**: 17.8 g

Ingredients:
- 1/2 tablespoon of kosher salt
- 1 pound of Italian sausage
- 1/4 tablespoon of black pepper
- 1 pound of ground beef
- 1 tablespoon of paprika
- 2 jalapenos
- 1 pound of bacon
- 1 cup of cheddar cheese
- 1 whole egg

Instructions
1. Slice the jalapenos, may or may not remove seeds.
2. Cut the bacon in half.
3. In a bowl, mix seasonings, meat, and egg. With clean hands, mix and set it aside.
4. Slice the cheese into 8 portions.
5. Divide the meat into 8 balls and place on parchment paper. Flatten them and add cheese and jalapeno and again shape them into a ball.
6. Wrap the balls in bacon slices, secure with a toothpick.
7. Place meatballs in Trager and cook for 1 hour at 225 °F
8. Raise the heat to 350 °F after 1 hour and cook until the internal temperature reaches 160°F.

5.31 Smoked Spicy Asian Pork Ribs

(**Ready in about**: 6 hours and 15 minutes| **Serving**: 15| **Difficulty**: Medium)
Nutrition per serving: Kcal: 612|**Fat**: 29 g| **Net Carbs**: 38 g| **Protein**:33 g

Ingredients:
- 1/2 cup of Togarashi seasoning
- 2 racks of baby back ribs
Sauce:
- 1/4 cup of rice wine vinegar
- 1/4 cup of soy sauce
- 1 tablespoon of Sriracha
- 2 tablespoons of garlic chili paste
- 1 cup of sweet chili sauce
- 1 teaspoon of powdered ginger
- 1/2 cup of pineapple juice

Instructions
1. Let the grill preheat to 180-190 °F or smoke setting.
2. Coat ribs with Togarashi mix and place on grill.
3. Smoke for 4-5 hours.
4. In a bowl, add all the sauce ingredients, mix well.
5. Put ribs in a pan and pour the sauce all over, cover with foil.
6. Put back on the grill and cook at 250-275 °F for 2-3 hours, but keep checking after every hour.

5.32 Grilled Bacon-Wrapped Pork Chops with Rosemary

(**Ready in about**: 30-30 minutes| **Serving**: 6| **Difficulty**: Medium)
Nutrition per serving: Kcal: 395|**Fat**: 22 g| **Net Carbs**: 2 g| **Protein**: 23 g

Ingredients:
- 6 slices of bacon
- 6 pork chops, center-cut
- 6 sprigs rosemary
- 2 tablespoons of Dry BBQ rub

Instructions
1. Let the Traeger preheat to 325°F. Coat the pork chops dry BBQ rub.
2. Put 1 rosemary sprig on each pork chop, wrap in bacon. Secure with a toothpick.
3. Cook for 10 minutes and turn it over. Cook until the internal temperature shows 145°F.
4. Remove and serve right away.

5.33 Traeger Pork Tenderloin with Mustard Sauce

(**Ready in about**: 25 minutes | **Serving**: 4| **Difficulty**: Medium)
Nutrition per serving: Kcal: 87|**Fat**: 6 g| **Net Carbs**: 2 g| **Protein**: 6 g

Ingredients:
- 1 pork tenderloin
- 1 and 1/2 tablespoons of cooking oil
- 1 teaspoon of red pepper flake
- 1 and 1/2 tablespoons of Dijon mustard
- 1 teaspoon of paprika
- 1/2 teaspoon of onion powder
- 3/4 teaspoon of salt
- 1/2 teaspoon of parsley flakes
- 1/2 teaspoon of granulated garlic
- 1 and 1/2 tablespoons of white vinegar
- 1/4 teaspoon of ground black pepper

Instructions
1. Let the pellet grill preheat to 350°F.
2. Combine all ingredients and rub onto pork well.
1. Put on grill cook for 20 minutes, turn every 5 minutes until internal temperature reaches 150°F.

5.34 Garlic Herb Grilled Pork Chops

(**Ready in about:** 10-15 minutes | **Serving:** 4 | **Difficulty:** Medium)
Nutrition per serving: Kcal: 323 | **Fat:** 6 g | **Net Carbs:** 4 g | **Protein:** 11 g

Ingredients:
- 1 cup of olive oil
- 1 tablespoon of Italian seasoning
- 6 pork chops, boneless
- 1/2 teaspoon of black pepper
- 2 tablespoons of lemon juice
- 1 teaspoon of salt
- 4 cloves of minced garlic

Instructions
1. In a bowl, mix Italian seasoning, pepper, olive oil, salt, minced garlic, and lemon juice.
2. Mix it well.
3. In a large sealable bag, add pork chops and pour marinade over and keep in the fridge for 1/2 an hour till 2 hours.
4. Let the Traeger preheat to 400°F.
5. Cook pork chops on the grill for 3 minutes on each side with the lid closed until the internal temperature reaches 145°F.

5.35 Pigs in Blanket

(**Ready in about:** 25 minutes | **Serving:** 6 | **Difficulty:** Medium)
Nutrition per serving: Kcal: 267 | **Fat:** 22 g | **Net Carbs:** 7 g | **Protein:** 9 g

Ingredients:
- 1 pack of biscuit dough, refrigerated
- 1 package of hotdogs, slice into thirds

Instructions
1. Let the Traeger preheat to 350°F.
2. Wrap the biscuit dough around cut hot dogs. Place on parchment paper.
3. Place the baking sheet on the grill cook for 20-25 minutes with the lid closed.
4. Cook until biscuits turn golden brown.

5.36 Traeger Smoked Stuffed Pork Tenderloin

(**Ready in about:** 80 minutes | **Serving:** 8 | **Difficulty:** Medium)
Nutrition per serving: Kcal: 610 | **Fat:** 31 g | **Net Carbs:** 5 g | **Protein:** 23 g

Ingredients:
- 1/2 cup of cheddar cheese
- 1 cup of spinach leaves
- 1 pork tenderloin
- 1 pound of sliced bacon
- 1/2 cup of provolone cheese

Rub:
- 1/2 teaspoon of granulated garlic
- 1 teaspoon of red pepper flake
- 1 teaspoon of salt
- 1 teaspoon of paprika
- 1/2 teaspoon of onion powder
- 1/4 teaspoon of cumin
- 1/2 teaspoon of pepper

Instructions
1. Let the grill preheat to 325°F.
2. In the center of the tenderloin, place spinach leaves on the whole length of the tenderloin.
3. Place cheese on top of tenderloin.
4. Roll the tenderloin, so the cheese and spinach are inside.
5. In a bowl, add all the ingredients of rub, coat the tenderloin in this rub mix.
6. Wrap the tenderloin in bacon.
7. Put wrapped tenderloin in the middle of the rack and cook for 1 hour until internal temperature reaches 145 °F
8. Take out from grill rest and slice.

5.37 Traeger Blackened Pork Chops

(**Ready in about:** 25 minutes | **Serving:** 6 | **Difficulty:** Medium)
Nutrition per serving: Kcal: 333 | **Fat:** 18 g | **Net Carbs:** 1 g | **Protein:** 25 g

Ingredients:
- 1/4 cup o blackening seasoning
- 6 pork chops
- Salt and pepper, to taste

Instructions
1. Let the grill preheat to 375 °F. Coat pork chops in the seasoning with salt and pepper.
2. Grill for 7-8 minutes, with the lid closed, and then flip
3. Cook until the internal temperature (as read by a meat thermometer) reaches 140-142°F.
4. Let it rest for 10 minutes before slicing.

5.38 Shake and Bake Pork Chops

(**Ready in about:** 25 minutes | **Serving:** 8 | **Difficulty:** Medium)
Nutrition per serving: Kcal: 276 | **Fat:** 12 g | **Net Carbs:** 30 g | **Protein:** 7 g

Ingredients:
- 8 6-8 ounces of bone-in pork chops
- 2 cups of plain breadcrumbs
- 1/2 teaspoon of garlic powder
- 2 cups of plain panko
- 1/3 cup of avocado oil
- 1/4 teaspoon of dried basil
- 1 and 1/2 teaspoons salt
- 1 teaspoon of paprika
- 1/2 teaspoon of dried parsley
- 1 teaspoon of onion powder
- 1/2 teaspoon of pepper
- 1/4 teaspoon of dried oregano

Instructions
1. Add all ingredients in a large sealable bad, mix to combine
2. Coat meat in flour, then in egg, then in shake and bake mix.
3. Let the grill preheat to 375 °F, and place breaded meat pieces in a baking tray.
4. Place tray on grill and cook for 20 minutes.
5. Serve hot.

CHAPTER 6
Traeger Grill Beef Recipes

Chapter 6: Traeger Grill Beef Recipes

6.1 Smoked Tri-Tip

(**Ready in about**: 2 hours and 15 minutes| **Serving**: 8| **Difficulty**: Medium)
Nutrition per serving: Kcal: 244| **Fat**: 13 g| **Net Carbs**: 0 g| **Protein**: 29 g
Ingredients:
- Roasted garlic blend
- 1 beef roast tri-ti

Instructions
1. Preheat the Traeger to 175°F.
2. Coat the beef with seasoning, generously.
3. Place on grill and cook for 90 minutes.
4. Transfer to a plate cover with foil.
5. Preheat the Traeger to 400-450°F.
6. Place the steak on the grill and cook until the doneness you want.
7. Rest it before serving.

6.2 T-Bone Grilled Steak

(**Ready in about**: 2 hours and 10 minutes| **Serving**: 6| **Difficulty**: Medium)
Nutrition per serving: Kcal: 656| **Fat**: 4 g| **Net Carbs**: 0 g| **Protein**: 56 g
Ingredients:
- Salt and pepper, to taste
- 2 pounds of T-bone steak

Instructions
1. Preheat the Traeger to 200°F.
2. Place the steak on the grill and cook till the internal temperature (as read by a meat thermometer) reaches 115°F.
3. Take off the grill and season with pepper and salt.
4. Sear on the skillet.
5. Let it rest for 5 minutes before serving.

6.3 Smoked Teriyaki Beef Jerky

Ready in about: 4 hours + 24 hours' marination | **Servings**: 16|
Difficulty: Medium)
Nutrition per serving: Kcal: 215| **Fat**: 11 g| **Net Carbs**: 2 g| **Protein**: 22 g
Ingredients:
- 1/3 cup of oil
- 1 tablespoon of minced garlic
- 1 and 1/2 cups of soy sauce
- 4 pounds of flank steak
- 1/2 cup of brown sugar
- 2 teaspoons of onion powder
- 1 cup of pineapple juice
- 1/2 teaspoon of garlic powder
- 1 teaspoon of powdered ginger
- 1/3 cup of apple cider vinegar
- 3 tablespoons of Sriracha

Instructions
1. Slice the steaks in strips with the grain.
2. In a large bowl, add all marinade ingredients. Mix well and pour in 2 separate zip lock bags.
3. Add meats in both pouches, coat well, and marinate for 1 day.
4. Preheat the Traeger to 160-180°F.
5. Take meat strips out and pat dry. Spray the racks with oil and place strips on the racks.
6. Smoke for 3-4 hours, or until cooked to your liking.
7. The more you cook, the drier they will get.

6.4 Meatball Stuffed Shells

(**Ready in about**: 2 hours and 10 minutes | **Serving**: 12| **Difficulty**: Medium)
Nutrition per serving: Kcal: 727| **Fat**: 24 g| **Net Carbs**: 80 g| **Protein**: 42 g
Ingredients:
- 2 pounds of ground beef
- 1/2 teaspoon of garlic powder
- 8 cups of marinara sauce
- 24 shells, pasta
- 1/2 teaspoon of onion powder
- 2 teaspoons of Italian seasoning blend
- 1/2 teaspoon of pepper
- 2 cups of shredded Italian blend cheese
- 1 whisked egg
- 2 cups of shredded mozzarella cheese
- 1 teaspoon of salt

Instructions
1. Preheat the Traeger to 350°F.
2. Cook pasta as per instructions.
3. Mix beef with all dry seasoning and egg.
4. Stuff every shell with the beef mix.
5. Place these shells in a baking pan.
6. Pour the sauce over and cheeses
7. Place the pan on the grill's top rack or on an inverted cake pan.
8. Bake for 30 to 45 minutes, until the internal temperature of the meat (as read by a meat thermometer) reaches 165 ° F.
9. Take off the grill. Let it rest, then serve.

6.5 Reverse-Seared Flat Iron Steak

(**Ready in about**: 2 hours and 10 minutes | **Serving**: 6| **Difficulty**: Medium)
Nutrition per serving: Kcal: 312| **Fat**: 9.1 g| **Net Carbs**: 2 g| **Protein**: 27 g
Ingredients:
- Salt and pepper, to taste
- 6 flat iron steaks

Instructions
1. Preheat the Traeger to smoke.
2. Place steak on the grill, and cook until internal temperature reaches 115°F.
3. Take off the grill, season with pepper and salt.
4. Place on a skillet over medium flame and sear on both sides.
5. Rest the steak and serve.

6.6 Tequila Lime Beef Tacos

(**Ready in about**: 3 hours | **Serving**: 12| **Difficulty**: Medium)
Nutrition per serving: Kcal: 335| Fat: 11 g| Net Carbs: 31 g| Protein: 27.7 g

Ingredients:
Roast:
- 2 tablespoons of pepper, salt, and garlic
- 4-pound of beef chuck roast
- 3 tablespoons chili margarita blend

Braising Liquid:
- 1 and 1/2 teaspoons of salt
- 4 ounces of silver tequila
- Puffy taco shells, 7-8 pieces
- Juice from 2 limes
- 2 cups beef broth
- 2 cans of el Pato
- 1 and 2/3 cup of warm water
- 2 and 1/2 cups of flour dough

Instructions
1. Preheat the Traeger to 225°F.
2. Season the meat with rub ingredients, place on grill.
3. Cook for 3 hours, flipping once halfway through.
4. Transfer meat in a baking dish.
5. Add all liquid braising ingredients and cover the dish.
6. Place on grill, cook at 325 °F for 1 hour.
7. Cook until it becomes shred able.
8. Place the meat shreds in puffy tacos serve with your favorite toppings.

6.7 Smoked and Seared Strip Steak

(**Ready in about**: 3 hours | **Serving**: 2| **Difficulty**: Medium)
Nutrition per serving: Kcal: 301| Fat: 10 g| Net Carbs: 2 g| Protein: 29.1 g

Ingredients:
- 2 strip steaks
- Olive oil, as needed
- Salt and pepper, to taste

Instructions
1. Coat the steaks in oil and season with salt and pepper.
2. Preheat the Traeger to 225 °F, place steaks on the grill, cook until internal temperature (as read by a meat thermometer) reaches 100°F.
3. Turn grill temperature to high, sear the steaks until the internal temperature reaches 120-130 °F, almost 3 minutes on each side.
4. Rest and serve.

6.8 Slow Smoked Beef Brisket

(**Ready in about**: 4 hours +24 Hours marination | **Servings**: 6-7|
Difficulty: Medium)
Nutrition per serving: Kcal: 311| Fat: 13 g| Net Carbs: 4 g| Protein: 30 g

Ingredients:
- 1/2 cup of BBQ sauce
- 12 pounds of beef brisket
- 1/2 cup of beef broth
- 2 tablespoons of vegetable oil
- 1/2 cup of apple juice
Rub:
- 2 teaspoons of chili powder
- 3 teaspoons of kosher salt
- 2 teaspoons of garlic powder
- 1 tablespoon of sugar
- 1 tablespoon of onion powder
- 3 tablespoons of coarse black pepper
- 2 teaspoons of chipotle powder
- 2 teaspoons of dry mustard

Instructions
1. In a bowl, mix all rub's ingredients. Keep safe in an air-tight jar.
2. Coat the brisket in olive oil, then in dry rub.
3. For 24 hours, marinate it. Put brisket fat side up on the grill.
4. Cook at 225 °F with the lid closed until the internal temperature reaches 150°F.
5. In a pan, add beef broth and apple juice with brisket. Cover with foil and place back on the grill.
6. Keep cooking until the internal temperature of the brisket (as read by a meat thermometer) reaches 190°F.
7. Turn the temperature of the grill to 190 °F. Cook meat for 3 hours.
8. Serve with BBQ sauce.

6.9 Chipotle Rubbed Tri-Tip

(**Ready in about**: 1 hour and 20 minutes | **Serving**: 4| **Difficulty**: Medium)
Nutrition per serving: Kcal: 287| Fat: 12 g| Net Carbs: 7 g| Protein: 29 g

Ingredients:
- 1 2-and-a-half-pound of beef tri-tip
- Olive oil, as needed

Spice Rub:
- 1 and 1/2 teaspoons of chipotle chili powder
- 1 tablespoon of coarse salt
- 1 teaspoon of granulated garlic
- 1 and 1/2 teaspoons of oregano
- 1/2 teaspoon of black pepper
- 1/2 teaspoon of ground cumin

Instructions
1. Preheat the Traeger to 225°F.
2. Mix all the spices of spice rub in a bowl.
3. Place the meat in a baking dish, and rub with spice rub. Press the seasoning in beef. Pour a little bit of olive oil and coat well.
4. Place meat on the grill, close the lid, and smoke for 45-60 minutes until internal temperature reaches 100 °F
5. Take the meat out on a plate and cover with aluminum foil.
6. Raise temperature to high, sear the meat for 3-4 minutes.
7. Serve.

6.10 The Perfect Cheeseburger

(**Ready in about**: 15 minutes | **Serving**: 6| **Difficulty**: Easy)
Nutrition per serving: Kcal: 251| Fat: 11 g| Net Carbs: 13 g| Protein: 27 g

Ingredients:
- 1 tomato cut into thin sliced
- 2 pounds of ground beef chuck
- Hamburger buns, 4 whole buns
- 1 thinly sliced onion
- Sharp cheddar, to taste
- 1 thinly sliced pickle
- Shredded iceberg lettuce, as needed

Instructions
1. Make ground beef into 4 patties. Season the patties with pepper and salt let them rest for a while.
2. Preheat the Traeger to smoke. Place patties on grill flip when they start to brown.
3. Cook to the doneness you like or until the internal temperature reaches 130-140°F.
4. Place sharp cheddar on patties, cook until it's melted.
5. Serve in buns with tomato, onion slices.

6.11 Pellet Grill Picanha

(**Ready in about**: 15 minutes | **Serving**: 6| **Difficulty**: Medium)
Nutrition per serving: Kcal: 286| Fat: 14 g| Net Carbs: 9 g| Protein: 29g

Ingredients:
- 1/2 teaspoon of black pepper
- 2 pounds of sirloin with the fat cap on
- 2 teaspoons of kosher salt

Instructions
1. Preheat the Traeger to 400-450°F.
2. Slice steaks into strips, 2" in width and 8" in length.
3. Coat the steak in salt (half) and black pepper.
4. Thread the meat on metal skewers. Thread fat cap first.
5. Make steak into C shape.
6. Use all slices of meat on different skewers.
7. Place skewers on the grill directly. Cook on each side for 3 minutes, flip and cook for another 3 minutes.
8. Cook until the internal temperature reaches 125°F.
9. Rest and serve with sprinkling the rest of the salt.

6.12 Beef Birria Tacos

(**Ready in about**: 5 hours and 15 minutes | **Serving**: 8| **Difficulty**: Medium)
Nutrition per serving: Kcal: 324| **Fat**: 12 g| **Net Carbs**: 14 g| **Protein**: 32 g

Ingredients:

Meat:
- 2 pounds of beef round tri-tip roast
- 4 tablespoons of adobo seasoning blend
- 2 pounds of beef chuck
- 1 teaspoon garlic powder
- 3 tablespoons of canola oil
- 1 teaspoon of salt

Braising Liquid:
- 1 tablespoon of beef bouillon
- 8 red chili peppers, mild
- 1 teaspoon garlic powder
- 3 cloves of garlic
- 1 teaspoon of salt
- 1 teaspoon of onion powder
- 1 tablespoon of chili powder
- 1/3 cup of apple cider vinegar
- 1 tablespoon of oregano
- 4 cups of hot water
- 1 diced onion
- 2 chipotle peppers

Instructions

1. Preheat the Traeger to 180-200°F.
2. Cut the beef into cubes and season with garlic powder, salt, and adobo.
3. In a skillet, brown the meat in a tablespoon of oil.
4. Place browned meat cubes in a Dutch oven.
5. Remove seeds for peppers and put them in a Dutch oven.
6. Smoke on the grill for 1 and 1/2 hours at 180-200°F.
7. Raise the grill's temperature to 300 °F, cook peppers for 1/2 an hour.
8. Take peppers out of the grill and put them in a blender with the rest of the ingredients.
9. Pulse on high until smooth. Pour over beef chunks.
10. Cover and cook for 2-4 hours, until beef is tender.
11. Shred the beef—place in tacos with cilantro, onion, tomato, and sour cream.

6.13 Smoked Prime Rib

(**Ready in about**: 3 hours and 40 minutes | **Serving**: 10| **Difficulty**: Medium)
Nutrition per serving: Kcal: 690| **Fat**: 60 g| **Net Carbs**: 3 g| **Protein**: 30 g

Ingredients:
- 1 tablespoon of black pepper
- 5 pounds of prime rib boneless, roast tied back
- 2 teaspoons of garlic powder
- 2 teaspoons of dried thyme
- 1 teaspoon of onion powder
- 2 tablespoons of brown sugar
- 2 teaspoons of dried rosemary
- 2 tablespoons of kosher salt

Instructions

1. In a bowl, add all ingredients except for meat. Mix well.
2. Coat the meat in this spice rub. Let it rest at room temperature for 60 minutes.
3. Preheat the Traeger to 225°F.
4. Place roast on grill fat side up, with the lid closed.
5. Smoke for 3 and 1/2 hours until the internal temperature reaches 120-130°F.
6. Rest and serve.

6.14 Philly Cheese Steak Sandwich

(**Ready in about**: 25 minutes | **Serving**: 4| **Difficulty**: Medium)
Nutrition per serving: Kcal: 673| **Fat**: 47 g| **Net Carbs**: 37 g| **Protein**: 47 g

Ingredients:
- 4 buns
- 1.5 pounds of thinly sliced rib-eye steak
- 1 thinly sliced onion
- 1 tablespoon of canola oil
- 1 thinly sliced bell pepper
- 4 slices of cheese
- 1/2 teaspoon of Pepper
- 1 teaspoon of salt

Instructions

1. Preheat the Traeger to 450°F.
2. Put a cast-iron pan on the grill and heat for 15 minutes. Add oil, green peppers, onion. Cook until translucent.
3. Add in seasoned steak with pepper and salt. Cook for 4 to 5 minutes.
4. Place in buns with cheese slices grill the whole sandwich for 3-4 minutes.

6.15 Mini Smoked Meatloaf

(**Ready in about**: 1 hour | **Serving**: 4| **Difficulty**: Medium)
Nutrition per serving: Kcal: 799| **Fat**: 46 g| **Net Carbs**: 53 g| **Protein**: 41 g

Ingredients:

Meatloaf:
- 1 pound of ground beef
- 1 egg
- 1/2 cup of chopped onion
- 1 cup of shredded cheddar cheese
- 3/4 cup of milk
- 1/2 cup of quick-cooking oats
- 1 teaspoon of salt

Toppings:
- 1 teaspoon of mustard
- 1/2 cup of ketchup
- 1/3 cup of brown sugar packed

Instructions

1. Preheat the Traeger to 350°F.
2. In a bowl, whisk milk and egg. Add in salt, oats, cheese, and onion. Mix well and add in the beef. Make into 8 mini loaves.
3. In a bowl, mix topping ingredients
4. Place loaves on the grill. Pour topping sauce over.
5. Cook for 45 minutes, with the lid, closed until no longer pink.
6. Serve hot.

6.16 Traeger Pot Roast

(**Ready in about**: 3 hours and 30 minutes| **Serving**: 8| **Difficulty**: Hard)
Nutrition per serving: Kcal: 423| **Fat**: 26 g| **Net Carbs**: 6 g| **Protein**: 39 g

Ingredients:
- 2 tablespoons of avocado oil
- 4 cups of beef broth
- 3-4 carrots
- 3-4 pounds of roast beef chuck
- 2 onions
- 1 cup of red wine
- Salt, garlic salt, pepper, seasoned salt, onion powder, as needed

Cornstarch Slurry;
- 1/3 cup of cold water
- 3 tablespoons of cornstarch

Instructions

1. In a cast-iron pan, add oil and place on medium flame.
2. Preheat the Traeger to 275°F.
3. Season meat with dry spices generously.
4. Brown the meat in cast iron for 4-5 minutes.
5. Add carrots, red wine, sliced onions, broth to pan.
6. Place pan on grill and cook for 2-3 hours.
7. Raise the temperature of Traeger to 325 °F until the internal temperature of beef reaches 200°F.
8. Take the pan off the grill and take out vegetables and meat and cover with foil.
9. Let the juices in the pan simmer. Add more broth to make it 3 cups.
10. Add cornstarch slurry to the pan. Mix until thickens.
11. Serve roast and vegetables with gravy.

6.17 Marinated Smoked Flank Steak

(**Ready in about**: 9 hours and 40 minutes| **Serving**: 4| **Difficulty**: Medium)
Nutrition per serving: Kcal: 264| **Fat**: 9 g| **Net Carbs**: 6 g| **Protein**: 38 g

Ingredients:
- 1 teaspoon of garlic powder
- 1 and a half-pound of flank steak
- 1 tablespoon of light brown sugar
- 1 tablespoon of soy sauce
- 1/2 teaspoon of black pepper
- 1 teaspoon of garlic salt

Instructions

1. In a bowl, add all ingredients, except for meat.
2. In a zip lock bag, add meat and marinade ingredients.
3. Mix well and keep in the fridge for 8 hours.
4. Preheat the Traeger to 225°F. Put the steak on the grill and cook for 1/2 an hour until the internal temperature reaches 135°F.
5. Serve hot.

6.18 Mexican Carne Asada

(**Ready in about**: 5 hours and 15 minutes| **Serving**: 6| **Difficulty**: Medium)
Nutrition per serving: Kcal: 519| **Fat**: 10 g| **Net Carbs**: 62 g| **Protein**: 41 g

Ingredients:
- 1 orange juice
- 1/4 cup of Worcestershire sauce
- 2 pounds of flank steak, thinly cut
- 2 tablespoons of white wine vinegar
- Salt and cumin to taste
- 4 garlic cloves
- 1/4 of an onion
- 2 tablespoons of black pepper

Instructions
1. In a zip lock bag, add all ingredients of the marinade and mix well. Add in steak.
2. Keep in the fridge for 5 hours. Do not over marinate.
3. Preheat the Traeger to 375°F.
4. Cook the steak directly on the grill. Flipping, so it does not become dry.
5. Serve in tortillas.

6.19 Baked Corned Beef Au Gratin

(**Ready in about**: 1 hour | **Serving**: 6| **Difficulty**: Medium)
Nutrition per serving: Kcal: 289| **Fat**: 12 g| **Net Carbs**: 14 g| **Protein**: 21 g

Ingredients:
- 1 pound of corned beef
- 2 tablespoons of butter, softened
- 1/2 cup of whole milk
- 2 tablespoons of all-purpose flour
- 4 cloves of minced garlic
- 3 pounds of russet potatoes
- 1 and 1/2 cups of heavy cream
- 1 teaspoon of kosher salt
- 1 sliced onion
- Black pepper, to taste

Instructions
1. Preheat the Traeger to 450°F.
2. Take a 9" cast iron pan, coat with butter. In a bowl, add minced garlic, cream, salt, black pepper, flour, and milk mix.
3. In the skillet, add onions, corned beef, and 1/3 of potatoes. Pour 1/3 cream mixture over potatoes.
4. Keep layering until all cream mix is used.
5. Bake for 1/2 an hour on the grill, cover with aluminum foil.
6. Take off foil and bake for 20 more minutes, until potatoes are brownish.
7. Add shredded cheese on top and bake for 3-5 minutes.
8. Serve.

6.20 Traeger Smoked Meatloaf

(**Ready in about**: 1 hour and 5 minutes | **Serving**: 12| **Difficulty**: Medium)
Nutrition per serving: Kcal: 198| **Fat**: 5 g| **Net Carbs**: 32 g| **Protein**: 19 g

Ingredients:
Meatloaf:
- 3 pounds ground beef
- 1 diced onion
- 2 egg yolks
- 1/4 cup of milk
- 3 whole eggs
- 1/2 cup of Ketchup
- 1/2 cup of panko breadcrumbs
- 1/2 teaspoon of salt
- 1/2 teaspoon of dry mustard
- 1/4 teaspoon of black pepper
- 1/4 teaspoon of garlic powder
- 1 teaspoon of dried parsley
- 1/2 teaspoon of onion powder
- 2 cups of saltine crackers, crushed
- 1 tablespoon of minced garlic

For Sauce:
- 1 and 1/2 cup of light brown sugar
- 1 and 1/2 cups of apple cider vinegar
- 1/4 cup of Ketchup
- 1 tablespoon of yellow mustard

Instructions
1. Preheat the Traeger to 325°F.
2. In a pan, mix all ingredients of the sauce. Let it simmer until it reduces and thickens.
3. In a bowl, add all other ingredients except for beef. Mix well, then add ground beef. Do not over mix.
4. In a foil pan, press the beef mixture. Leave some space between the pan and loaf.
5. Pour 1/3 of the sauce over.
6. Place on grill and cook for 1/2 an hour or until it sets and completely cooked.
7. Flip onto grill and brush with glaze cook with lid closed for 10 minutes. Baste with sauce again cook for 10 to 15 minutes until internal temperature reaches 160°F.
8. Take off the grill, rest, and serve.

6.21 Grilled Steak Fajitas

(**Ready in about**: 20-30 minutes | **Serving**: 8| **Difficulty**: Medium)
Nutrition per serving: Kcal: 448| **Fat**: 19 g| **Net Carbs**: 37 g| **Protein**: 30 g

Ingredients:
- 2 pounds of flank steak
- 1/4 cup of light sodium soy sauce
- 2 lemons, juiced
- 2 limes, juiced
- 1 teaspoon of cumin
- 1/3 cup of olive oil
- 2 tablespoons of brown sugar
- 3 cloves of minced garlic
- 1 teaspoon of chili powder

Instructions
1. In a bowl, add all ingredients except for beef. Mix well.
2. In a zip lock bag, add beef and pour over the marinade. Coat well and keep in the fridge for 1/2 an hour or more.
3. Preheat the Traeger to 400-500°F.
4. Place marinated steak on the grill, with the lid closed. Cook for 6-10 minutes, flip and cook for more than 6-10 minutes.
5. Take off the grill and rest 10 minutes, then serve in tortillas.

6.22 Grilled Mexican Style Surf and Turf

(**Ready in about**: 70 minutes | **Serving**: 2| **Difficulty**: Medium)
Nutrition per serving: Kcal: 543| **Fat**: 39 g| **Net Carbs**: 0 g| **Protein**: 48 g

Ingredients:
- 2 steaks boneless Angus beef
- 2 8-ounce lobster tails
- 1 teaspoon of paprika
- 2 cloves of minced garlic
- 1 teaspoon of kosher salt
- Zest and juice from 1 lime
- 1 teaspoon of chili powder
- 1/2 cup of softened unsalted butter
- 1/4 cup of fresh cilantro, chopped
- 1 teaspoon of ground cumin

Instructions
1. Wash and trim lobster tails. Release the meat, and keep the tail end attached.
2. Preheat the Traeger to medium-high.
3. In a pan, add cilantro, butter, lime zest, a pinch of salt, garlic and lime juice.
4. Cook on low heat until butter melts. Turn off the heat.
5. In a separate bowl, mix chili powder, paprika, 1 teaspoon of salt, and cumin.
6. Season the tail and steaks with this spice rub.
7. Place steaks on the grill, flip once, and cook until the internal temperature reaches 135°F.
8. Take off steaks and let them rest.
9. Take 2 limes and cut in half, and place on grill middle side down.
10. Place lobster tails on the grill, pour over melted butter and cook until lobster temperature reaches 140°F.
11. Serve with cilantro butter.

6.23 Traeger Grilled Tomahawk

(**Ready in about**: 70 minutes | **Serving**: 1| **Difficulty**: Medium)
Nutrition per serving: Kcal: 615| **Fat**: 41 g| **Net Carbs**: 0 g| **Protein**: 58 g

Ingredients:
- Salt & Pepper, to taste
- 1 tomahawk steak

Instructions
1. Preheat the Traeger to 180°F.
2. Season the steak with salt and pepper and place it on the grill directly.
3. Cook until the internal temperature of the meat reaches 100°F.
4. Take off the grill, and raise the temperature to 450°F.
5. Place meat on the grill again, rotate, and flip every 2 minutes until the internal temperature (as read by a meat thermometer) reaches 125°F.
6. Rest and serve.

6.24 Prime Rib Sandwich Pinwheel

(**Ready in about**: 55 minutes | **Serving**: 4| **Difficulty**: Medium)
Nutrition per serving: Kcal: 788| **Fat**: 60 g| **Net Carbs**: 24 g| **Protein**: 37 g

Ingredients:
- 3 cups of cubed prime rib
- 1 sliced shallot into thin rounds
- 2 tablespoons of butter
- 3 tablespoons of horseradish sauce
- 2 cups of cheddar cheese
- 1 roll of crescent dough

Instructions
1. Preheat the Traeger to 350°F.
2. In a pan, add 2 tablespoons of butter and sauté onions for 10-15 minutes, until caramelized.
3. Turn off the heat, set it aside.
4. Roll the dough, spread horseradish on the dough.
5. Add cubed meat and cheese, and onion.
6. Roll into sandwiches. Place on grill.
7. Cook for 20-25 minutes at 350°F.
8. Let it rest for 5 minutes, then serve.

6.25 Grilled Beef Bulgogi

(**Ready in about**: 20-30 minutes | **Serving**: 12| **Difficulty**: Medium)
Nutrition per serving: Kcal: 468| **Fat**: 32 g| **Net Carbs**: 7 g| **Protein**: 38 g

Ingredients:
- 1/4 cup of sesame oil
- 4 pounds of ribeye, cut into thin slices
- 1/2 of Asian pear
- 1/4 cup of Gochujang
- 1 cup of soy sauce
- 7 cloves of minced garlic
- 1 cup of sugar
- 1/2 teaspoon of black pepper

Instructions
1. In a blender, add sugar, sesame oil, pear, garlic, gochujang, pepper, and soy. Pulse until combined
2. Drizzle over meat, coat, and keep in the fridge for 4 hours or overnight. Keep mixing in time of marination.
3. Preheat the Traeger to 400°F.
4. Place meat on the grill, cook for 5-6 minutes. Flip and cook for 2-3 minutes.
5. Do not char it.
6. Drizzle marinade over and serve.

6.26 Carne Asada

(**Ready in about**: 20 minutes | **Serving**: 8| **Difficulty**: Medium)
Nutrition per serving: Kcal: 337| **Fat**: 10 g| **Net Carbs**: 23 g| **Protein**: 33 g

Ingredients:
- Marinade:
- 1 tablespoon of garlic
- 1 cup of Margarita mix
- 1/2 cup of soy sauce
- 1/4 cup of cilantro, chopped
- 1/2 cup of orange juice
- 2 ounces of Tequila
- Steak:
- 4 tablespoons of chili margarita rub
- 3-pound of flank steak

Instructions
1. In a large sealable bag, add all the marinade ingredients, put the steak in. coat well, and keep it in the fridge.
2. Preheat the Traeger to 425-450°F.
3. Take the meat out and pat dry, season with spice rub generously.
4. Place on grill and cook on each side for 6 minutes.
5. Rest it for 10 minutes before serving.

6.27 Grilled New York Strip

(**Ready in about**: 20 minutes | **Serving**: 6| **Difficulty**: Medium)
Nutrition per serving: Kcal: 198| **Fat**: 14 g| **Net Carbs**: 0 g| **Protein**: 17 g

Ingredients:
- Salt and pepper, to taste
- 3 New York strips

Instructions
1. Keep the steak at room temperature for 1/2 an hour before cooking.
2. Preheat the Traeger to 450°F.
3. Coat the meat with salt and pepper and place it on the grill.
4. Cook each side for 5 to 7 minutes
5. Cook until the internal temperature reaches 125-128°F.
6. Rest the meat and serve.

6.28 Smoked Beef Ribs

(**Ready in about**: 5 hours and 15 minutes | **Serving**: 6| **Difficulty**: Medium)
Nutrition per serving: Kcal: 954| **Fat**: 65 g| **Net Carbs**: 35 g| **Protein**: 53 g

Ingredients:
- 3 cups of Barbecue sauce
- 5 pounds of beef ribs
- 3 tablespoons of Beef rub

Instructions
1. Season the ribs with a dry rub, and Preheat the Traeger to 180 °F, or Smoke mode.
2. Put seasoned meat on grill and cook for 2 hours.
3. Raise the temperature of the grill to 275 °F, cook the meat for 2 hours more.
4. Raise the temperature of the grill to 325 °F, now baste with BBQ sauce every 10-15 minutes, in the last hour, until meat is fork-tender.
5. Let it rest for 10 minutes, then serve.

6.29 Grilled Beef Short Rib Lollipop

(**Ready in about**: 3 hours and 30 minutes | **Serving**: 4| **Difficulty**: Medium)
Nutrition per serving: Kcal: 264| **Fat**: 9 g| **Net Carbs**: 1 g| **Protein**: 22 g

Ingredients:
- Barbecue sauce, half cup or as needed
- 4 short rib beef lollipops
- BBQ rub, as needed

Instructions
1. Preheat the Traeger to 275°F.
2. Season meat lollipop with spice rub generously.
3. Put on the grill and cook for 3-4 hours.
4. Keep basting with BBQ sauce in the last 1/2 an hour.
5. Serve hot.

6.30 Brisket Chili

(**Ready in about**: 60 minutes | **Serving**: 12| **Difficulty**: Medium)
Nutrition per serving: Kcal: 385| **Fat**: 8 g| **Net Carbs**: 17 g| **Protein**: 31 g

Ingredients:
- 15 ounces of tomato sauce
- 4 cups of cooked brisket, diced
- 1 can of chili beans
- 2 cans of stewed tomatoes
- 8 cups of water
- Sour cream, to your taste
- 1 package of chili kit
- 1 can drain of pinto beans
- Cheese, as needed

Instructions
1. In a pot, add all ingredients except for beans.
2. Let it simmer on low heat for 45 minutes. Add in beans.
3. Preheat the Traeger to 375°F.
4. Place the pot on the grill and cook for 1/2 an hour.
5. Serve with cheese and sour cream.

6.31 Smoked Brisket

(**Ready in about**: 1 hour and 25 minutes | **Serving**: 15| **Difficulty**: Medium)
Nutrition per serving: Kcal: 797| **Fat**: 51 g| **Net Carbs**: 0 g| **Protein**: 76 g

Ingredients:
- 1/2 cup of salt, garlic and pepper
- 15-18 pound of beef brisket

Instructions
1. Season the meat generously on each side with the dry spice rub; make sure the meat is at room temperature.
2. Preheat the Traeger grill to 220°F.
3. Place the meat directly on the grill, with the lid closed, and cook until the internal temperature reaches 180 to 190°F.
4. In pink butcher paper wrap, the meat and place on grill. Lower the grill temperature to 165°F.
5. Cook until the internal temperature of the meat (as read by a meat thermometer) reaches 204-205°F.
6. Take off the grill, let it wrapped in butcher paper and clean towels, place in cooler for 1/2 an hour to 60 minutes.
7. Unwrap and serve.

6.32 Grilled Filet Mignon

(**Ready in about**: 20 minutes | **Serving**: 3| **Difficulty**: Medium)
Nutrition per serving: Kcal: 229| **Fat**: 15 g| **Net Carbs**: 0 g| **Protein**: 23 g

Ingredients:
- Salt and pepper, to taste
- 3 filet mignons

Instructions
1. Preheat the Traeger to 450°F.
2. Coat the meat with pepper and salt. Season well.
3. Put on the grill directly and cook on each side for 5 minutes, or until internal temperature (as read by a meat thermometer) reaches 125 °F for rare and 145 °F for medium.
4. Rest and serve.

6.33 Traeger Smoked Mississippi Pot Roast

(**Ready in about:** 5 hours and 15 minutes | **Serving:** 8| **Difficulty:** Medium)
Nutrition per serving: Kcal: 314| **Fat:** 13 g| **Net Carbs:** 4 g| **Protein:** 39 g

Ingredients:
- 1 stick of salted butter
- 5 pounds of beef roast chuck
- 1 teaspoon of black pepper
- 1 teaspoon of paprika
- 1 teaspoon of onion powder
- 8 pepperoncini peppers
- 1/4 cup of carrots, chopped
- 1 packet of au jus mix
- 1 teaspoon of salt
- 1/2 teaspoon of granulated garlic
- 1 packet of dressing dry ranch mix
- 1/2 a cup of water

Instructions
1. Coat the roast with all dry spices.
2. Sear the roast in cast iron on each side.
3. Preheat the Traeger grill to 275°F.
4. In a large grill-safe pan, add seared meat with butter, ranch mix, pepperoncini, water, carrots, jus, and garlic. Place this pan on the grill and close the lid.
5. Let it cook and monitor so it would not burn after every hour.
6. Cook until it becomes fork tender or internal temperature (as read by a meat thermometer) reaches 200-205°F.
7. Serve with bread and mashed potatoes.

6.34 Grilled Curried Flank Steak

(**Ready in about:** 20-30 minutes | **Serving:** 6| **Difficulty:** Medium)
Nutrition per serving: Kcal: 300| **Fat:** 20 g| **Net Carbs:** 5 g| **Protein:** 40 g

Ingredients:
- 3 pounds (1.5 kg) flank steak

Marinade:
- 2 tablespoons of curry powder
- 1 cup vegetable oil
- 4 minced garlic cloves
- 1 whole lemon (juice)
- 2 tablespoon of soy sauce
- 1 teaspoon of ground black pepper
- 1 teaspoon of salt

Instructions
1. Mix all the ingredients, except the steak, in container.
2. Put the meat in a bowl with half the marinade.
3. Marinate for 8 hours or overnight.
4. Refrigerate the remaining marinade in an airtight container.
5. Pour the remaining marinade into a small saucepan and let simmer until reduced by half. Keep warm.
6. Preheat your Traeger at 350°F during 10 minutes.
7. Drain the steak.
8. Arrange the steaks on the grill and cook each side for 7 to 10 minutes.
9. Retire steaks from grill and let it cool for 5 minutes.
10. Slice the stakes and serve with the remaining marinade.

6.35 Beef Sirloin and Tomato Vinaigrette

(**Ready in about:** 30-40 minutes | **Serving:** 6| **Difficulty:** Medium)
Nutrition per serving: Kcal: 300| **Fat:** 25 g| **Net Carbs:** 5 g| **Protein:** 40 g

Ingredients:
- 3 beef sirloin steaks
- Extra-virgin olive oil, as needed
- Salt and pepper, to taste

Vinaigrette:
- 3 tablespoons of vinegar
- 8 tomatoes
- 1 teaspoon of minced thyme

Instructions
1. Apply olive oil and salt and pepper to taste to rub both sides of tenderloin.
2. Put the sirloin in a roasting pan.
3. Preheat grill to 500°F (260°C) lid closed for 20 minutes.
4. Place the sirloin on the grill and roast for 10 minutes.
5. Lower the temperature to 350°F (177°C) and roast for an additional 15 minutes until reaching the desired doneness.
6. Make the vinaigrette by combining the tomatoes, olive oil,
7. Vinegar, and thyme in a food processor. Add salt and pepper to taste.
8. Retire the sirloin from the grill and accompany with the vinaigrette.

6.36 Spicy Tenderloin Steaks

(**Ready in about:** 1 hour | **Serving:** 4| **Difficulty:** Easy)
Nutrition per serving: Kcal: 190| **Fat:** 10 g| **Net Carbs:** 2 g| **Protein:** 20 g

Ingredients:
- 2 tenderloin steaks
- 1/2 teaspoon of chili pepper
- 1 teaspoon of ground mustard
- ½ tablespoon of onion powder
- 2 tablespoons of ground black pepper
- ½ tablespoon of garlic powder
- 2 tablespoons of salt

Instructions
1. Mix all the ingredients, except the steaks, in a container.
2. Apply plenty of the rub mixture to the steaks.
3. Preheat your Traeger to 225°F (107°C) 20 minutes.
4. Put the steaks directly on the grill and smoke until the internal temperature (as read by a meat thermometer) reaches 120°F (49°C), 40 minutes to 1 hour.
5. Remove the steaks from the grill and let it rest.
6. Raise the grill temperature to 450°F (200°C). Put the steaks back to the grill and cook each side for 5 to 10 minutes
7. Withdraw the steaks from the grill; let it cool for 5 minutes before serving.

CHAPTER 7
Traeger Grill Poultry Recipes

Chapter 7: Traeger Grill Poultry Recipes

7.1 Traeger Smoked Turkey

(**Ready in about**: 4 hours and 15 minutes| **Serving**: 12| **Difficulty**: Medium)
Nutrition per serving: Kcal: 418|**Fat**: 4 g| **Net Carbs**: 3 g| **Protein**: 41 g

Ingredients:
- 1/4 cup of olive oil
- 1 10-13-pound turkey. rinsed and patted dry
- 1 and 1/2 teaspoons of salt
- 2 teaspoons of Traeger chicken rub
- 2 teaspoons of poultry seasoning

Instructions
1. Mix seasonings and oil, coat the turkey with this rub.
2. Rub under turkey's skin also.
3. Preheat the Traeger to 250 °F with the lid closed for 15 minutes.
4. Place turkey on the pan and put on the grill. Cook for 2 hours and close the lid.
5. After 2 hours, cover the turkey and raise the temperature to 325°F.
6. Cook for 2 to 4 hours until the internal temperature reaches 165°F.
7. Let it rest before slicing and serving.

7.2 Brined Smoked Turkey

(**Ready in about**: 7 hours and 20 minutes| **Serving**: 7| **Difficulty**: Medium)
Nutrition per serving: Kcal: 545|**Fat**: 13 g| **Net Carbs**: 10 g| **Protein**: 37 g

Ingredients:
- 15 pounds of turkey
- Salt and pepper, to taste
- 2 tablespoons of olive oil

Brine:
- 1 tablespoon of black peppercorns
- 4 cups of hot water
- 2 cups of apple cider
- 1 tablespoon of rosemary fresh
- 21 tablespoon of steak seasoning
- 1 cup of kosher salt
- 1 tablespoon of thyme fresh

Rub:
- 2 teaspoons of dried thyme
- 1/2 cup of butter, softened
- 2 teaspoons of dried rosemary
- 1 teaspoon of black pepper
- 1/2 teaspoon of garlic powder
- 1 teaspoon of dried sage
- tablespoons of ground black pepper
- ½ tablespoon of garlic powder
- 2 tablespoons of salt

Instructions
1. Remove neck and giblets and clean the cavity.
2. In a large pot, add all ingredients of brine mix until salt dissolves.
3. Add turkey to the brine, cover the container, keep in the fridge overnight.
4. Submerge the whole turkey add more water if needed.
5. After 12 hours or more, rinse the turkey and pat dry.
6. Put the turkey in a roasting pan
7. Preheat the Traeger to 250 °F with the lid closed for 15 minutes.
8. In a bowl, add all ingredients of spice rub.
9. Coat the turkey and under the skin too.
10. Spread olive oil on turkey.
11. Add black pepper and salt to the turkey cavity.
12. Smoke for 1/2 an hour for each pound or until the internal temperature reaches 165°F.
13. Rest and slice.

7.3 Smoked Chicken Breasts

(**Ready in about**: 40 minutes| **Serving**: 4| **Difficulty**: Easy)
Nutrition per serving: Kcal: 135|**Fat**: 3 g| **Net Carbs**: 1 g| **Protein**: 24 g

Ingredients:
- 2-3 tablespoons of BBQ chicken rub
- 1 pound of skinless, boneless chicken breasts

Instructions
1. Preheat the Traeger to 250 °F with the lid closed for 15 minutes.
2. Pound the chicken to half-inch thickness—coat chicken with rub.
3. Place chicken on smoker and smoke for 1/2 an hour, or until internal temperature reaches 165°F.
4. Rest for 10 minutes, then serve.

7.4 Smoked Whole Chicken

(**Ready in about**: 3 hours and 10 minutes| **Serving**: 4| **Difficulty**: Medium)
Nutrition per serving: Kcal: 418|**Fat**: 8 g| **Net Carbs**: 1 g| **Protein**: 35 g

Ingredients:
- 3 tablespoons of BBQ chicken rub
- 1 whole chicken

Instructions
1. Preheat the Traeger to the smoker or 250°F.
2. Coat the trimmed chicken with a dry rub. Cover all spots and add spice rub under the skin too.
3. Place chicken on the grill and close the lid. Cook until the internal temperature (as read by a meat thermometer) reaches 165°F.
4. Rest and serve.

7.5 Alabama Chicken Leg Quarters

(**Ready in about**: 4 hours and 45 minutes| **Serving**: 6| **Difficulty**: Medium)
Nutrition per serving: Kcal: 287|**Fat**: 11 g| **Net Carbs**: 5 g| **Protein**: 37 g

Ingredients:
- 1/2 cup of all-purpose rub
- 1 bottle of Italian dressing
- 4-6 chicken leg quarters

Alabama Sauce:
- 1 teaspoon of horseradish
- 2 cups of mayonnaise
- 1/2 cup of apple cider vinegar
- 2 tablespoons of all-purpose rub
- 1 tablespoon of sugar
- Juice of 2 lemons

Instructions
1. Trim excess skin and fat.
2. Place chicken in a large zip lock bag, and add Italian dressing. Coat chicken well. Keep in the fridge for 4 hours or overnight.
3. Preheat the Traeger to 275-300°F.
4. Take chicken out coat with rub, place chicken on grill skin side up.
5. Keep monitoring chicken so it won't burn.
6. Flip chicken after 45 minutes.
7. Cook until internal temperature (as read by a meat thermometer) reaches 170-180 °F
8. In a bowl, mix all Alabama sauce ingredients.
9. Serve with grilled chicken.

7.6 Chicken Lollipops

(**Ready in about**: 50 minutes| **Serving**: 6| **Difficulty**: Medium)
Nutrition per serving: Kcal: 243|**Fat**: 19 g| **Net Carbs**: 3 g| **Protein**: 35 g

Ingredients:
- 6-12 chicken drumsticks
- 2-3 cups of Barbecue sauce
- Poultry rub, as needed

Instructions
1. Trim chicken into a lollipop.
2. Wrap the chicken bone in foil, season with poultry rub.
3. Let it rest for 1/2 an hour or 1 hour in the fridge
4. Smoke for 1/2 an hour at 225 degrees F.
5. Cook at 350 °F for 30-45 minutes or until the meat's temperature reaches 165°F.
6. dip chicken in barbecue sauce
7. Cook at degrees for 10 minutes, until the internal temperature reaches 175°F.
8. Serve hot.

7.7 Smoked Chicken Thighs

(**Ready in about**: 60 minutes| **Serving**: 6| **Difficulty**: Medium)
Nutrition per serving: Kcal: 432|**Fat**: 32 g| **Net Carbs**: 1 g| **Protein**: 37 g

Ingredients:
- 1 jar of teriyaki sauce
- 3 pounds of chicken thighs, bone-in

Instructions
1. In a large zip lock bag, add teriyaki sauce with chicken. Coat the chicken well.
2. Keep in the fridge for 3 hours or more.
3. Preheat the grill to 350 degrees F.
4. Place chicken directly on grill bone side up.
5. Cook for 25 minutes with lid closed at 300°F.
6. Flip the pieces over. Cook for another 25 minutes until the internal temperature reaches 165°F.
7. Let it rest for 10 minutes, then serve.

7.8 Traeger Chicken Teriyaki

(**Ready in about**: 20-30 minutes| **Serving**: 6| **Difficulty**: Medium)
Nutrition per serving: Kcal: 146|**Fat**: 2 g| **Net Carbs**: 8 g| **Protein**: 22 g

Ingredients:
- 3 tablespoons of Maui Wowee seasoning
- 3 chicken breasts
- 2 tablespoons of green onions
- 1 cup of Teriyaki sauce

Instructions
1. Preheat the Traeger to 350°F. Cut the chicken in 1/2 to make it slimmer.
2. Coat the chicken with a seasoning rub.
3. Put the chicken on the grill and cook on each side for 5-6 minutes or until internal temperature reaches (as read by a meat thermometer) 165 °F
4. Serve with teriyaki sauce.

7.9 Smokey Wings

(**Ready in about**: 2 hours and 30 minutes| **Serving**: 6-7| **Difficulty**: Medium)
Nutrition per serving: Kcal: 278|**Fat**: 9 g| **Net Carbs**: 10 g| **Protein**: 25 g

Ingredients:
- 2 pounds of chicken wings
- 1 tablespoon of sesame seeds
- 2 tablespoons of soy sauce
- 1/2 teaspoon of ginger powder
- 3 tablespoons of hoisin sauce
- 1 tablespoon of honey
- 2 cloves of minced garlic
- 1 teaspoon of sesame oil

Instructions
1. Preheat the Traeger to 225°F.
2. Smoke chicken wings for 1 and a half hours with the lid closed.
3. Raise grill temperature to 375°F.
4. Put wings in a large bowl.
5. In a cup, add soya sauce, ginger powder, garlic, honey, sesame oil, hoisin sauce. Mix well and pour over wings; coat well.
6. Place coated wings on a foiled baking sheet and cook on the grill for 1/2 an hour or until the internal temperature reaches 165°F.
7. Serve hot.

7.10 Chicken Sausage Rolls

(**Ready in about**: 40 minutes| **Serving**: 6-7| **Difficulty**: Medium)
Nutrition per serving: Kcal: 214|**Fat**: 12 g| **Net Carbs**: 18 g| **Protein**: 19 g

Ingredients:
- 1 pound of ground chicken
- 1 whisked egg
- 1 grated zucchini
- 1 cup of bread crumbs
- 1 tablespoon of sesame seeds
- 1 carrot, grated
- ¼ cup of Thai chili sauce
- 1/2 onion, grated
- 1 teaspoon of dried thyme
- 1/2 teaspoons of garlic powder
- 1/2 cup of chopped flat-leaf parsley
- 4 sheets of puff pastry

Instructions
1. Place parchment paper on 2 baking sheets
2. In a bowl, mix lightly beaten egg, onion, carrot, chicken, zucchini, and breadcrumbs. Mix with clean hands until well-combined.
3. Roll puff pastry into 6 by 12 rectangle. Slice in 1/2 and add 1/8th of the mixture in each piece.
4. Roll the dough with the filling inside. Seal the edges.
5. Cook at 350 °F for 30-45 minutes or until the meat's temperature reaches 165°F.
6. dip chicken in barbecue sauce
7. Cook at degrees for 10 minutes, until the internal temperature reaches 175°F.
8. Serve hot.

7.11 Traeger Grilled Chicken Breast

(**Ready in about**: 30 minutes| **Serving**: 6| **Difficulty**: Medium)
Nutrition per serving: Kcal: 120|**Fat**: 4 g| **Net Carbs**: 2 g| **Protein**: 19 g

Ingredients:
- 3 chicken breasts
- 1/4 teaspoon of onion powder
- 3/4 teaspoon of salt
- 1 tablespoon of avocado oil
- 1/4 teaspoon of garlic powder
- Black pepper, to taste

Instructions
1. Preheat the Traeger to 375 °F with the lid closed for 15 minutes.
2. Coat chicken breast in oil.
3. Season chicken with onion, salt, garlic powder, and pepper.
4. Place directly on the grill and cook each side for 5-7 minutes, or until the internal temperature reaches 165°F, as read by a meat thermometer.
5. Serve hot.

7.12 Grilled BBQ Orange Chicken

(**Ready in about**: 3 hours | **Serving**: 12| **Difficulty**: Medium)
Nutrition per serving: Kcal: 354|**Fat**: 19.8 g| **Net Carbs**: 17 g| **Protein**: 37 g

Ingredients:
- 1 5 pounds of a whole chicken
- 2 tablespoons of red pepper flakes
- 3 tablespoons of BBQ sauce
- 1 24-ounce jar of orange marmalade
- 1/4 cup of all-purpose rub
- 1 tablespoon of fresh ginger

Instructions
1. Preheat the Traeger to 275 °F with the lid closed for 15 minutes.
2. In a pan, on low flame, melt orange marmalade. Mix with ginger and BBQ sauce.
3. Coat chicken with rub and put on the grill. Flip and cook the other side cook until the internal temperature reaches 165°F. It will take almost 2 hours.
4. In the last 20 minutes, pour marmalade mix on the bird after every 10 minutes.
5. Rest and serve

7.13 Chicken Wings

(**Ready in about**: 20-30 minutes | **Serving**: 12| **Difficulty**: Medium)
Nutrition per serving: Kcal: 319|**Fat**: 11 g| **Net Carbs**: 9 g| **Protein**: 37 g

Ingredients:
- 5 pounds of chicken wings
- 3 cups of Zesty Italian dressing
- All-purpose rub, enough to coat wings
- 1/2 cup of soy sauce

Ranch Dip:
- 1/4 cup of buffalo sauce
- Buttermilk ranch dressing
- 1-2 tablespoons of all-purpose rub
- 1/3 cup of blue cheese, crumbled

Instructions
1. In a large zip lock bag, add Italian dressing and soy sauce of marinade, add chicken wings and coat them well.
2. Keep in the fridge for 2-8 hours.
3. Later, place chicken wings on a rack, pat dry with a paper towel, season with all-purpose rub generously.
4. Preheat the Traeger to 275 °F with the lid closed for 15 minutes.
5. Place away from heat and cook for 20 minutes with lid closed. Flip and cook until the internal temperature reaches 185°F.
6. Mix sauce ingredients. Brush wings with sauce until they are charred.
7. Serve with blue cheese dip.

7.14 Whole BBQ Chicken

(**Ready in about**: 4 hours | **Serving**: 12| **Difficulty**: Medium)
Nutrition per serving: Kcal: 343|**Fat**: 19 g| **Net Carbs**: 18 g| **Protein**: 40 g

Ingredients:
- 1 4-5-pound whole chicken, cut up
- 2 tablespoons of poultry seasoning
- 3 tablespoons of BBQ rub
- Blue cheese dressing
- 1/4 cup of buttermilk
- 1 cup of blue cheese buffalo
- 2 tablespoons of lemon juice
- 1 tablespoon of Worcestershire sauce
- 1 cup of mayonnaise
- 2 tablespoons of chives, chopped
- 1 cup of sour cream

Sauce:
- 2 tablespoons of lemon juice
- 3/4 cup of butter
- 1 tablespoon of onion powder
- 1 cup of hot sauce
- 1 tablespoon of garlic powder
- 1/8 teaspoon of cayenne
- 1/2 teaspoon of ground black pepper
- 1 and 1/2 tablespoons of Worcestershire sauce

Instructions
1. Cut the chicken into different pieces.
2. Mix all rub ingredients and coat the chicken; let it rest for 1/2 an hour or longer.
3. Preheat the Traeger to 275 °F with the lid closed.
4. Place chicken on the grill and cook until internal temperature (as read by a meat thermometer) reaches 165 F flip so will cook evenly.
5. For the dressing, mix all ingredients of cheese dressing and keep in the fridge for 2 hours.
6. For the sauce, mix all ingredients with melted butter, let it simmer. Turn off the heat and let it cool.
7. Brush the chicken at 160 °F with sauce and serve with cheese sauce.

7.15 Citrus Turkey

(**Ready in about**: 4 hours | **Serving**: 12| **Difficulty**: Medium)
Nutrition per serving: Kcal: 351|**Fat**: 13 g| **Net Carbs**: 9 g| **Protein**: 37 g

Ingredients:
- 1 15–pound Turkey
- 3 oranges
- 1 tablespoon of garlic powder
- 3 lemons
- 1 tablespoon of onion powder
- 3 tablespoons of salt
- 2 tablespoons of Italian seasoning
- 3 limes
- Italian seasoning, as needed
- Poultry seasoning, as needed
- Minced Fresh herbs: One teaspoon

Instructions
1. In a bowl, add Italian seasoning, garlic, onion powder, and salt. Mix well. Coat the bird well in a dry rub for 1-3 days.
2. On the grill, layer limes, herbs, oranges, and lemon in a pan. Place the bird on top.
3. Season the bird with spices and butter.
4. Preheat the Traeger to 275 °F with the lid closed for 15 Minutes.
5. Cook for 3 and a half hours until the internal temperature of the bird reaches 165 F.
6. Serve hot.

7.16 Herb Buttered Chicken

(**Ready in about**: 3 hours | **Serving**: 6| **Difficulty**: Medium)
Nutrition per serving: Kcal: 323|**Fat**: 15 g| **Net Carbs**: 8 g| **Protein**: 32 g

Ingredients:
- 1 whole chicken
- 1 butter stick
- 2 teaspoons of chipotle chili powder
- Basil, 1 teaspoon
- 2 teaspoons of garlic powder
- Thyme, 1 teaspoon

Instructions
1. Cut the chicken open, lay it flat.
2. Melt 1 stick of butter mix well with chipotle chili and garlic powder.
3. Fill up the seasoning injection and inject into chicken breast till it swells, then in legs and thighs.
4. Sprinkle with basil and thyme.
5. Preheat the Traeger to 275 °F with the lid closed for 15 minutes. Place chicken on grill and smoke for 45 with the lid closed.
6. After 45 minutes, raise the temperature to 350 °F, cook for 1 hour or until the internal temperature reaches 165 °F
7. Before slicing the chicken, let it rest and serve.

7.17 Smoked Hassel Back Pesto Chicken

(**Ready in about**: 3 hours | **Serving**: 12| **Difficulty**: Medium)
Nutrition per serving: Kcal: 345|**Fat**: 17 g| **Net Carbs**: 9 g| **Protein**: 39 g

Ingredients:
- Pesto sauce, enough to coat chicken breasts
- 2 Chicken breasts
- Mozzarella, to taste
- Italian seasoning, enough to coat chicken breasts

Instructions
1. Rub chicken with Italian seasoning and score the chicken.
2. Preheat the Traeger to 350 °F with the lid closed for 15 minutes.
3. Place chicken directly on grill cook until internal temperature reaches 150°F.
4. Put on mozzarella cheese on top, cook until melted.
5. Serve hot.

7.18 Smoked Herb Butter Turkey

(**Ready in about**: 4 hours | **Serving**: 12| **Difficulty**: Medium)
Nutrition per serving: Kcal: 437|**Fat**: 21.3 g| **Net Carbs**: 11 g| **Protein**: 37 g

Ingredients:
- 2 Butter sticks
- Different fresh herbs mixture
- Italian seasoning
- Chicken seasoning
- 1 whole turkey

Instructions
1. In a bowl, mix fresh chopped herbs with room temperature butter, mix well, spread parchment paper, and roll into a log. Keep in the freezer.
2. Preheat the Traeger to 200 °F with the lid closed for 15 minutes.
3. Put the turkey on a grill with herb butter under the turkey's skin.
4. Smoke for 1/2 an hour at 200°F.
5. Cook at 325 F for 2 to 3 hours until the meat's internal temperature reaches 165°F.
6. Rest and serve.

43

7.19 Grilled Chicken Salad

(**Ready in about**: 2 hours and 20 minutes | **Serving**: 12| **Difficulty**: Easy)
Nutrition per serving: Kcal: 367| **Fat**: 19.3 g| **Net Carbs**: 21 g| **Protein**: 36 g

Ingredients:
- 1/2 cup of plain yogurt
- 4 green onions
- 1 whole chicken
- 1/2 cup of mayonnaise
- 1 lemon
- Cumin
- 1 tablespoon brown sugar
- 4 stalks of celery
- 1 cup of red grapes
- Fresh dill
- 1 cup of green grapes

Instructions
1. Break the chicken down into breasts, thighs, legs, and wings
2. Rub the chicken with poultry seasoning.
3. Smoke at 250 °F until internal temperature reaches 165°F.
4. Take all bones out of cooked chicken and shred.
5. Chop celery, green onions into bite-size pieces
6. Cut grapes in half.
7. In a large bowl, add all chopped-up ingredients.
8. In another bowl, add 1/2 cup mayo, 1/2 cup yogurt, lemon juice, dill, sugar, salt, cumin, and pepper. Mix well
9. Pour dressing over chopped ingredients, mix well, and serve.

7.20 Honey Balsamic Chicken Legs

(**Ready in about**: 5 hours and 20 minutes | **Serving**: 12| **Difficulty**: Medium)
Nutrition per serving: Kcal: 367| **Fat**: 19.3 g| **Net Carbs**: 21 g| **Protein**: 36 g

Ingredients:
- 10-12 chicken legs
- 2 teaspoons of minced garlic
- 1 cup of honey
- 1 cup of balsamic vinegar
- 1/2 cup of dark brown sugar
- 1 cup of pineapple juice
- 1 cup of soy sauce
- 1 teaspoon of Sriracha

Instructions
1. In a bowl, add all ingredients, mix well.
2. Coat chicken legs in marinade and place in a large zip lock bag with marinade.
3. Keep in the fridge for 4 hours or overnight.
4. Preheat the Traeger to 325 °F, and place the chicken directly on grates. Do not discard marinade.
5. Let the chicken cook and add marinade into a saucepot. Simmer for 20-30 minutes and reduce by half.
6. Cook chicken for 35-45 minutes; raise the temperature to 450 °F for the last 15 minutes.
7. Serve with sauce.

7.21 Mayo & Herb Roasted Turkey

(**Ready in about**: 4 hours and 20 minutes | **Serving**: 8| **Difficulty**: Medium)
Nutrition per serving: Kcal: 342| **Fat**: 13 g| **Net Carbs**: 13 g| **Protein**: 35 g

Ingredients:
- 1 12-pound turkey
- 1 and 1/4 cup of mayonnaise
- 1/4 teaspoon of honey
- Salt and pepper, to taste
- 1/3 cup of fresh herbs, chopped

Instructions
1. Preheat the Traeger to 425 °F with the lid closed for 15 minutes
2. In a bowl, mix herbs and mayo. Add ¼ teaspoon of honey mix well.
3. Clean the turkey and pat dry.
4. Coat the turkey with mayo mix. Season with pepper and salt.
5. Add fresh rosemary, thyme in the bird cavity, tie the legs together.
6. Roast turkey for 1/2 an hour-45 minutes.
7. As turkey is cooking, lower temperature to 350°F.
8. Continue roasting until internal temperature (as read by a meat thermometer) reaches 160 °F in the breast part and 175 °F in the thigh.
9. Rest before slicing.

7.22 Honey Lime Chicken Adobo Skewers

(Ready in about: 30 minutes | **Serving**: 6| **Difficulty**: Medium)
Nutrition per serving: Kcal: 298| Fat: 10 g| Net Carbs: 9 g| Protein: 30 g

Ingredients:
- 4 chicken breasts, cut into cubes
- 2 teaspoon of onion powder
- 3/4 cup of rice vinegar
- 1/4 cup of soy sauce
- Salt and black pepper, to taste
- 1 tablespoon of vegetable oil
- 2 teaspoons of minced garlic
- 3 tablespoons of honey

Instructions
1. In a bowl, add all ingredients, mix well.
2. Cover it and keep it in the fridge overnight.
3. Preheat the Traeger to high, with the lid closed for 15 minutes
4. Thread the chicken on skewers, grill for 12-15 minutes keep turning.
5. Serve hot with limes.

7.23 Baked Chicken Pot Pie

(**Ready in about**: 50 minutes | **Serving**: 5| **Difficulty**: Medium)
Nutrition per serving: Kcal: 353| Fat: 11 g| Net Carbs: 19 g| Protein: 29 g

Ingredients:
- 1 yellow onion, diced
- 2 tablespoons of flour
- 2 tablespoons of butter
- 1/2 cup of milk
- 2 cup of chicken stock
- 1 and 1/2 cups of peas and carrots
- 1/2 teaspoon of Traeger Pork & Poultry rub
- 1/4 teaspoon of dried thyme leaves
- 4 cups of cooked diced chicken
- 1 egg, whisked with 1 tablespoon of water
- 1 diced stalk of celery
- 2 teaspoons dry sherry, optional
- Salt and pepper, to taste
- 1 sheet of frozen puff pastry

Instructions
1. Preheat the Traeger to 400 °F with the lid closed for 15 minutes.
2. In a pan, add butter sauté celery, onion cook for 3-5 minutes, on medium flame until translucent.
3. Sprinkle 2 tablespoons of flour and mix.
4. Gradually add the stock, whisk well, add milk, and let it simmer.
5. Add in dry sherry.
6. Add carrots, poultry rub, peas, chicken, and thyme. Let it simmer for 5-10 minutes.
7. Add salt and pepper.
8. In a well-oiled skillet, add pot pie filling you just made.
9. Cover with lightly floured puff pastry, pierce with a knife, so steam will not trap inside, brush with egg wash.
10. Bake in Traeger for 1/2 an hour.

7.24 Braised Brunswick Stew

(Ready in about: 2 hours and 30 minutes | **Serving**: 6| **Difficulty**: Medium)
Nutrition per serving: Kcal: 598| Fat: 14 g| Net Carbs: 17 g| Protein: 36 g

Ingredients:
- 1 onion
- 1 bell pepper, chopped
- 2 stalks of celery
- 8 tablespoons of butter
- 4 cloves of minced garlic
- 1 teaspoon of smoked paprika
- 1/2 teaspoon of cayenne pepper
- 1 pound of beef brisket
- 1 tablespoon of Worcestershire sauce
- 1 pound of pulled chicken
- 1 45-ounce can of diced tomatoes
- 1 cup of Traeger BBQ sauce
- 1 cup of chicken broth
- 1 cup of frozen okra
- 1 cup of frozen lima beans
- 1 cup of frozen corn
- 1 tablespoon of apple cider vinegar
- Hot sauce
- Salt and black pepper, to taste

Instructions
1. In a Dutch oven on medium flame, sauté celery, onion, and bell pepper for 5-8 minutes, until translucent.
2. Add garlic, sauté for two minutes. Add Worcestershire sauce, paprika, barbecue sauce, tomatoes, and cayenne.
3. Let it cook for 5 minutes.
4. Add in the chicken, smoked beef brisket, and chicken broth, let it boil.
5. Preheat the Traeger to 300 °F, with the lid closed for 15 minutes
6. Transfer the covered Dutch oven to the grill. Cook for 1 and a half hours; add more broth if required.
7. Add okra, lima beans, and corn. Take the lid off and cook for 1/2 an hour or until vegetables are soft.
8. Add salt and black pepper to your liking.
9. Add vinegar and serve hot.

7.25 Skillet-Roasted Bird

(Ready in about: 1 hour | Serving: 6| Difficulty: Medium)
Nutrition per serving: Kcal: 356| Fat: 11 g| Net Carbs: 12 g| Protein: 29 g

Ingredients:
- 4 pounds of game birds
- 1 bunch of fresh rosemary
- 4 tablespoons of butter
- 1 bunch of fresh thyme
- Salt and black pepper, to taste
- 1 bunch of fresh parsley
- 2 lemons, cut in halves

Instructions
1. Preheat the Traeger to high, with the lid closed and a cast-iron skillet inside
2. Coat the birds with butter and add pepper and salt to the inside of the birds.
3. Add all herbs, one-1/2 lemon inside the birds
4. Tie the birds' legs together. Add 2 tablespoons of butter in skillet and place bird in and roast for 40-45 minutes until internal temperature reaches 165°F.
5. Serve and enjoy.

7.26 Pretzel Mustard Chicken

(Ready in about: 45 minutes| Serving: 4| Difficulty: Medium)
Nutrition per serving: Kcal: 312| Fat: 10 g| Net Carbs: 14 g| Protein: 26 g

Ingredients:
- 4 skinless, boneless chicken breasts
- 1/4 pound of pretzel sticks
- 3 tablespoons of apple cider
- 1 tablespoon of honey
- 3 tablespoons of Dijon mustard
- 1 and 1/2 teaspoons of fresh thyme

Instructions
1. In a blender, crush the pretzel sticks until they look like breadcrumbs.
2. In a bowl, mix cider, thyme, mustard, and honey.
3. Coat chicken in the mustard mix, then in crushed pretzels, and place on a wire rack. Spray coated chicken with oil.
4. Preheat Traeger to 375 °F with the lid closed.
5. Place a pan on the grill with chicken inside and bake for 20-25 minutes, until internal temperature reads 165°F.
6. Let chicken rest before serving.

7.27 Grilled Sweet Cajun Wings

(Ready in about: 30-45 minutes| Serving: 4| Difficulty: Medium)
Nutrition per serving: Kcal: 289| Fat: 13 g| Net Carbs: 5 g| Protein: 22 g

Ingredients:
- Traeger Pork & Poultry rub
- 2 pounds of chicken wings
- Traeger Cajun shake

Instructions
1. Coat the wings with a Cajun shake and sweet rub.
2. Set the Traeger to 350 °F, with the lid closed.
3. Cook for 1/2 an hour until the internal temperature reaches 165°F.
4. Serve and enjoy.

7.28 Smoked and Braised Duck Legs

(Ready in about: 2-3 hours| Serving: 4| Difficulty: Medium)
Nutrition per serving: Kcal: 352| Fat: 18 g| Net Carbs: 9 g| Protein: 24 g

Ingredients:
- 2 tablespoons of black pepper
- 6 duck legs
- 2 tablespoons of salt
- 2 stalks of celery
- 1 rosemary sprigs
- Vegetable oil
- 1 tablespoon of brown sugar
- 2 onions
- 12 cups of any Stock
- 1/2 tablespoon of fresh thyme
- 2 carrots
- 4 garlic cloves
- 2 dried bay leaves
- 2 cups of red wine
- 1 bunch of fresh thyme

Instructions
1. A day before, mix sugar, salt, thyme, and pepper. Coat duck legs with spice rub and keep in the fridge overnight.
2. Next day rinse duck legs with cold water and pat dry.
3. Set the grill to high and keep the lid closed for 15 minutes.
4. Place a skillet on the grill and let it preheat for 15-20 minutes. Add 1 tablespoon of oil.
5. Add duck legs to a pan, close the lid and cook until skin is crispy or for 10-15 minutes.
6. Flip and cook for 5 more minutes.
7. Add chopped onion, carrots, celery, enough stock to submerge 3/4 of duck, garlic, rosemary, red wine, bay leaves, thyme.
8. Lower grill temperature to 350 °F, cook for 2 hours until meat is tender.
9. In the last 19 minutes of cooking, lower temperature to 180°F.
10. Take out from the grill and cover with foil.
11. Strain the sauce and cook until reduced and thickened—season with pepper and salt.
12. Serve with duck.

7.29 Roast Chicken and Pimento Potatoes

(Ready in about: 1 hour and 15 minutes | Serving: 8| Difficulty: Medium)
Nutrition per serving: Kcal: 324| Fat: 21 g| Net Carbs: 8 g| Protein: 25 g

Ingredients:
- 2 whole chickens
- 2 tablespoons of salt
- 5 tablespoons olive oil
- 6 cloves of minced garlic
- 2 lemon cut into halves
- 2 bunches of fresh thyme
- 3 pound of Yukon gold potatoes
- 3 tablespoons of Spanish smoked paprika
- 1/2 cup of chopped flat-leaf parsley
- Black pepper

Instructions
1. Wash the chicken inside and out, pat dry with a paper towel. Tie the legs of the chicken and tuck wings behind the back.
2. In a bowl, add smoked paprika, salt, herbs, and garlic mix well. Add in 3 tablespoons of oil. Spread this mix over the chicken's outside. Keep in the fridge for 6 hours or overnight.
3. Season potatoes with pepper and salt. Coat with 3 tablespoons of oil. Place on a baking sheet.
4. Place marinated chicken with potatoes and drizzle lemon juice over chicken and a little bit on potatoes.
5. Preheat Traeger to 400-450 F
6. Roast the lemons, potatoes, and chicken for 1/2 an hour.
7. Lower temperature to 350 °F, cook until internal temperature reaches 165°F.
8. Serve chicken with vegetables.

7.30 Grilled Nashville Hot Chicken Mac & Cheese

(Ready in about: 55 minutes | Serving: 8| Difficulty: Medium)
Nutrition per serving: Kcal: 455| Fat: 28 g| Net Carbs: 27 g| Protein: 22 g

Ingredients:
- 2 cups of shredded cheddar
- 4 cups of water
- 1/2 teaspoon of salt
- 1 packet of Ranch seasoning mix
- 1/4 cup of salted butter
- 1 pound of rotini
- 1/2 cup of heavy cream
- 1 cup of milk
- 2 cups cubed chicken
- 2 tablespoons Nashville chicken seasoning
- 1/2 cup of plain breadcrumbs

Instructions
1. In a pot, add salt, milk, rotini, butter, water, and ranch mix. Let it boil and cook for 7-8 minutes until pasta is tender.
2. Turn off the heat and add in the cream. Add in cheese mix until melted.
3. Add in hot chicken seasoning, and add cubed chicken.
4. Transfer in a grill -safe dish
5. In a bowl, mix breadcrumbs with 2 tablespoons of melted butter. Cover the top of mac and cheese with the breadcrumb mix. Add 1 tablespoon of Hot Chicken seasoning on top.
6. Turn the Traeger to 325 °F bake the mac and cheese until bubbly and hot.

7.31 Traeger Grilled Nashville Hot Chicken

(Ready in about: 1 hour and 20 minutes | Serving: 6| Difficulty: Medium)
Nutrition per serving: Kcal: 765| Fat: 39 g| Net Carbs: 5 g| Protein: 59 g

Ingredients:
- 1/2 cup of Nashville hot chicken rub
- 1/2 cup of oil
- 5 pounds of a whole chicken

Instructions
1. Set the grill to smoke, keep the lid open.
2. Keep the temperature high; now, keep the lid closed.
3. Tie the chicken legs, coat with oil, and rub. Place directly on the grill.
4. Make sure the breast side is up.
5. Cook until the internal temperature reaches 165°F, as read by a meat thermometer.
6. Rest the chicken before serving.

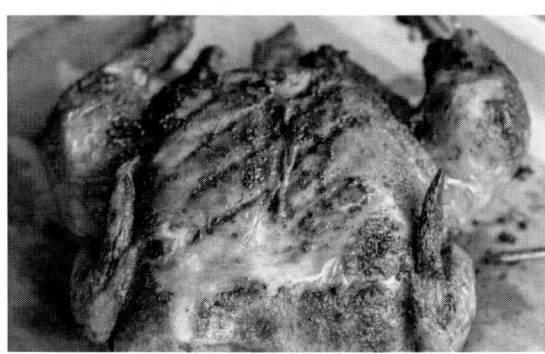

7.32 Sweet Chili Chicken Leg Quarters

(Ready in about: 45 minutes | Serving: 8| Difficulty: Medium)
Nutrition per serving: Kcal: 475 | Fat: 23 g| Net Carbs: 2 g| Protein: 56 g

Ingredients:
- Sweet chili sauce
- 3 tablespoons of oil
- 8 quarters of chicken leg
- Seasoning rub

Instructions
1. Let the grill preheat to 350-400°F.
2. Coat chicken with oil and generously season with seasoning rub.
3. Place chicken directly on grill skin side up and cook for 15-20 minutes
4. Flip it and cook for another 10-20 minutes.
5. When the internal temperature chicken reaches 150 °F, turn the temperature to high until it reaches 165°F, as read by a meat thermometer.
6. In the last 5 minutes, brush the sweet chili sauce.
7. Serve and enjoy.

7.33 Traeger Smoked Turkey Legs

(Ready in about: 3-5 hours | Serving: 12| Difficulty: Medium)
Nutrition per serving: Kcal: 601 | Fat: 35 g| Net Carbs: 20 g| Protein: 70 g

Ingredients:
- 1/2 cup of canola oil
- 8-12 Turkey legs
- Brine:
- 1 cup of Barbecue rub
- 2 gallons of warm water
- 1 cup of curing salt
- 1 cup of dark brown sugar
- 1 cup of poultry seasoning
- 2 tablespoons of black peppercorns
- 1 gallon of cold water
- 8 cups of ice
- 4 bay leaves

Instructions
1. In a large pot, add all ingredients of brine, except for ice and cold water. Let it boil and simmer for 5 minutes; mix the salt well.
2. Turn off the heat and let it come to a room temperature
3. Remove from the burner, let cool to room temperature.
4. Add in cold water and ice and keep in the fridge.
5. Add meat to brine, cover, and keep in the fridge for 24 hours.
6. Let the grill preheat to 200°F.
7. Take the lamb out and rinse. Pat dry.
8. Coat the lamb leg with a light layer of oil and smoke for 3-5 hours.
9. Cook until the internal temperature reaches 165-180°F.
10. Let it rest before serving.

7.34 Traeger Smoked Cornish Hens

(Ready in about: 1 hour and 10 minutes | Serving: 6| Difficulty: Medium)
Nutrition per serving: Kcal: 676 | Fat: 35 g| Net Carbs: 6 g| Protein: 51 g

Ingredients:
- 6 Cornish hens
- 6 tablespoons of poultry rub
- 2-3 tablespoons of avocado oil

Instructions
1. Preheat Traeger to 275°F.
2. Rub the hens with oil.
3. Smoke for 1/2 an hour at 275°F.
4. Flip the chicken over, keep the breast side up and grill at 400°F. until internal temperature reaches 165°F.
5. Rest for 10 minutes before serving.

7.35 Sweet Tea BBQ Chicken Thighs

(Ready in about: 12 hours and 25 minutes | Serving: 4| Difficulty: Medium)
Nutrition per serving: Kcal: 376 | Fat: 15 g| Net Carbs: 23 g| Protein: 21 g

Ingredients:
Sweet Tea Brine:
- 5 slices of lemon
- 1/2 teaspoon of black pepper
- 4 cups of sweet tea
- 4 slices of orange
- 1/2 teaspoon of garlic powder
- 2 teaspoons of salt
- 1/2 teaspoon of Italian seasoning

Sweet tea BBQ sauce:
- 1/4 cup of sweet tea
- 1 cup of Barbecue sauce

BBQ Chicken Thighs:
- 1/2 teaspoon of garlic powder
- 2 and 1/2 pounds of boneless chicken thighs
- 1/2 teaspoon of Italian seasoning
- 1/2 teaspoon of each salt and black pepper

Instructions
1. In a pot, add all ingredients of sweet tea brine, mix well, and submerged the chicken inside. Keep in the fridge, covered, for 12-24 hours.
2. In a mug, mix 1/4 cup of sweet tea with BBQ sauce. Set it aside.
3. Let the Traeger heat to 400-500 °F
4. In a bowl, add pepper, Italian Seasoning, salt, and garlic powder. Mix well.
5. Take chicken out and sprinkle with the dry spice rub, then rush with tea BBQ sauce.
6. Grill chicken for 7-8 minutes.
7. Flip chicken and brush with more BBQ tea sauce, cook for another 6-7 minutes until internal temperature reaches 165°F..

7.36 Savory Grilled Chicken

(Ready in about: 1 hour | Serving: 6| Difficulty: Medium)
Nutrition per serving: Kcal: 378 | Fat: 28 g| Net Carbs: 2 g| Protein: 38 g

Ingredients:
- 2 and 1/2 pounds of skinless, boneless chicken breasts
- 1 tablespoon of Worcestershire sauce
- 1/4 cup of white wine vinegar
- Juice from 1/2 lemon
- 3 tablespoons of mayonnaise
- 1/2 cup of olive oil
- 2 teaspoons of fresh thyme
- 1 teaspoon of smoked paprika
- 1 teaspoon of salt and black pepper, each
- 1/2 tablespoons of onion powder
- 1 clove of minced garlic

Instructions
1. In a bowl, add all ingredients except for chicken, mix well.
2. In a large zip lock bag, pour marinade and chicken. Coat the chicken well.
3. Marinade for 1/2 an hour or a whole day
4. Let the grill preheat to 400-500 °F
5. Grill the chicken until cooked through or for 5 minutes on each side.

7.37 Greek Chicken Marinade

(Ready in about: 1 hour and 5 minutes | Serving: 2| Difficulty: Medium)
Nutrition per serving: Kcal: 313 | Fat: 24 g| Net Carbs: 6.8 g| Protein: 35 g

Ingredients:
- 3 pounds of chicken thighs or drumsticks
- 1 and 1/2 cups plain yogurt
- 2 teaspoons of salt
- 1/2 cup of olive oil
- 1 teaspoon of black pepper
- 1 teaspoon of fresh chopped thyme
- 1 teaspoon of lemon zest
- 1/3 cup of fresh lemon juice
- 2 teaspoons of fresh chopped dill
- 8 cloves of minced garlic
- 1 teaspoon of fresh chopped rosemary
- 1 teaspoon of oregano

Instructions
1. In a bowl, add lemon juice, yogurt, garlic, pepper, herbs, salt, and olive oil. Mix well
2. Add in chicken and coat well; keep in the fridge for 2 hours or all night.
3. Preheat Traeger to 400°F.
4. Place chicken on a baking sheet and place the sheet on grill cook for until internal temperature reaches 170 °F, as read by a meat thermometer.
5. Serve hot.

7.38 Easy Grilled Curry Chicken

(Ready in about: 30 minutes | Serving: 2| Difficulty: Medium)
Nutrition per serving: Kcal: 336 | Fat: 21 g| Net Carbs: 7 g| Protein: 37 g

Ingredients:
- 2 teaspoons of smoked paprika
- 2 teaspoons of curry powder
- 2 tablespoons of apple sauce
- 1/2 teaspoon of salt
- 3 tablespoons of coconut milk
- 2 tablespoons of corn oil
- 1/2 teaspoon of turmeric powder
- Two chicken breasts
- 1 teaspoon of black pepper

Instructions
1. In a bowl, add turmeric, pepper, smoked paprika, curry powder, oil, salt, and corn oil, mix well.
2. Add in coconut milk, apple sauce to make a paste.
3. Coat the chicken well with this paste.
4. Preheat the Traeger to 375°F.
5. Cook chicken directly on the grill for 5 to 8 minutes until the thermometer reaches 165°F.
6. Serve hot.

7.39 Gold BBQ Grilled Chicken

(Ready in about: 20-30 minutes | Serving: 4| Difficulty: Easy)
Nutrition per serving: Kcal: 276 | Fat: 9 g| Net Carbs: 15 g| Protein: 32 g

Ingredients:
- 1-1.5 skinless, boneless chicken breasts
- Grilling & Finishing sauce of Carolina Gold

Marinade:
- 1/4 cup of apple cider vinegar
- 1/4 cup of olive oil
- 1 teaspoon of lemon juice
- 1 teaspoon of sugar
- 1/4 teaspoon of white pepper
- 1 teaspoon of Worcestershire sauce
- 2 cloves of minced garlic
- 1 teaspoon of onion powder
- 1 teaspoon of kosher salt

Instructions
1. In a large sealable, add all the marinade ingredients, add chicken mix, and keep in the fridge for 4 hours.
2. Preheat the Traeger to 375°F.
3. Take chicken out and pound it so it comes to the same thickness all over.
4. Place pieces directly on the grill.
5. Cook for 6 to 8 minutes on each side, until cooked through or until internal temperature reaches 165°F.
6. In the last 3 minutes of cooking, brush gold sauce over chicken.
7. Let it rest before serving.

7.40 Smoked Buttermilk Fried Chicken

(Ready in about: 2 hour and 45 minutes+ brine 12 hours| Serving: 8| Difficulty: Medium)
Nutrition per serving: Kcal: 418 | Fat: 16 g| Net Carbs: 19 g| Protein: 46 g

Ingredients:
- Buttermilk Brine
- 4 pounds of chicken pieces
- 1/2 teaspoon of ground pepper
- 1/2 teaspoon granulated garlic
- 1/4 cup of hot sauce
- 2 cups of buttermilk
- 1/2 teaspoon of salt
- Breading:
- 1 teaspoon of salt
- black pepper: 1/2 teaspoon
- 2 cups of all-purpose flour
- 1 teaspoon of paprika
- 1 teaspoon mustard powder
- 1 teaspoon baking soda
- 1 teaspoon onion powder
- 1/2 teaspoon cayenne pepper
- 1/2 teaspoon granulated garlic
- 1 teaspoon baking powder
- 1/2 teaspoon of ground thyme
- Egg Wash:
- 1/4 cup of whole milk
- 4 whole eggs

Instructions
1. In a large pot, add all ingredients of buttermilk brine, mix well, and keep chicken inside. Keep in the fridge overnight.
2. Set the Traeger to smoke or 180°F. Smoke the brined chicken for 2 hours.
3. Take off from the grill and let it cool completely.
4. Meanwhile, prepare the egg wash, and combine all the ingredients of breading.
5. In a skillet, add 4 to 5 cups of oil keep to 350 °F on the grill. Keep monitoring the temperature of oil using a thermometer.
6. Coat the chicken in the flour mix—place in a rack.
7. Fry chicken pieces a few at a time until crispy.
8. Cook until the internal temperature reaches 165°F.
9. Serve hot.

7.41 Pellet Grill Jerk Chicken Thighs

(Ready in about: 1 hour and 20 minutes | Serving: 6| Difficulty: Easy)
Nutrition per serving: Kcal: 619 | Fat: 44 g| Net Carbs: 7 g| Protein: 32 g

Ingredients:
- 6 chicken skin-on thighs
- 1/2 teaspoon of cinnamon
- 4 cloves of garlic
- 3 tablespoons of olive oil
- Jerk chicken marinade
- 4 teaspoon salt
- 1 and 1/2 teaspoons of black pepper
- 2 tablespoons of soy sauce
- 1/2 teaspoon of ground nutmeg
- 2 teaspoon of fresh thyme leaves
- 4-5 habanero peppers
- 1 teaspoon of ground allspice
- 1/4 cup of fresh lime juice
- 1 onion
- 1 tablespoon of chopped green onion
- 1 tablespoon of brown sugar

Instructions
1. In a blender, add all ingredients except for chicken, pulse to combine.
2. In a large sealable bag, add marinade and chicken coat well and keep in the fridge overnight.
3. Let the grill preheat to 375°F. Place chicken on grill skin side down.
4. Cook chicken for 20-25 minutes, flip and grill more until internal temperature shows 165°F.
5. In a large pan, add 1/2 a cup of oil on medium flame, take the chicken out from the grill.
6. Fry in hot oil to crisp up skin for 2-3 minutes.
7. Serve hot.

7.42 Beer Can Chicken

(Ready in about: 1 hour and 40 minutes | Serving: 6| Difficulty: Easy)
Nutrition per serving: Kcal: 718| Fat: 44 g| Net Carbs: 8 g| Protein: 37 g

Ingredients:
- 1/2 cup of chicken rub, dry
- 1 4-5-pound chicken
- 1 can of beer

Instructions
1. Let the grill set to smoke for 4 -5 minutes; keep the lid open. Keep the temperature to high until it reaches 450°F.
2. Rub chicken with dry rub generously.
3. Keep the chicken whole and add 1/2 beer of can inside the chicken.
4. Cook until the internal temperature reaches 165°F.
5. Slice and serve.

7.43 Traeger Chicken Wings with Spicy Miso

(Ready in about: 40 minutes | Serving: 6| Difficulty: Easy)
Nutrition per serving: Kcal: 608| Fat: 34 g| Net Carbs: 24 g| Protein: 27 g

Ingredients:
- 2 pounds of chicken wings
- 1/8 cup of gochujang
- 3/4 cup of soy sauce
- 1 tablespoon of Sriracha
- Togarashi
- 1/8 cup of miso
- 1/2 cup of oil
- 1/2 cup of pineapple juice
- 1/2 cup of water

Instructions
1. In a bowl, add all ingredients, mix well, and coat the wings well.
2. Keep in the refrigerator for 8-12 hours.
3. Let the grill preheat to 375°F.
4. Place wings directly on Traeger, with the lid closed.
5. Grill until the internal temperature reaches 165 °F, or for 25 minutes.
6. Before serving, sprinkle with Togarashi.

7.44 Traeger Turkey Breast

(Ready in about: 40-50 minutes | Serving: 5| Difficulty: Easy)
Nutrition per serving: Kcal: 150| Fat: 5 g| Net Carbs: 2 g| Protein: 20 g

Ingredients:
- 4 pounds (2.3 kg) turkey breasts, cooked
- 10 slices bacon
- 20 ounces of scallion, chopped
- 1/2 cup of white wine
- Salt and black pepper to taste

Instructions
1. Slice the turkey breast horizontally. Lay the breast flat.
2. In a skillet, cook the bacon until crispy.
3. Cook the scallions in the wine and cook until wine dries.
4. Combine the bacon with salt, pepper, and the scallions.
5. Put the mixture in the refrigerator to cool during 15 to 20 minutes.
6. Once chilled, spread the mixture over the turkey breast, pressing lightly to make sure it adheres.
7. Roll the turkey breast tightly and tie with cooking twine.
8. Preheat your Traeger temperature to 400°F (200°C) for 15 minutes.
9. Season the outside of the turkey breast with salt and pepper.
10. Place on the grill and cook for 40 minutes.
11. Remove the turkey from the grill and let it rest for 10 minutes before serving.

7.45 Grilled Marinated Chicken

(Ready in about: 12 minutes | Serving: 6| Difficulty: Easy)
Nutrition per serving: Kcal: 165| Fat: 5 g| Net Carbs: 1 g| Protein: 4 g

Ingredients:
- 6 (1/2 pound) chicken breasts
- Marinade
- 2 cups of olive oil
- 2 tablespoons of white vinegar
- 1 tablespoon of lemon juice
- 1 orange (the juice)
- 1 tablespoon of minced garlic
- 1-1/2 tablespoon of chopped thyme
- 2 tablespoons of fresh chives, chopped
- 1 red bell pepper
- 1/2 tablespoon of ground pepper
- 1-1/2 tablespoon of salt

Instructions
1. Mix all the marinade ingredients then add the chicken until well covered.
2. Marinate for 40 minutes in the refrigerator.
3. When ready to cook, preheat your Traeger to 450°F for 15 minutes.
4. Grill for 15 minutes on each side or until reaching your preferred doneness.
5. Set aside. Serve and enjoy.

CHAPTER 8
Traeger Grill Seafood Recipes

Chapter 8: Traeger Grill Seafood Recipes

8.1 Traeger Halibut with Parmesan

(**Ready in about**: 25 minutes | **Serving**: 6| **Difficulty**: Medium)
Nutrition per serving: Kcal: 291| **Fat**: 15 g| **Net Carbs**: 1 g| **Protein**: 37 g

Ingredients:
- 2 pounds of skinless fillet of halibut
- 1/2 cup of shredded parmesan
- 1 tablespoon of mayonnaise
- 1/4 cup of softened salted butter
- 1 tablespoon of sour cream
- 3 tablespoons of chopped chives

Instructions
1. Preheat the Traeger to 375°F.
2. Mix all ingredients except for fish.
3. Coat the fish fillet in the cheese mix. Place on grill-safe pan.
4. Cook for 15-20 minutes.
5. Broil for 1-2 minutes, serve hot.

8.2 Traeger Cioppino

(**Ready in about**: 1 hour and 5 minutes | **Serving**: 8| **Difficulty**: Medium)
Nutrition per serving: Kcal: 711| **Fat**: 26 g| **Net Carbs**: 22 g| **Protein**: 76 g

Ingredients:
- Soup Base:
- 6 cups of fish stock
- 1 sliced fennel bulb
- 1/4 cup of butter
- 1 diced carrot
- 4 diced shallots
- 1 diced onion
- 5 cloves of minced garlic
- 2 teaspoons of dried oregano
- 3 sprigs of fresh thyme
- 2 15-ounce cans of diced tomatoes with juices
- 2 cups of dry white
- 1 6-ounce can of tomato paste
- 2 bay leaves
- 1 tablespoon of salt
- 1 teaspoon of red pepper flakes
- Seafood:
- 2 pounds of skinless fresh fish, cut into one-inch pieces
- 2 crabs, halved and steamed
- 1 pound of prawns
- 1 pound of cleaned mussels
- 1 pound of cleaned steamer clams

Instructions
1. Preheat the Traeger to 375°F.
2. In a Dutch oven, add butter on medium flame. Add in diced carrot, a sliced fennel bulb, shallots, and diced onion.
3. Sauté for 2 to 3 minutes, till the vegetables softened.
4. Add garlic and sauté for 30 seconds.
5. Add tomatoes with juice, herbs, fish stock, seasonings, and tomato paste. Let it simmer.
6. Place Dutch oven on the grill, let it simmer for 15 minutes until the stew's internal temperature reaches 180 to 211°F.
7. Add all seafood.
8. Cook for 10 minutes.
9. Serve hot.

8.3 Blackened Catfish Tacos

(**Ready in about**: 25 minutes | **Serving**: 5| **Difficulty**: Medium)
Nutrition per serving: Kcal: 515| **Fat**: 27 g| **Net Carbs**: 21 g| **Protein**: 46 g

Ingredients:
- All-purpose rub
- 1 pound of catfish:
- 1 cup of shredded cabbage
- 5 tortillas
- Lemon cut into wedges
- 1 cup of shredded cheese
- Tartar Sauce:
- 1 cup of mayo
- 1 diced cucumber
- 3 tablespoons of wasabi paste
- Juice from 2 lemons
- 1 brick of cream cheese
- 1 diced onion
- 1/4 cup of dill pickle relish

Instructions
1. Coat the fish in seasoning rub. Keep in the fridge.
2. In a bowl, add onion, cream cheese, mayo, and mix well.
3. Add in wasabi paste, 1/4 cup of dill pickle relish, cucumber, lemon juice of 1 lemon, salt, and pepper. Mix well. Keep in the fridge.
4. Preheat the Traeger to 350°F., and place the fish on grill grates. Cook on one side for 10 minutes.
5. Take off grill and serve in tacos with tartar sauce, cabbage and cheese.

8.4 Traeger Honey Garlic Salmon

(**Ready in about**: 25 minutes | **Serving**: 6| **Difficulty**: Medium)
Nutrition per serving: Kcal: 619| **Fat**: 36 g| **Net Carbs**: 17 g| **Protein**: 49 g

Ingredients:
Sauce:
- 3 tablespoons of butter
- 3 tablespoons of soy sauce
- 1/3 cup of honey
- 2 tablespoons of white wine
- 2 tablespoons of minced garlic
- 3 tablespoons of balsamic vinegar

Salmon:
- Olive oil
- 6 small salmon filets
- Garlic powder
- Salt and pepper
- Onion powder

Instructions
1. Preheat the Traeger to 350 °F
2. In a bowl, add all ingredients of the sauce.
3. Pour this mix into a grill-safe dish
4. Coat salmon with olive oil and sprinkle with seasoning; place salmon in foil pan.
5. Place both pans on the grill and cook for 10-20 minutes or until salmon's internal temperature reaches 145°F.
6. Cook the sauce for 10 minutes. Do not burn.
7. Take both pans out of the grill.
8. Pour sauce over salmon and serve.

8.5 Traeger Lobster Rolls

(**Ready in about**: 15 minutes | **Serving**: 4| **Difficulty**: Easy)
Nutrition per serving: Kcal: 234| **Fat**: 16 g| **Net Carbs**: 16 g| **Protein**: 8 g

Ingredients:
- 4 rolls
- 4 lobster tails, grilled but cooled down
- 2 tablespoons of lemon juice
- 1 teaspoon of kosher salt
- 2 tablespoons of chopped parsley
- 1 tablespoon of chopped green onion
- 1 stalk of celery stalk, chopped
- 1/4 cup of mayo
- 1/2 teaspoon of ground black pepper

Instructions
1. In a bowl, add parsley, lemon juice, mayo, green onions, salt, celery, and black pepper mix well. Let it rest for 5-10 minutes.
2. Remove shells from lobster and cut into small pieces
3. Slowly mix the sauce and lobster and the sauce.
4. Toast the buttered buns in a pan. Place lobster and mixture on top.
5. Smoke in Traeger for 10 minutes at 250 °F until heated through.
6. Serve right away.

8.6 Traeger Tuna Melt Flatbread

(**Ready in about**: 20 minutes| **Serving**: 6| **Difficulty**: Easy)
Nutrition per serving: Kcal: 321| **Fat**: 15 g| **Net Carbs**: 12 g| **Protein**: 23 g

Ingredients:
- 6 flatbreads
- 2 cans of water-packed tuna
- 1/4 teaspoon of garlic powder
- 1/2 teaspoon of salt
- 1/4 teaspoon of onion powder
- 1/2 cup of mayo
- Microgreens
- 3 tablespoons of chopped dill pickles
- 1/4 teaspoon of pepper
- 2 cups of shredded cheese

Instructions
1. Mix all ingredients.
2. Let the Traeger preheat to smoke (180 °F).
3. Place on 6 flatbreads and smoke for 10 minutes in Trager
4. Put microgreens on top
5. Serve and enjoy.

8.7 Traeger Chimichurri Shrimp

(**Ready in about**: 18 minutes| **Serving**: 6| **Difficulty**: Easy)
Nutrition per serving: Kcal: 388| **Fat**: 17 g| **Net Carbs**: 4 g| **Protein**: 52 g

Ingredients:
- 3 tablespoons of avocado oil
- 3 tablespoons of chimichurri seasoning blend
- 3 pounds of peeled shrimp, deveined

Instructions
1. Preheat the Traeger to 375 F.
2. Thread shrimps on skewers and drizzle oil.
3. Season with chimichurri spice rub.
4. Put on the grill and cook on each side for 2-3 minutes, until cooked.
5. Serve right away.

8.8 Traeger Spicy Fried Shrimp

(**Ready in about**: 35 minutes| **Serving**: 6| **Difficulty**: Medium)
Nutrition per serving: Kcal: 327| **Fat**: 17 g| **Net Carbs**: 18 g| **Protein**: 24 g

Ingredients:
- 1/3 cup of oil
- 1 pound of shrimps, peeled and deveined
- 2 tablespoons of Nashville hot rub
- 1/2 teaspoon of onion powder
- 1 tablespoon of paprika
- 1 cup of flour
- 4 whole eggs
- 1/4 teaspoon of white pepper
- 1 teaspoon of salt
- 1/2 teaspoon of garlic powder

Instructions
1. Preheat the Traeger to 400°F.
2. Pat the shrimps dry.
3. In a bowl, add all dry ingredients, mix well.
4. In a bowl, add eggs and whisk.
5. Coat shrimps in flour, then in the dry spice mix, then in egg wash, back again in flour.
6. Thread breaded shrimps on skewers.
7. Keep in the fridge for 15-20 minutes.
8. Place skewers on an oiled grill cook for 3 minutes with the lid closed.
9. Take off grill and brush with oil place again on grill cook for 5 minutes.
10. Serve hot.

8.9 Smoked Lobster Tails

(**Ready in about**: 1 hour | **Serving**: 4| **Difficulty**: Medium)
Nutrition per serving: Kcal: 765| **Fat**: 38 g| **Net Carbs**: 1 g| **Protein**: 99 g

Ingredients:
- 4 teaspoons of olive oil
- Salt and pepper, to taste
- 4 lobster tails

Instructions
1. Preheat the Traeger to 225°F.
2. Season the tails with pepper, olive oil, and salt.
3. Place tails on the smoker, slit side up for 60 minutes.
4. Serve hot.

8.10 Traeger Grilled Crab Legs

(**Ready in about**: 55 minutes | **Serving**: 6| **Difficulty**: Medium)
Nutrition per serving: Kcal: 765| **Fat**: 38 g| **Net Carbs**: 1 g| **Protein**: 99 g

Ingredients:
- 1 cup of melted butter
- 4-6 pounds of snow crab legs
- 2 cloves of minced garlic
- 3 tablespoons of chopped fresh parsley
- 2-3 tablespoons of Old Bay seasoning
- 1/4 cup of dry white wine

Instructions
1. Preheat the Traeger to 375°F.
2. Put Crab in foil pan. Mix all other ingredients and pour over crab.
3. Place on grill cook with closed lid.
4. Cook for 10 minutes, baste with juices, cook for another 10 minutes.
5. Baste again and cook for 5-10 minutes.
6. Serve right away.

8.11 Foil Packet Salmon

(**Ready in about**: 30 minutes | **Serving**: 4| **Difficulty**: Easy)
Nutrition per serving: Kcal: 155| **Fat**: 11 g| **Net Carbs**: 1 g| **Protein**: 13 g

Ingredients:
- 4 teaspoons of butter
- 1 salmon filet slice into 4 pieces
- 1 tablespoon of fin and feather seasoning
- 4 slices of lemon

Instructions
1. Preheat the Traeger to 350-375°F.
2. Take 4 large and thick pieces of foil, spray with non-stick spray.
3. Place salmon on foil, sprinkle the rub and place lemon slice with 1 tablespoon of butter on top.
4. Wrap salmon loosely in foil and seal.
5. Place on grill cook on indirect heat. Cook until internal temperature (as read by a meat thermometer) reaches 120-135 °F, or for 15 to 20. °F
6. Serve right away.

8.12 Easy Shrimp Diablo

(**Ready in about**: 15 minutes | **Serving**: 8| **Difficulty**: Medium)
Nutrition per serving: Kcal: 180| **Fat**: 3 g| **Net Carbs**: 2 g| **Protein**: 34 g

Ingredients:
- 2 pounds of shrimp without tail or shells
- 1 sliced green pepper
- 1 can of El Pato green
- 1 chopped sweet onion
- 1 jalapeno remove seeds and sliced
- 1 can of El Pato yellow

Instructions
1. For the whole night, marinate vegetables and shrimp in both El Pato yellow.
2. Preheat the Traeger to 350°F.
3. Cook shrimp and vegetables in a pan, on the grill in the marinade.
4. Let it simmer for 5 minutes until shrimp cooks
5. Serve hot with tortillas.

8.13 Salmon Miso Poke Bowl

(**Ready in about**: 2 hours and 15 minutes | **Serving**: 4| **Difficulty**: Easy)
Nutrition per serving: Kcal: 481| **Fat**: 30 g| **Net Carbs**: 33 g| **Protein**: 23 g

Ingredients:
For Salmon:
- 1/2 teaspoon sesame oil
- 2 cups of fresh salmon, cut into cubes
- 1 tablespoon of red miso
- 3 tablespoons of soy sauce
- 1/2 teaspoon of ginger, minced
- 3 tablespoons of green onions, white parts only
- 1 tablespoon of rice wine vinegar
- Sushi rice
- 1/2 teaspoon of minced garlic

Toppings:
- Sliced avocados
- Shelled edamame
- Sriracha
- Nori slices
- Diced green onions
- Diced cucumbers
- Sesame seeds

Instructions
1. In a bowl, add all marinade ingredients with salmon and keep in the fridge for 1-2 hours.
2. Preheat your smoker to 350ºF.
3. After totally unfreezing the salmon, grill for 90 minutes or until salmon reaches your desired brown color.
4. Add it on sushi rice and serve with the desired topping.

8.14 Salmon Orzo Pasta Salad

(**Ready in about**: 50 minutes | **Serving**: 8| **Difficulty**: Easy)
Nutrition per serving: Kcal: 365| **Fat**: 11 g| **Net Carbs**: 45 g| **Protein**: 20 g

Ingredients:
- 1 grilled salmon fillet
- 2 cups of orzo, uncooked
- 1 handful of baby spinach
- 1/4 cup of diced red bell peppers
- 1 cup of crumbled feta
- 1 cup sliced in half, cherry tomatoes
- 1 cucumber, diced
- 1 cup of Greek freak dressing
- 1/4 cup of Kalamata olives

Instructions
1. Cook pasta in well-salted water. Rinse with cold water.
2. In the meantime, preheat your smoker to 350ºF.
3. In a large bowl, mix the pasta with baby spinach, bell peppers, cherry tomatoes, feta, olives, and cucumber.
4. Grill for 30 minutes or until salmon reaches your desired doneness.
5. Pour over dressing mix gently to the pasta.
6. Add grilled salmon, mix lightly, and serve.

8.15 Grilled Salmon Sandwich

(**Ready in about**: 60 minutes | **Serving**: 4| **Difficulty**: Medium)
Nutrition per serving: Kcal: 652| **Fat**: 33 g| **Net Carbs**: 25 g| **Protein**: 50 g

Ingredients:
Salmon Sandwiches:
- Fin & Feather Traeger rub
- 4 salmon sandwich-sized filets
- 1 teaspoon of salt
- 1 tablespoon of olive oil
- Lettuce
- 4 toasted buns

Dill Aioli:
- 1/4 teaspoon of salt
- 1/2 cup of mayonnaise
- 1/2 teaspoon of minced fresh dill
- 2 teaspoons of lemon juice
- 1/2 teaspoon of lemon zest

Instructions
1. In a bowl, add all ingredients of dill mayo, mix well, and keep in the fridge.
2. Preheat the Traeger to 425-450 ºF
3. Coat fish filet with olive oil, salt, and then seasoning rub.
4. Place fish on grill cook until the internal temperature of fish reaches 130-135 ºF
5. Let it rest for 5 minutes before placing it in a bun.
6. Top with aioli, lettuce, and serve.

8.16 Traeger Grilled Shrimp Scampi

(**Ready in about**: 15 minutes | **Serving**: 4| **Difficulty**: Medium)
Nutrition per serving: Kcal: 298| **Fat**: 24 g| **Net Carbs**: 2 g| **Protein**: 16 g

Ingredients:
- 1 pound of the colossal tail-on raw shrimp
- 1/2 teaspoon of chopped fresh garlic
- 1/2 cup of melted salted butter
- 1/2 teaspoon of garlic powder
- 1/4 cup of dry white wine
- 1/2 teaspoon of salt
- 1 tablespoon of lemon juice

Instructions
1. Preheat the Traeger to 400 ºF with the cast iron skillet.
2. In a bowl, mix garlic, melted butter, lemon juice, and white wine.
3. Pour in the cast iron pan, let it heat for 3-4 minutes.
4. Coat the shrimp with salt and garlic powder—place in cast iron skillet.
5. Grill for 10 minutes with lid closed; make sure not to overcook shrimp.
6. Serve right away.

8.17 Red Snapper Recipe

(**Ready in about**: 20-30 minutes | **Serving**: 4| **Difficulty**: Medium)
Nutrition per serving: Kcal: 281| **Fat**: 13 g| **Net Carbs**: 4 g| **Protein**: 25 g

Ingredients:
- 1 lime
- 1 teaspoon of black pepper
- 4 large red snapper filets
- 1/3 cup of olive oil
- 2 onions
- 1 teaspoon of minced garlic
- 1 teaspoon of salt
- 1/2 teaspoon of cumin
- 3 teaspoons of fresh cilantro
- 1/4 cup of Ponzu sauce
- 1 teaspoon of ancho chili powder
- 1/2 teaspoon of lime zest

Instructions
1. Cut the lime into slices. Cut onions into rings and break them apart.
2. In the olive oil, whisk all ingredients.
3. Preheat the Traeger to 350ºF.
4. On top of lime and onion slice, place the fish and coat with olive oil mix.
5. After every 15 minutes, baste the fish. Cook until flaky and firm.
6. Serve right away.

8.18 BBQ Salmon with Bourbon Glaze

(**Ready in about**: 2 hours | **Serving**: 4| **Difficulty**: Medium)
Nutrition per serving: Kcal: 281| **Fat**: 18 g| **Net Carbs**: 2 g| **Protein**: 22 g

Ingredients:
- 4 salmon fillets
- 1 tablespoon of olive oil
- 1 cup of ketchup
- 1 cup of Jim beam bourbon
- 1/4 cup of apple cider vinegar
- 3 teaspoons of Worcestershire sauce
- 1/2 cup of brown sugar
- 1 tablespoon of lemon juice
- 1 tablespoon of yellow mustard
- 1/2 teaspoon of minced garlic
- 1/2 teaspoon of black pepper
- 1 teaspoon of salt
- 2 tablespoon of dry rub seasoning

Instructions
1. Preheat the Traeger to 350ºF.
2. Coat dry fish with olive oil and rub with seasoning.
3. In a bowl, add the rest of the ingredients and mix well.
4. Put salmon on the grill, cook for 5 minutes, and brush with glaze generously, and cook for 10 minutes.
5. Again, brush with glaze, flip the fish and glaze the other side.
6. Cook until the internal temperature reaches 145°F.
7. Serve right away.

8.19 Smoked Trout

(**Ready in about**: 2 hours | **Serving**: 4| **Difficulty**: Medium)
Nutrition per serving: Kcal: 276| **Fat**: 19.9 g| **Net Carbs**: 3 g| **Protein**: 21 g

Ingredients:
- 4 skin-on trout fillets
- 2 tablespoons of brown sugar
- 1/2 teaspoons of onion powder
- 1 teaspoon of dried oregano
- 1 and 1/2 teaspoons of kosher salt
- 1/2 teaspoon of dried thyme
- 1/4 teaspoon of black pepper
- 1/2 teaspoon of chili powder

Instructions
1. Pre-heat the Traeger to 225 ºF
2. Take bones out of fish fillet.
3. In a bowl, mix oregano, brown sugar, chili powder, pepper, salt, onion powder, and thyme. Rub this spice mix on the surface of fish.
4. Place fish on the grill with the lid closed and cook for 1 and a half hours until the internal temperature reaches 140°F.
5. Drizzle lemon juice before serving.

8.20 Lemon Ginger Grilled Shrimp

(**Ready in about**: 30 minutes | **Serving**: 4| **Difficulty**: Easy)
Nutrition per serving: Kcal: 214| **Fat**: 9 g| **Net Carbs**: 4 g| **Protein**: 20 g

Ingredients:
- 3 pounds of jumbo shrimp, deveined and peeled
- 2 teaspoons of sesame oil
- 2 cloves of garlic
- 1/4 cup of lemon juice
- 1 diced onion
- 1/2 cup of olive oil
- 3 tablespoons of All-Purpose rub
- 2 tablespoons of cilantro
- 2 tablespoons of grated ginger root

Instructions
1. In a blender, add cilantro, olive oil, ginger, rub, lemon juice, and garlic. Pulse on high until smooth.
2. Take two tablespoons of mix safe.
3. Pour the rest over shrimp and coat well; keep in the fridge for 1-2 hours.
4. Preheat the Traeger to 250°F. Add shrimp on skewers with head and tail.
5. Grill the shrimps for 3-4 minutes on each side, brush the reserved marinade over shrimps, and serve.

8.21 Sesame Crusted Halibut with Tahini Mayonnaise

(**Ready in about**: 30 minutes | **Serving**: 4| **Difficulty**: Easy)
Nutrition per serving: Kcal: 281| **Fat**: 21 g| **Net Carbs**: 2 g| **Protein**: 19 g

Ingredients:
Halibut:
- 1 tablespoon vegetable oil
- 1 and a half-pound of halibut fillet, slice into 4 pieces
- 1/2 cup of pickled ginger
- 1/2 teaspoon of kosher salt
- 1/2 cup of sesame seeds
- 1 teaspoon of sesame oil

Mayonnaise:
- 1/4 cup of tahini paste
- 2 yolks only
- 1 and 1/2 cups of vegetable oil
- 1 tablespoon of soya sauce
- 2 tablespoons of lemon juice

Instructions
1. In a grinder, crush salt with sesame seeds. Do not make powder.
2. Coat the fish with all oils.
3. Coat oiled fish with crushed sesame seeds.
4. Preheat the Traeger to 225°F.
5. Place fish on the grill and cook for two and a half hours until internal temperature reaches 145 °F
6. In a blender, add all ingredients of mayo except for oil. Blend well. Gradually add oil while the blender is on.
7. Serve fish with picked ginger and tahini mayo.

8.22 Grilled Teriyaki Salmon

(**Ready in about**: 30 minutes | **Serving**: 4| **Difficulty**: Easy)
Nutrition per serving: Kcal: 276| **Fat**: 25 g| **Net Carbs**: 3 g| **Protein**: 14 g

Ingredients:
- 1/8 cup of olive oil
- 1 large salmon fillet
- 1/4 teaspoon of pepper
- 1/2 teaspoon of salt
- 1 teaspoon of sesame seeds
- 1/4 teaspoon of garlic salt
- 1/4 cup of butter, cut into pats
- 1/4 cup of teriyaki sauce

Instructions
1. Preheat the Traeger to 400°F.
2. Place fish in a make-shift foil pan.
3. Pour olive oil and season with seasonings, and place butter pieces on top.
4. Place foil on the grill. Cook for 8 minutes and brush with teriyaki sauce after 5 minutes.
5. Cook until the internal temperature reaches 145°F.
6. Sprinkle sesame seeds and serve.

8.23 Lemon Pepper Traeger Grilled Salmon

(**Ready in about**: 30 minutes | **Serving**: 4| **Difficulty**: Easy)
Nutrition per serving: Kcal: 211| **Fat**: 8 g| **Net Carbs**: 2 g| **Protein**: 29 g

Ingredients:
- 1/8 cup of olive oil
- 1 salmon fillet
- 1/4 cup of butter, cut into pats
- 2-3 tablespoons of lemon pepper seasoning

Instructions
1. Preheat the Traeger to 400°F.
2. Place fish in a make-shift foil pan.
3. Pour olive oil and season with seasonings, and place butter pieces on top.
4. Cook fish in foil on the grill and cook for 15 minutes with lid closed, until internal temperature reaches 145°F.
5. Serve right away.

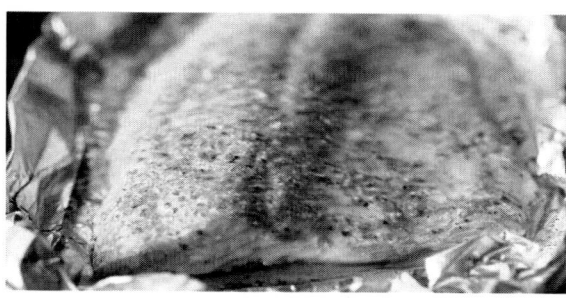

8.24 Traeger Grilled Lemon Dill Salmon

(**Ready in about**: 30 minutes | **Serving**: 2| **Difficulty**: Easy)
Nutrition per serving: Kcal: 485| **Fat**: 6 g| **Net Carbs**: 4 g| **Protein**: 26 g

Ingredients:
- 1/4 cup of olive oil
- 1 salmon filet, large
- 1/2 teaspoon of dried dill
- Lemon juice
- 1 teaspoon of kosher salt

Instructions
1. Preheat the Traeger to smoke, then raise the temperature to 350 °F and now close the lid.
2. Place fish skin side on foil and coat with olive oil, season with 1 teaspoon of lemon juice, dill, and salt.
3. Place fish in foil on the grill and cook for 15-20 minutes, or until fish is flaky.
4. Before serving, rest for 5 minutes.

8.25 Traeger Grilled Salmon with Togarashi

(**Ready in about**: 25 minutes | **Serving**: 3| **Difficulty**: Easy)
Nutrition per serving: Kcal: 119| **Fat**: 10 g| **Net Carbs**: 1 g| **Protein**: 6 g

Ingredients:
- 1 large salmon filet
- 1 tablespoon of Togarashi seasoning
- 1/4 cup of olive oil
- 1/2 cup of kosher salt

Instructions
1. Preheat the Traeger to 400°F.
2. Put salmon on a foil skin side down.
3. Cover fish in olive oil and season with Togarashi and salt.
4. Put fish with foil on the grill, cook for 15-20 minutes with lid closed, until internal temperature reaches 140 to 145°F.
5. Serve right away.

8.26 Traeger Smoked Salmon

(**Ready in about**: 3-4 hours | **Serving**: 8| **Difficulty**: Easy)
Nutrition per serving: Kcal: 101| **Fat**: 2 g| **Net Carbs**: 16 g| **Protein**: 4 g

Ingredients:
Brine:
- 1/3 cup of kosher salt
- 4 cups of water
- 1 cup of brown sugar

Salmon:
- Maple syrup
- Large salmon filet

Instructions
1. In a large pot, add all ingredients of brine mix until sugar dissolves. Place salmon fillet in brine cover and keep in the fridge for 10-12 hours.
2. Take fish out, rinse and pat dry. Keep it at room temperature for 1-2 hours.
3. Preheat the Traeger to smoke, place fish on the oiled rack, and put the rack on the grill.
4. Cook fish with the lid closed off and Brush with maple syrup once in an hour.
5. Do not let the temperature of the grill rises above 180°F.
6. Cook for 3-4 hours, or until it becomes flaky.

8.27 Sriracha Salmon Stuffed Mushrooms

(**Ready in about**: 20 minutes | **Serving**: 8| **Difficulty**: Easy)
Nutrition per serving: Kcal: 161| **Fat**: 10 g| **Net Carbs**: 8 g| **Protein**: 10 g

Ingredients:
- 15-20 mushrooms, trimmed and cleaned
- 1/2 cup of panko bread crumbs
- 2 teaspoons of diced garlic
- Sriracha
- 1/4 teaspoon of garlic powder
- 1 6-ounce drained can of Sockeye salmon
- 1 tablespoon of butter
- 1 egg, whisked
- 1/4 cup of softened cream cheese
- 1/4 teaspoon of salt
- 1/2 cup of shredded parmesan
- 1/8 teaspoon of pepper

Instructions
1. Preheat the Traeger to 350°F.
2. Dice the stems of mushroom sauté them with garlic and butter.
3. Mix this sautéed mix with salmon, pepper, salt, egg, panko, cream cheese, parmesan, garlic powder. Mix well and stuff the mushroom cap with this mix.
4. Put a dash of Sriracha on top. Bake for 15-20 minutes.

8.28 Smoked Salmon Dip

(**Ready in about**: 20 minutes | **Serving**: 10| **Difficulty**: Easy)
Nutrition per serving: Kcal: 113| **Fat**: 9 g| **Net Carbs**: 2 g| **Protein**: 5 g

Ingredients:
- 8 ounces of smoked salmon
- 1/2 cup of softened cream cheese
- 1/4 teaspoon of garlic powder
- 1 tablespoon of lemon juice
- 1 cup of sour cream
- 1 teaspoon of fresh dill
- 2 teaspoons of prepared horseradish
- 1/4 teaspoon of cayenne pepper

Instructions
1. Add all ingredients to a bowl and combine well.
2. Preheat the pellet grill to smoke.
3. Smoke the dip for 10 minutes.
4. Enjoy with tortilla chips.

8.29 Traeger Grilled Rockfish

(**Ready in about**: 30 minutes | **Serving**: 6| **Difficulty**: Easy)
Nutrition per serving: Kcal: 270| **Fat**: 9 g| **Net Carbs**: 2 g| **Protein**: 28 g

Ingredients:
- 6 tablespoons of butter
- 6 filets of rockfish
- 2 teaspoons chopped fresh dill
- 1 lemon cut into slices
- 1/2 teaspoon of onion powder
- 3/4 teaspoon of Himalayan salt
- 1/2 teaspoon of garlic powder

Instructions
1. Preheat the grill to 375°F.
2. Put fish in the grill-safe pan, season fish with dill, garlic powder, salt, and onion powder.
3. Put 1 tablespoon of butter on each fillet and lemon slices.
4. Put the baking pan on the grill with the lid closed. Cook until fish becomes flaky or for 20 minutes.
5. Let it rest for 5 minutes before serving.

8.30 Grilled Lingcod

(**Ready in about**: 25 minutes | **Serving**: 4| **Difficulty**: Easy)
Nutrition per serving: Kcal: 245| **Fat**: 2 g| **Net Carbs**: 2 g| **Protein**: 33 g

Ingredients:
- 1/2 teaspoon of white pepper
- 2 pounds of lingcod filets
- 1/4 teaspoon of cayenne
- Lemon cut into wedges and slices
- 1/2 teaspoon of salt

Instructions
1. Preheat the Traeger to 375°F.
2. Season cod with cayenne pepper, salt, and pepper and place lemon slices on top.
3. Place the fish on a grill mat or parchment paper.
4. Lightly season the fish with the pepper and, and top with a lemon slice.
5. Put the fish on the grill, cook until internal temperature reaches 145 °F
6. Serve with lemon wedges.

8.31 Pan Seared Lingcod

(**Ready in about**: 22 minutes | **Serving**: 4| **Difficulty**: Easy)
Nutrition per serving: Kcal: 112| **Fat**: 7 g| **Net Carbs**: 3 g| **Protein**: 10 g

Ingredients:
- 1 tablespoon of olive oil
- 4 pieces of cod filets
- 1/2 teaspoon of onion powder
- 3 cloves of garlic
- 1 tablespoon of butter
- 1/2 teaspoon of paprika
- 1 sprig of fresh thyme
- 1/2 teaspoon of salt
- 1/4 teaspoon of black pepper

Pan Sauce:
- 1 teaspoon of chopped Italian parsley
- 1 lemon

Instructions
1. Preheat the Traeger to 375 °F with a cast iron pan inside.
2. Season fish with paprika, salt, onion powder, and black pepper.
3. In a cast-iron pan, add oil and butter on medium-low heat.
4. Place fish with garlic and thyme in the pan, let it cook for 4-5 minutes, with the lid closed, until a golden-brown crust appears.
5. Flip fish and cook for 4-5 minutes until internal temperature reaches 145°F. Do not burn the garlic.
6. Take fish out with pan and cover with foil, let it rest.
7. Deglaze pan with lemon juice and pour over fish and serve.

8.32 Molasses Glazed Salmon

(**Ready in about**: 20 minutes | **Serving**: 2| **Difficulty**: Medium)
Nutrition per serving: Kcal: 151| **Fat**: 9 g| **Net Carbs**: 8.8 g| **Protein**: 19 g

Ingredients:
- 1/4 cup of pastrami rub
- 2 salmon filets
- 1 cup of Molasses glaze

Molasses Glaze:
- 2 tablespoons of white cooking wine
- 1/4 cup of Molasses
- A pinch of pepper flakes
- 1/4 cup of dark soy sauce

Pastrami Rub:
- 1/4 cup of black pepper
- 1 teaspoon of onion powder
- 1 tablespoon of granulated garlic
- 2 tablespoons of kosher salt
- 1 tablespoon of coriander
- 1 teaspoon of ground mustard
- 2 tablespoons of raw sugar

Instructions
1. To make molasses glaze. Add all ingredients to a pot, heat for 2-3 minutes. Whisk well. Set it aside.
2. Preheat the Traeger to 325°F.
3. Brush fish pieces with cool molasses glaze and keep in the fridge for 1/2 an hour.
4. For pastrami seasoning, mix all ingredients and coat the salmon in pastrami rub.
5. Place on grill and cook until internal temperature reaches 135°F.
6. Before serving, rest salmon for 5-10 minutes.

8.33 Traeger Teriyaki Smoked Shrimp

(**Ready in about**: 20 minutes | **Serving**: 6| **Difficulty**: Medium)
Nutrition per serving: Kcal: 87| **Fat**: 8 g| **Net Carbs**: 2 g| **Protein**: 16 g

Ingredients:
- 2 tablespoons of minced green onion
- 1/2 teaspoon of onion powder
- 1 pound of uncooked shrimp with tail
- 4 tablespoons of teriyaki sauce
- 1/2 teaspoon of salt
- 1/2 teaspoon of garlic powder
- 4 tablespoons of Sriracha mayo

Instructions
1. Peel shrimp keep the tail attached and deveined. Wash and pat dry.
2. Season with salt, onion powder, and garlic powder.
3. Preheat the Traeger to 450°F.
4. Place seasoned shrimp on the grill, cook each side for 5-6 minutes.
5. Coat cooked shrimp with teriyaki sauce. Serve with green onions and Sriracha mayo.

8.34 Grilled Crab Cakes

(**Ready in about**: 15 minutes | **Serving**: 6| **Difficulty**: Medium)
Nutrition per serving: Kcal: 251| **Fat**: 14 g| **Net Carbs**: 15 g| **Protein**: 16 g

Ingredients:
- 1 tablespoon of avocado oil
- 2 tablespoons of mayonnaise
- 1/2 teaspoon of salt
- 1 egg white
- 16 ounces of crab
- 2 teaspoons of minced garlic
- 1/2 cup of cornflake crumbs
- Roasted pepper aioli for serving
- Pepper Aioli, to taste

Instructions
1. Preheat the Traeger to 375-425 °F with a cast iron pan.
2. In a bowl, mix all ingredients lightly.
3. Shape into patties—spray oil on cast iron pan.
4. Place the patties in the pan.
5. Turn over after 5-6 minutes, cook until internal temperature reaches 155°F.
6. Serve with pepper aioli.

53

8.35 Crab-Stuffed Lingcod

(**Ready in about**: 50 minutes | **Serving**: 6 | **Difficulty**: Medium)
Nutrition per serving: Kcal: 476 | **Fat**: 33 g | **Net Carbs**: 6 g | **Protein**: 38 g

Ingredients:

Lemon Cream Sauce:
- 1/4 cup of white wine
- 1/4 teaspoon of black pepper
- 2 tablespoons of olive oil
- 1 teaspoon of salt
- 4 cloves of garlic, minced
- 2 tablespoons of lemon juice
- 3 tablespoons of butter
- 1 shallot, chopped
- 1 teaspoon of lemon zest
- 1 leek, chopped
- 1 cup of heavy whipping cream

Crab Mix:
- Green onion: chopped
- 1/3 cup of mayonnaise
- 1/3 cup of sour cream
- 1 pound of crab meat
- 1/2 teaspoon of old bay seasoning
- 1/3 cup of lemon cream sauce
- 1/4 teaspoon of black pepper

Fish:
- 1 tablespoon of olive oil
- 1 tablespoon of chopped Italian parsley
- 2 pounds of lingcod fillets
- 1 teaspoon of salt
- 1 tablespoon of chopped green onion
- 1 teaspoon of paprika

Instructions

For Lemon Cream Sauce:
1. Put in a pan, then sauté garlic, leek, and shallot in oil, pepper, butter, and salt. Cook until translucent.
2. Pour white wine and gradually add cream.
3. Let it simmer on low heat for 2-3 minutes.
4. Turn off the heat and add zest and lemon juice.
5. Add sauce to the blender, pulse on high until smooth. Take 1/3 of the cup for crab mix.

For Crab Mix:
1. In a bowl, add all ingredients of crab mix. Mix well. Set it aside.

For Fish:
1. Preheat the Traeger to high.
2. Cut fish into 6-ounce pieces.
3. Make pocket/ pouches in the middle of the fish fillet.
4. Rub fish with olive oil—season with salt.
5. Overstuff the crab mixture into each pocket.
6. Sprinkle paprika on top and place on grill.
7. Cook on high for 15 minutes.
8. Take off the grill and pour the rest of the lemon sauce and serve with green onion.

8.36 Smoked Scalloped Potatoes

(**Ready in about**: 1 hour and 15 minutes | **Serving**: 8 | **Difficulty**: Medium)
Nutrition per serving: Kcal: 335 | **Fat**: 15 g | **Net Carbs**: 38 g | **Protein**: 12 g

Ingredients:
- 1 cup of scallops
- 4 Russet potatoes, cut into ¼ inch of thickness
- 1 diced onion
- 1/2 cup of sharp shredded cheddar cheese
- 1/3 cup of grated parmesan cheese
- 1/2 cup of mozzarella shredded cheese
- 1 tablespoon of chives
- 2 tablespoons of all-purpose flour
- 2 tablespoons of softened butter
- 2 cloves of minced garlic
- 1 and 1/2 cups of half-and-half
- 1/2 teaspoon of salt
- 1/2 teaspoon of black pepper
- 2 teaspoons of seasoned salt

Instructions

1. Preheat the Traeger to 375°F.
2. Spread butter on a cast-iron skillet.
3. In a bowl, mix garlic and 1/2 and 1/2 and set it aside.
4. Cut potatoes into slices of 1/8th inch thickness.
5. In a skillet, layer onions, scallops, and potatoes, add 1/2 of the seasoning and pour 1/2 of the sauce.
6. Repeat with onion, potato, scallops, seasoning, and sauce layers.
7. Bake for 40-45 minutes uncovered on the grill. Turn it and move to the other side of the grill.
8. Mix all cheeses in a bowl, add a layer on top. Cook for 10-15 minutes.
9. Top with chives and serve.

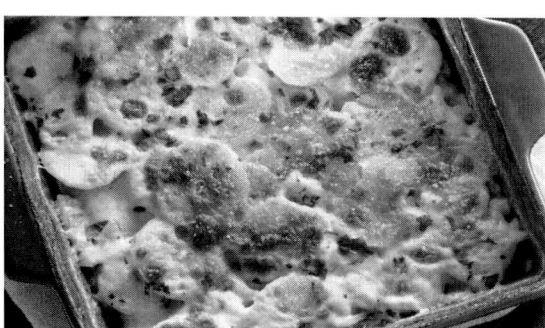

8.37 Shrimp Ceviche

(**Ready in about**: 1 hour and 35 minutes | **Serving**: 12 | **Difficulty**: Medium)
Nutrition per serving: Kcal: 88 | **Fat**: 2 g | **Net Carbs**: 6 g | **Protein**: 11 g

Ingredients:
- 1 8-ounce can of tomato sauce
- 2 pounds of raw shrimp, peeled and deveined
- 1/2 cup of lime juice
- 3 diced tomatoes
- 1 diced onion
- 3 diced jalapeño peppers, without seeds
- 1 diced cucumber
- 1/2 cup of chopped cilantro
- 1 tablespoon of olive oil
- 1 tablespoon of salt
- 1 and 1/2 teaspoons of onion powder
- 1 teaspoon of hot sauce
- 1 and 1/2 teaspoons of granulated garlic
- 1/4 cup of clam juice

Instructions

1. Preheat the Traeger to 450°F.
2. In a bowl, add shrimp, olive oil, and 1/2 of each salt, granulated garlic, and onion powder, mix well,
3. Place shrimp on grill cook for 4 minutes, flipping halfway.
4. Let the shrimp get cool.
5. Meanwhile, in a bowl, add onion, cucumbers, tomatoes, jalapeno. Chop shrimp and also add in the bowl.
6. Add lime juice and the rest of the ingredients and mix well.
7. Keep in the fridge, covered, for 1 to 2 hours. Serve with tortilla chips.

8.38 Smoked Salmon Eggs Benedict

(**Ready in about**: 15 minutes | **Serving**: 2 | **Difficulty**: Hard)
Nutrition per serving: Kcal: 464 | **Fat**: 35 g | **Net Carbs**: 14 g | **Protein**: 22 g

Ingredients:
- 4 whole eggs
- 2 split English muffins, toasted
- 8 ounces of smoked salmon
- 4 yolks only
- Pinch of cayenne
- 1/2 cup of salted butter

- Hollandaise Sauce:
- 1 tablespoon of lemon juice

Instructions

1. On medium flame, put a medium pot of water and let it simmer gently.
2. Melt the butter.
3. In a bowl, whisk egg yolks vigorously with lemon juice until thickens in volume.
4. Butter the toasted muffins
5. Pour butter in whisked yolk lemon mixture and whisk until jam-like consistency but should not be too thick may add a table of warm water if needed.
6. Make sure salmon is at room temperature, place on muffins smokes in Traeger for 10 minutes.
7. Poach whole eggs in the water. Place on top of salmon.
Pour over hollandaise sauce.

8.39 Garlic Dill Smoked Salmon

(**Ready in about**: 20 hours and 15 minutes | **Serving**: 12 | **Difficulty**: Medium)
Nutrition per serving: Kcal: 139 | **Fat**: 5 g | **Net Carbs**: 16 g | **Protein**: 9 g

Ingredients:
- 2 salmon filets
  Brine:
- 1 cup of brown sugar
- 1/3 cup of kosher salt
- 4 cups of water
- Seasoning
- 1 tablespoon of chopped fresh dill
- 3 tablespoons of minced garlic

Instructions

1. In a pot, add all brine ingredients. Mix until salt and sugar are dissolved, pour in a large zip lock bag. Add in salmon and keep in the fridge for 16 hours. Make sure to remove any bones from salmon.
2. After marination, take salmon out, rinse and dry. Keep in the fridge, uncovered for 2 to 4 hours (must-do-step.)
3. When it's time to cook, season salmon with dill and garlic.
4. Preheat the Traeger to smoke with the lid closed
5. Place on the grill and close the lid.
6. Smoke until the internal temperature reaches 175 °F, cook for 4 hours.
7. Serve right away.

8.40 Smoked Salmon Chowder

(Ready in about: 50 minutes| Serving: 8| Difficulty: Medium)
Nutrition per serving: Kcal: 449| Fat: 26 g| Net Carb 25 g| Protein: 28 g

Ingredients:
- 3 tablespoons of bacon fat
- 1 cup of diced carrots
- 1 pound of baby potatoes, cut into quarters
- 1 cup of diced celery
- 1/2 pound of bacon, thick-cut
- 1/2 cup of diced onion
- 1 pound of smoked salmon
- 1/2 teaspoon of white pepper
- 2 teaspoons of fresh thyme
- 8 cups of chicken stock
- 1/2 cup of heavy cream

Instructions
1. Preheat the Traeger to 375°F.
2. Cook bacon on the stovetop until crispy. Add 3 tablespoons of bacon fat into a Dutch oven.
3. Sauté on grill onion, celery, and carrots in bacon fat for 5 minutes.
4. Add in potatoes, chicken stock— Cook for 35 minutes, or until potatoes are tender.
5. Add in cream, pepper, salmon, thyme cook until all combined.
6. Serve right away.

8.41 Grilled Salmon in Onion Sauce

(**Ready in about**: 4 hours| **Serving**: 5| **Difficulty**: Medium)
Nutrition per serving: Kcal: 250| Fat: 60 g| Net Carb 19 g| **Protein**: 10 g

Ingredients:
- 5 Salmon fillets
- 2 cups garlic sauce
- 1 cup brown sugar
- ⅓ tablespoon salt
- 4 cups water

Instructions
1. In a recipient, add water, sugar, and salt until dissolved.
2. Add the salmon and refrigerate for 4 hours.
3. After 4 hours, remove the salmon and wash it.
4. Preheat your grill at 400°F for 10 minutes.
5. Add garlic sauce to the salmon.
6. Put the salmon in the grill, lower the heat to 250°F.
7. Smoke for 4 hours.
8. Remove salmon from grill, let it cool for 5 minutes, then serve.

8.42 Grilled Shrimp in Chives

(**Ready in about**: 15 minutes | **Serving**: 4| **Difficulty**: Easy)
Nutrition per serving: Kcal: 150| **Fat**: 1.4 g| **Net Carbs**: 1.3 g| **Protein**: 19 g

Ingredients:
- 4 pounds shrimps, cleaned
- 2 tablespoons oil
- ½ tablespoons of salt
- 10 ounces of chives
- ⅛ tablespoons of pepper
- ½ tablespoons of garlic powder

Instructions
1. Preheat your grill to 400°F.
2. Mix all the ingredients, except chives and shrimps in a bowl.
3. Chop the chives finely.
4. Wash the shrimps.
5. Preheat your oven at 300°F.
6. Add the chives and shrimps to the mixture.
7. Grill for 30 minutes. Remove when the shrimp gets pink/light red.

8.43 Grilled Curried Sardines

(**Ready in about**: 20-30 minutes | **Serving**: 4| **Difficulty**: Easy)
Nutrition per serving: Kcal: 150| **Fat**: 10 g| **Net Carbs**: 0 g| **Protein**: 22 g

Ingredients:
- 8 large sardines, clean, no head.
- 1 tablespoon of olive oil
- 1 tablespoon of curry powder
- 3 teaspoons of soy sauce
- 1 tablespoon of lemon juice
- 1 tablespoon of mustard
- 1/2 teaspoon of minced garlic
- 1/2 teaspoon of black pepper
- 1 teaspoon of salt

Instructions
1. Rub sardines with curry.
2. In a bowl, add all the ingredients, except sardines and curry, and mix well.
3. Add sardines to the mixture, marinade for 10 minutes.
4. Preheat the Traeger to 350°F during 10 minutes.
5. Put sardines on a pan and into the grill, cook for 5-7 minutes per side.
6. Retire from grill and let it rest for 5 minutes before serving.

CHAPTER 9
Traeger Grill Lamb Recipes

Chapter 9: Traeger Grill Lamb Recipes

9.1 Ground Meat Kebabs

(**Ready in about**: 50 minutes | **Serving**: 2-4| **Difficulty**: Easy)
Nutrition per serving: Kcal: 154| **Fat**: 9 g| **Net Carbs**: 12 g| **Protein**: 18.4 g

Ingredients:
- 1 and a half-pound of chilled ground lamb
- 2 cloves of minced garlic
- 1 teaspoon of salt
- 3 tablespoons of chopped cilantro
- 1/4 cup of minced onion
- 1 tablespoon of fresh mint
- 1 tablespoon of ground cumin
- 1/4 teaspoon of ground cinnamon
- 1 teaspoon of paprika
- 1/2 teaspoon of ground coriander
- Pita bread, for serving

Instructions
1. In a bowl, add all ingredients. Mix well and shape into balls.
2. Thread meatballs on a skewer. With cold washed hands shaped into kebabs.
3. Keep in the fridge covered for 1/2 an hour or overnight.
4. Preheat the grill to 350°F. Keep the lid closed for 10 minutes.
5. Grill kebabs for 1/2 an hour or until the internal temperature of the kebab reaches 160°F.
6. Serve with pita bread.

9.2 Braised Lamb Shank

(**Ready in about**: 4 hours | **Serving**: 4| **Difficulty**: Medium)
Nutrition per serving: Kcal: 324| **Fat**: 14 g| **Net Carbs**: 10 g| **Protein**: 22 g

Ingredients:
- 4 lamb shanks, whole
- 4 sprig fresh thyme and rosemary
- Traeger Prime rib rub
- 1 cup of red wine
- 1 cup of beef broth

Instructions
1. Coat the Lamb with prime rib rub.
2. Let the Traeger preheat to 500 °F, keep the lid closed for 15 minutes.
3. Put coated lamb shanks on the grill and cook for 20-25 minutes.
4. Place the grilled shank in a Dutch oven. Add in herbs, beef broth, and wine. Cover tightly and place on the grill again at 325°F.
5. Let it cook for 3-4 hours until the meat thickest part internal temperature reaches 180°F.

9.3 Lamb Wraps BBQ Style

(**Ready in about**: 3 hours | **Serving**: 4| **Difficulty**: Medium)
Nutrition per serving: Kcal: 314| **Fat**: 19 g| **Net Carbs**: 18.9 g| **Protein**: 23 g

Ingredients:
- Juice from 1 lemon
- Traeger Big game rub
- 1 lamb leg
- 1 red onion, cut into slices
- 2 cups of Greek yogurt
- Olive oil
- 2 cucumbers
- Juice and zest from 2 lemons
- 4 tablespoons of fresh dill chopped
- 2 cloves of garlic
- 3 Roma tomatoes, diced
- 2 tablespoons of fresh mint leaves
- 12 pitas
- 1 cup of feta cheese
- Kosher salt and black pepper, to taste

Instructions
1. Rub olive oil, lemon juice on lamb leg (should be at room temperature.) Coat with a big game rub.
2. Set the Traeger to high and keep the lid closed for 15 minutes.
3. Roast lamb leg for 1/2 an hour at 500°F.
4. Lower the temperature to 350 °F and keep cooking until the thickest part of the lamb leg reaches 140°F.
5. Meanwhile, add the rest of the ingredients except for cheese and diced tomato in a bowl and mix well. Keep in the fridge.
6. Slice the Lamb, and place in warmed pita top with Tzatziki sauce, feta cheese, and diced tomato.
7. Serve and enjoy.

9.4 Leg of Lamb Gyros

(**Ready in about**: 3 hours | **Serving**: 8-10| **Difficulty**: Medium)
Nutrition per serving: Kcal: 298| **Fat**: 16 g| **Net Carbs**: 16 g| **Protein**: 22 g

Ingredients:
- 1 tablespoon of black pepper
- 1 cup and 1 tablespoon of grapeseed oil
- 1/4 cup of Dijon mustard
- 1/2 cup of cremini mushrooms
- 8 cloves of minced garlic
- 1 tablespoon of dried rosemary
- 1/2 tablespoon and 1 teaspoon dried oregano
- 1/3 cup of lemon juice
- Red onion cut into a large wedge
- 5 pounds of sirloin bone-in leg of lamb
- 2/3 cup of chopped scallions
- 3 tablespoons of coarse sea salt
- 1 diced tomato
- 1/2 tablespoon of dried thyme
- Tzatziki sauce:
- 8-10 pitas

Instructions
1. Preheat the grill to smoke mode.
2. Add mustard, rosemary, grapeseed oil, thyme, pepper, lemon juice, salt, garlic, and scallions. Pulse until thick paste forms.
3. On top of the lamb, score the top. Spread 2/3 of paste over lamb leg.
4. Wrap the leg in aluminum foil and let it rest at room temperature for 60 minutes.
5. Hang the Lamb by hook and smoke for 45 minutes.
6. Switch the temperature to 225°F.
7. Smoke the Lamb for 3 hours at 135°F.
8. Meanwhile, thread the mushrooms and red onion on a skewer. Brush with remaining paste (marinade) grill for 3-5 minutes.
9. Take out the lamb leg and cover it with aluminum foil. Rest for 1/2 an hour, then slice.
10. Serve with warm pita, roasted vegetables, and Tzatziki sauce.

9.5 Grilled Lamb Burger

(**Ready in about**: 50 minutes | **Serving**: 4| **Difficulty**: Medium)
Nutrition per serving: Kcal: 256| **Fat**: 20 g| **Net Carbs**: 25 g| **Protein**: 24 g

Ingredients:
- 2 pound of ground lamb
- 5 cloves of garlic, mince only 2 cloves
- Salt and pepper, to taste
- 6 chopped scallions
- 1 red bell pepper
- 2 tablespoons of fresh mint
- 1 cup of mayonnaise
- 2 tablespoons of fresh dill
- 4 brioche buns
- 4 slices of cheese
- 2 teaspoon of fresh lemon juice

Instructions
1. Set the grill to High, and keep the lid closed for 15 minutes.
2. In a bowl, add salt, jalapeno, dill, Lamb, pepper, mint, scallions, and garlic, mix well.
3. Make into patties of 3/4 "thickness.
4. Grill the red bell pepper for 20 minutes, flip every 5 minutes until charred well.
5. Keep the charred pepper in a sealable bag for 10 minutes, take peel skin off, and remove seeds.
6. In a blender, add lemon juice, pepper, red pepper, salt, mayo, and garlic. Pulse until creamy.
7. Place burgers on the grill and cook for 5 minutes, cook until you are satisfied with doneness.
8. In the end, place cheese on patties until it melts.
9. Add mayo, onion, tomato on buns, and cheese patty. Enjoy.

9.6 Grilled Lamb Lollipops with Mango Chutney

(**Ready in about**: 40 minutes | **Serving**: 4| **Difficulty**: Medium)
Nutrition per serving: Kcal: 237| **Fat**: 18.9 g| **Net Carbs**: 9 g| **Protein**: 25 g

Ingredients:
- 3 cloves of chopped garlic
- 6 Frenched lamb chops
- 3 sprigs of cilantro, roughly chopped
- 1 tablespoon of lime juice
- 1 teaspoon of salt
- 1/2 of the habanero pepper, chopped and remove seeds
- 1 mango, cut into cubes
- 2 tablespoons of olive oil
- 1/2 teaspoon of black pepper
- 5 tablespoons of cracked black pepper
- 2 tablespoons of chopped mint
- 1/2 tablespoon of coarse salt

Instructions
1. Rub sardines with curry.
2. In a bowl, add all the ingredients, except sardines and curry, and mix well.
3. Add sardines to the mixture, marinade for 10 minutes.
4. Preheat the Traeger to 350°F during 10 minutes.
5. Put sardines on a pan and into the grill, cook for 5-7 minutes per side.
6. Retire from grill and let it rest for 5 minutes before serving.

9.7 Lamb Burgers with Pickled Onions

(**Ready in about**: 60 minutes | **Serving**: 4| **Difficulty**: Medium)
Nutrition per serving: Kcal: 236| **Fat**: 14 g| **Net Carbs**: 13 g| **Protein**: 17 g

Ingredients:
- 1 pound of ground lamb
- Red onion, 1/2 cut into slices and 1/2 diced
- 1/2 teaspoon of kosher salt
- 1 cup of Greek yogurt
- 2 tablespoons of lemon juice
- 6 tablespoons of lime juice
- 5 cloves of minced garlic
- 2 tablespoons of chopped herbs like mint, parsley, and dill
- 1 tablespoon of olive oil
- 1/2 teaspoon of raw cane sugar
- 1 and 1/2 teaspoons of ground cumin
- 2 tablespoons of minced fresh dill
- 1 cup of ground pork
- 3 tablespoons of minced parsley
- Cucumber, cut into pieces
- 1 teaspoon of ground coriander
- 3 tablespoons of minced fresh mint
- Black pepper
- 6 buns
- Tomato slices
- Butter lettuce

Instructions
1. In a bowl, add lime juice, 1/2 teaspoon of sugar, 1/2 teaspoon of salt, thinly sliced onion. Mix well and let it sit for 2 hours in the fridge.
2. In another bowl, add yogurt, ¼ teaspoon of minced garlic, lemon juice, mixed chopped herbs, 1/2 teaspoon of salt, mix well and cover it, keep in the fridge.
3. In a pan, in warm olive oil, sauté onion for 7 minutes.
4. In a bowl, mix coriander, pork, parsley, cooled sautéed onion, mint, lamb, salt, pepper, garlic, dill, cumin. Mix well but do not over mix.
5. Make 6 meat patties. Cook right away or keep in the fridge for 8 hours.
6. Preheat the grill to high.
7. Put burgers on the grill and cook for 2-3 minutes on each side until cooked well.
8. Rest the burgers for 5 minutes off the grill.
9. Serve burgers in buns with yogurt sauce, pickled onion slices of vegetables.

9.8 Slow Roasted BBQ Lamb Shoulder

(**Ready in about**: 5 hours| **Serving**: 4| **Difficulty**: Medium)
Nutrition per serving: Kcal: 312| **Fat**: 15 g| **Net Carbs**: 9 g| **Protein**: 25 g

Ingredients:
- 1/4 teaspoon of cumin seeds
- 1 tablespoon of smoked paprika
- 1 tablespoon of lemon juice
- 1/4 teaspoon of coriander seeds
- 3 cloves of garlic
- 1 tablespoon of mint, chopped
- 2 tablespoons + 1/2 cup of water:
- 4 tablespoons of olive oil
- 1/4 teaspoon of caraway seeds
- 1 tablespoon of salt
- 3 pound of lamb shoulders
- 1 and 1/2 cups of Greek yogurt
- 2 ounce of ancho chilies, dried, remove seeds
- 1 tablespoon of fresh chopped dill
- 1/4 cup cucumber, grated
- Juice and zest of 1 lemon
- Salt and pepper, to taste

Instructions
1. In a grinder, add all seeds finely grind them.
2. In a bowl, add ancho chilies and 2 tablespoons of water and microwave for 2 minutes on high.
3. Add this chili mix to a blender and add lemon juice, 2 tablespoons of oil, 2 garlic cloves, ground spices, 1 tablespoon of salt, paprika. Pulse on high until pureed.
4. In a pan, place Lamb and rub 1/2 of the pureed sauce all over. Let it rest at room temperature for 2 hours.
5. Preheat the Traeger to 325 °F; keep the lid closed for 15 minutes.
6. Pour 1/2 cup of water into pan cover with foil. Cook for 2 and a half hours.
7. Keep adding water in the pan if required.
8. Uncover and let it cook for 2 and a half hours, till lamb is tender and brown. Baste often with juice at the bottom of the pan.
9. Let it rest for 20 minutes off the grill.
10. In a bowl, add the rest of the ingredients, mix well.
11. Serve the shredded pork with yogurt sauce.

9.9 Braised Irish Lamb Stew

(**Ready in about**: 3 hours| **Serving**: 4| **Difficulty**: Medium)
Nutrition per serving: Kcal: 352| **Fat**: 13 g| **Net Carbs**: 14 g| **Protein**: 26 g

Ingredients:
- 4 pound of boneless lamb shoulder, cut into 1" pieces
- 2 tablespoons of olive oil
- 1 diced onion
- 1/2 cup of white wine
- 1 cup of chopped bacon
- 4 cup of beef stock
- 2 cloves of minced garlic
- 2 carrots, cut into cubes
- 2 sprigs of fresh thyme
- 1 sprig of fresh rosemary
- 2 bay leaves
- 1/4 cup of flour
- 2 potatoes, cut into cubes
- Salt and pepper, to taste
- 1/4 cup of butter, at room temperature

Instructions
1. Preheat the Traeger to 350 °F, keep the lid closed for 15 minutes.
2. Sprinkle salt and pepper to season the lamb. In a Dutch oven, add 2 tablespoons of olive oil, brown the lamb on all sides set it aside.
3. Cook bacon for 15-20 minutes, until crispy and browned. Keep safe 2 tablespoons of bacon fat.
4. Sauté onion in bacon fat until translucent. Add garlic cook for 30 seconds.
5. Add lamb back to Dutch oven, add white wine, and deglaze.
6. Add carrots, stock, potatoes, and herbs, let it simmer.
7. Cover it and place it on the grill at 350°F.
8. Let it for 1 and a half to 2 hours, until Lamb is falling-apart tender.
9. Take out from the grill and place back on the stovetop. Mix flour and butter, and pour into the stew— Cook for 5-10 minutes. Add pepper and salt.
10. Take out bay leaves and sprigs and serve..

9.10 Grilled Butterflied Leg of Lamb

(**Ready in about**: 40 minutes| **Serving**: 8| **Difficulty**: Medium)
Nutrition per serving: Kcal: 323| **Fat**: 9 g| **Net Carbs**: 6 g| **Protein**: 27 g

Ingredients:
- Juice from 1 lemon
- 5 pounds of boneless lamb's leg, butterflied
- 1/4 cup of red wine vinegar
- 2 and 1/2 teaspoons of rosemary minced
- 1 teaspoon of thyme
- 4 cloves of minced garlic
- 1 teaspoon of salt
- 1 cup of olive oil
- 1 onion, cut into rings
- 1 teaspoon of ground black pepper

Instructions
1. Add lemon juice, pepper, thyme, salt, red wine vinegar, rosemary, garlic. Mix until salt dissolves. Add in olive oil and mix.
2. Place lamb in a large freezer bag. Add in the marinade, onions, and lemon rinds. Mix well and keep in the fridge overnight or for several hours.
3. Take out the Lamb and pat dry.
4. Preheat the Traeger to 500 °F, place the lamb on the grill, fat side down. Cook for 1/2 an hour on each side or until the meat's internal temperature reaches 135°F.
5. Let it rest for 5 minutes before slicing.

9.11 Roasted Rack of Lamb

(**Ready in about**: 40 minutes| **Serving**: 4| **Difficulty**: Medium)
Nutrition per serving: Kcal: 313| **Fat**: 10.7 g| **Net Carbs**: 9 g| **Protein**: 24 g

Ingredients:
- 1 teaspoon of black pepper
- 1 cup of panko breadcrumbs
- 1 rack of frenched lamb
- 1 tablespoon of salt
- 1 teaspoon of minced rosemary
- 1/2 cup of yellow mustard
- 1 tablespoon of chopped Italian parsley
- 1 teaspoon of minced sage

Instructions
1. Rub mustard of lamb and season with black pepper and salt.
2. In a dish, add herbs and breadcrumbs. Mix and coat the lamb with breadcrumbs.
3. Let the Traeger preheat to 500°F.
4. Place Lamb on the grill, bone side down, and cook until Lamb's internal temperature (as read by a meat thermometer) reaches 120 °F or for 20 minutes.
5. Let it rest before slicing.

9.12 Lamb Stew

(**Ready in about**: 1 hour and 45 minutes| **Serving**: 4| **Difficulty**: Medium)
Nutrition per serving: Kcal: 298| **Fat**: 11 g| **Net Carbs**: 13 g| **Protein**: 25 g

Ingredients:
- 2 tablespoons of olive oil
- 3 pounds of lamb, cut into half-inch chunks
- Salt and pepper, to taste
- 2 cup of beef stock
- 1 diced turnip
- 4 cloves of chopped garlic
- 2 bay leaves
- 2 cups of diced onion
- 1 and 1/2 cups of stout beer
- 1 parsnip, cut into cubed
- 1/4 cup of tomato paste
- 3 diced carrot
- 1 cup of mashed potatoes
- 2 tablespoons of dried thyme

Instructions
1. Preheat the Traeger to 450 °F, keep the lid closed for 15 minutes.
2. With salt and pepper, season the Lamb. In a pan, brown lamb on all sides.
3. Sauté garlic for two minutes. Add tomato paste, cook for 1 minute. Add thyme, salt, beef stock, pepper, bay leaves, and beer—cook on high.
4. Place vegetables on the grill, add in the stew, serve with mashed potatoes.

9.13 Grilled Lamb Chops with Rosemary Sauce

(**Ready in about**: 40 minutes| **Serving**: 6| **Difficulty**: Medium)
Nutrition per serving: Kcal: 312| **Fat**: 10.3 g| **Net Carbs**: 9 g| **Protein**: 25 g

Ingredients:
- 1/4 cup of roughly chopped onion
- 2 tablespoons of soy sauce
- 1/2 cup of olive oil
- 2 teaspoon of Dijon mustard
- 2 tablespoons of balsamic vinegar
- 2 cloves of minced garlic
- 1 teaspoon of Worcestershire sauce
- 1 tablespoon of fresh rosemary
- 4 lamb chops
- Salt and pepper, to taste

Instructions
1. In a pan, sauté the garlic and onion in olive oil on medium flame. Do not let it brown.
2. Add garlic, onion to a blender. Add Worcestershire sauce, soy sauce, rosemary, mustard, and vinegar. Blend it.
3. Add black pepper. While the blender is on, add olive oil slowly.
4. Add water if the sauce is too thick.
5. Let the Traeger preheat to 500°F.
6. Brush olive oil on lamb chops, season with salt and pepper on both sides.
7. Cook until the internal temperature reaches 135°F.
8. Serve with sauce.

9.14 Greek Style Roast Leg of Lamb

(**Ready in about**: 2 hours and 40 minutes| **Serving**: | **Difficulty**: Medium)
Nutrition per serving: Kcal: 299| **Fat**: 13 g| **Net Carbs**: 8.9 g| **Protein**: 24 g

Ingredients:
- 1 6-7 pound of lamb's leg, bone-in
- Kosher salt and ground black pepper
- 2 sprigs of fresh rosemary
- 8 cloves of garlic
- juice from 2 lemons
- 1 sprig of fresh oregano
- 6 tablespoons of olive oil

Instructions
1. With a sharp knife, make slits in lamb leg.
2. In a processor, add oregano, garlic, and rosemary roughly chop them.
3. Stuff into lamb's slit.
4. Coat lamb's leg with lemon juice, olive oil.
5. With plastic wrap, cover the leg and keep it in the fridge for 8 hours.
6. Before cooking, let the Lamb come to room temperature. Season with pepper and salt.
7. Place lamb on a pan—preheat the grill to 450°F.
8. Place lamb in the pan, on the grill and cook for 1/2 an hour, then reduce heat to 350°F.
9. Cook until the internal temperature reaches 130°F. It will take almost 90 minutes.
10. Rest before serving.

9.15 Lamb Sausage Smoked

(**Ready in about**: 3 hours and 10 minutes| **Serving**: 6 | **Difficulty**: Medium)
Nutrition per serving: Kcal: 171| **Fat**: 14 g| **Net Carbs**: 9.9 g| **Protein**: 21 g

Ingredients:
- 2 pounds of lamb shoulders
- 1/2 teaspoon of cayenne pepper
- 1 teaspoon of cumin
- 1 teaspoon of paprika
- 2 tablespoons of fennel ground
- 1 tablespoon of cilantro finely chopped
- 1 tablespoon of garlic minced
- 2 tablespoons of salt
- 1 tablespoon of parsley minced
- 3 cups of Greek yogurt
- Juice from 1 lemon
- 1 teaspoon of black pepper
- 1 hog casings
- 1 peeled cucumber
- 1 tablespoon of fresh dill
- 1 clove of garlic

Instructions
1. Grind the lamb shoulder.
2. In a bowl, add minced meat, minced garlic, paprika, fennel, cumin, parsley, cilantro, cayenne pepper, black pepper, and salt. Mix well and keep in the fridge.
3. Make sausages by sausage horn and hog casing.
4. Prick the casing so the air bubbles will release.
5. In another bowl, add yogurt, cucumber, dill, garlic, lemon juice, salt, and black pepper, to taste.
6. Preheat the Traeger to 225°F.
7. Place sausages on grill and smoke for 60 minutes.
8. Remove links and preheat to 500°F.
9. Once the temperature is established, cook for 5 minutes on each side.
10. Serve with yogurt sauce and potatoes.

9.16 Pistachio Crusted Roasted Lamb

(**Ready in about**: 60 minutes| **Serving**: 6 | **Difficulty**: Medium)
Nutrition per serving: Kcal: 278| **Fat**: 13 g| **Net Carbs**: 15 g| **Protein**: 26 g

Ingredients:
- 2 racks of lamb
- 1 teaspoon herbs de Provence
- 1 bunch of different color carrots, chopped
- 1 clove of minced garlic
- 1 pound of fingerling potatoes
- 2 tablespoons of vegetable oil
- 3 tablespoons of Dijon mustard
- 2 tablespoons of olive oil
- 2 tablespoons of breadcrumbs
- Salt and black pepper, to taste
- 2 teaspoons of thyme minced
- 2/3 cup of pistachios, chopped
- 1 tablespoon of butter

Instructions
1. Set the Traeger to high, keep the lid closed for 15 minutes.
2. Add 1 tablespoon of vegetable oil to an iron skillet and place on grill. Preheat for 20 minutes with lid closed.
3. Season the lamb rack with salt, herbs de Provence, and pepper.
4. In a bowl, add chopped carrots, olive oil, thyme, salt, potatoes, garlic, and black pepper. Mix well.
5. Put the lamb in a skillet, brown on every side, cook for 6-8 minutes. Take out the Lamb in a baking pan.
6. In a bowl, mix olive oil, salt, pepper, bread crumbs, pistachios, and butter.
7. Spread mustard on the rack of lamb and coat with pistachio mixture.
8. Place coated lamb on the grill directly. Add seasoned carrots and potatoes in the previous skillet on the grill.
9. Keep the lid close, cook for 15 minutes.
10. Stir vegetables after 15 minutes, cover the lamb with foil.
11. Cook for 5-10 minutes more, until the internal temperature of the meat reaches 125°F.
12. Let the lamb rest on the grill. Take out vegetables if tender.
13. Serve the lamb with roasted vegetables.

9.17 Rosemary Lamb

(**Ready in about**: 3 hours| **Serving**: 6 | **Difficulty**: Easy)
Nutrition per serving: Kcal: 266| **Fat**: 9.9 g| **Net Carbs**: 6 g| **Protein**: 22 g

Ingredients:
- 1 bunch of asparagus
- 2 tablespoons of olive oil
- 1/2 cup of butter
- Black pepper
- Salt, to taste
- 1 dozen baby potato
- 1 rack of lamb ribs
- 2 rosemary springs

Instructions
1. Preheat the Traeger to 225°F.
2. Trim the membrane of ribs and coat with olive oil and rosemary
3. In a baking dish, mix butter with potatoes.
4. Place ribs on the grill with potatoes.
5. Smoke until internal temperature reaches 145 °F or for 3 hours.
6. In the last 20 minutes of cooking, add asparagus to potatoes until tender.
7. Serve the lamb with vegetables.

9.18 Chipotle Lamb

(**Ready in about**: 2 hours| **Serving**: 6 | **Difficulty**: Easy)
Nutrition per serving: Kcal: 256| **Fat**: 9.2 g| **Net Carbs**: 9 g| **Protein**: 24 g

Ingredients:
- 3/4 cup of olive oil
- 2 tablespoons fresh thyme
- 2 tablespoons Italian parsley
- 1 tablespoon chipotle peppers crushed
- 1 rack of lamb ribs
- Black pepper
- 1/4 cup bacon rub
- 2 tablespoons fresh rosemary
- 3 cloves of garlic
- 2 tablespoons fresh sage

Instructions
1. Let the Traeger preheat to 275°F.
2. In a bowl, add thyme, rosemary, Italian parsley, oregano, cilantro, ¼ cup olive oil, sage, 1/4 bacon rub, garlic cloves.
3. Spread the rub on lamb ribs.
4. Smoke ribs until internal temperature reaches 120-125°F.
5. Raise the temperature to 425 °F and cook until internal temperature (as read by a meat thermometer) reaches 135-145°F.
6. Let it rest before serving.

9.19 Rosemary Citrus Grilled Lamb Chops

(**Ready in about**: 2 hours| **Serving**: 6 | **Difficulty**: Medium)
Nutrition per serving: Kcal: 289| **Fat**: 10 g| **Net Carbs**: 8 g| **Protein**: 26 g

Ingredients:
- 2 pounds of lamb loin
- 1/4 cup of red wine vinegar
- 1/4 cup of olive oil
- 4 cloves of minced garlic
- 2 tablespoons of steak seasoning
- Juice of 1/2 lime
- 3 tablespoons of orange juice

Instructions
1. In a bowl, mix all ingredients and 2 tablespoons of steak rub.
2. Place the lamb in a baking pan, cover the lamb with marinade.
3. Cover with foil, let it marinate for 4-12 hours.
4. Let the Traeger preheat to 400°F.
5. Place Lamb directly on the grill, cook for 5-7 minutes on each side.
6. Lower temperature to 350 °F, cook for 5-7 minutes more.
7. Cover the lamb in foil, rest for 5 minutes.
8. Slice and serve.

9.20 Grilled Rack of Lamb

(**Ready in about**: 1 hour | **Serving**: 8| **Difficulty**: Medium)
Nutrition per serving: Kcal: 288| **Fat**: 9.8 g| **Net Carbs**: 7 g| **Protein**: 25 g

Ingredients:
- 1 tablespoon of fresh parsley, chopped
- Steak rub
- 2 tablespoons of Dijon mustard
- 1 teaspoon of roughly chopped rosemary
- 2 racks of lamb, bones removed and trimmed

Instructions
1. Coat the lamb with Dijon mustard.
2. Sprinkle steak seasoning all over with rosemary and parsley.
3. Let the Traeger preheat to 400°F.
4. Sear the lamb for 6 minutes.
5. Lower the grill's temperature to 300°F.
6. Make the lamb stand against each other and cook for 20 minutes until the internal temperature becomes 200°F.
7. Let it rest for 10 minutes before serving. Enjoy.

9.21 Easy Lamb Chops

(**Ready in about**: 20 minutes | **Serving**: 4| **Difficulty**: Easy)
Nutrition per serving: Kcal: 370| **Fat**: 18 g| **Net Carbs**: 2 g| **Protein**: 20 g

Ingredients:
- 4 (5-ounces) lamb chops
- 3 tablespoons olive oil
- 4 ounces of oregano
- Ground black pepper
- Salt to taste

Instructions
1. Mix well all the ingredients and then add the chops.
2. Let it marinade for 30 minutes
3. Preheat the grill to 350°F.
4. Put the chops in the grill and cook for about 5-10 minutes per side.

CHAPTER 10
Traeger Grill Vegetables Recipes

Chapter 10: Traeger Grill Vegetables Recipes

10.1 Roasted Broccoli Cheese Soup

(Ready in about: 2 hours and 25 minutes| **Serving:** 4| **Difficulty:** Easy)
Nutrition per serving: Kcal: 44| **Fat** 5 g| **Net Carb** 1 g| **Protein:** 0 g

Ingredients:
- 3 cups of broccoli florets
- 2 cups of half-and-half
- 1 cup broccoli stems, cut into slices
- Olive oil
- 1/4 cup of all-purpose flour
- 2 carrots, cut into thin rounds
- 6 tablespoons of butter
- 2 cups of chicken stock
- 1 clove of garlic
- 1 yellow onion, diced
- 1/2 teaspoon of paprika
- 1/2 cup of grated cheddar cheese
- 1/2 teaspoon of mustard powder:
- Pinch of cayenne powder
- 3/4 teaspoon of salt and black pepper, each

Instructions
1. Preheat the grill to 425°F. Cut broccoli into bite-size pieces, place on a baking tray, coat with olive oil, and season with salt.
2. Roast for 5 minutes on the grill. Take off the grill and set it aside.
3. Preheat a cast-iron skillet on the grill, with the lid closed.
4. Sauté onion with 1 tablespoon of butter for 4 minutes. Add garlic and cook for 30 seconds.
5. Transfer the mixture to a plate.
6. Lower the grill's temperature to 375 °F with a cast iron skillet inside.
7. Add 4 tablespoons of butter and flour, cook for 20 minutes, stirring every 5 minutes.
8. Add stock and whisk, then keep mixing. Cook until thickens, or for 45 minutes.
9. Add garlic, onion and broccoli, cayenne, paprika, pepper, mustard powder, and salt.
10. Let it simmer for 20-25 minutes. Add cheese, cook until melted.
11. Serve right away.

10.2 Traeger Grilled Vegetables

(Ready in about: 35 minutes| **Serving:** 8| **Difficulty:** Easy)
Nutrition per serving: Kcal: 44| **Fat:** 5 g| **Net Carb** 1 g| **Protein:** 0 g

Ingredients:
- 1-2 tablespoons of Traeger Veggie seasoning
- 1 tray of mixed vegetables, your choice
- 1/4 cup Vegetable oil

Instructions
1. Preheat the Traeger to 375°F.
2. Toss the vegetables in oil and vegetable rub. Place on a baking sheet.
3. Put on the grill, cook for 10-15 minutes. Serve and enjoy.

10.3 Roasted Carrots with Pistachio and Pomegranate Relish

(Ready in about: 40 minutes| **Serving:** 6| **Difficulty:** Medium)
Nutrition per serving: Kcal: 211| **Fat:** 8.8 g| **Net Carb** 4 g| **Protein:** 21 g

Ingredients:
- 2 teaspoons of kosher salt
- 2 teaspoons of Fennel seed
- 2 Bunch of rainbow carrots
- 1 teaspoon of sugar
- 1/2 teaspoon of cumin
- 2 tablespoons + 1/3 cups of olive oil
- 1/2 cup of Pomegranate seeds
- 1/2 cup of chopped pistachios
- 2 teaspoons of kosher salt
- 2 teaspoons of Fennel seed
- 2 Bunch of rainbow carrots
- 1 teaspoon of sugar
- 1/2 teaspoon of cumin
- 2 tablespoons + 1/3 cups of olive oil
- 1/2 cup of Pomegranate seeds
- 1/2 cup of chopped pistachios
- 2 cloves of minced garlic
- 1/4 cup of chopped flat-leaf parsley
- 1 teaspoon of coriander
- 1/4 cup of chopped mint
- Salt
- Zest and juice of 1 lime

Instructions
1. Preheat the Traeger to 450°F.
2. In a bowl, add all spices, garlic, sugar, salt with 2 tablespoons of olive oil. Add carrots and coat them well.
3. Roast for 1/2 an hour on a sheet tray. Take out from grill, sprinkle with zest.
4. In a bowl, add ¼ of olive oil, herbs, lime juice, salt, pomegranate seeds, and pistachios. Whisk well and adjust seasoning.
5. Serve carrots with pomegranate relish.

10.4 Smoked Pumpkin Soup

(Ready in about: 2 hours and 30 minutes| **Serving:** 6| **Difficulty:** Medium)
Nutrition per serving: Kcal: 315| **Fat:** 11 g| **Net Carb** 19.4 g| **Protein:** 24 g

Ingredients:
- 5 pounds of the whole pumpkin
- 1 diced onion
- 2 cloves of minced garlic
- 1/8 teaspoon of ground allspice
- 3 tablespoons of butter
- 1 tablespoon of brown sugar
- 5 cups of chicken broth
- 1 teaspoon of paprika
- 1 teaspoon of ground cinnamon
- 1/2 cup of whipped cream
- 1/8 teaspoon of ground nutmeg
- Fresh parsley
- 1/2 cup of apple cider

Instructions
1. Cut the pumpkin into quarters and take out the seeds.
2. Preheat the Traeger to 165°F.
3. Smoke pumpkin for 60 minutes on the grill cut side down.
4. Raise the temperature to 300 °F, and cook pumpkin until tender, for 90 minutes.
5. Take it out and peel the skin off.
6. In a large pot, melt butter. Sauté garlic, onion for 5 minutes until soft.
7. Add in all dry spices and sugar. Add apple cider vinegar cook until syrup-like and reduced.
8. Add chicken broth and roasted pumpkin. Simmer for 1/2 an hour.
9. Puree the soup in a blender, add more broth if it is too thick, and season with pepper and salt to your liking.
10. Serve with heavy cream and parsley.

10.5 Mashed Red Potatoes

(Ready in about: 55 minutes| **Serving:** 4| **Difficulty:** Easy)
Nutrition per serving: Kcal: 289| **Fat:** 15 g| **Net Carb** 21 g| **Protein:** 13 g

Ingredients:
- 8 red potatoes
- Salt and black pepper, to taste
- 1/2 cup of heavy cream
- 1/4 cup of butter

Instructions
1. Preheat the Traeger to 450°F.
2. Cut potatoes in quarters. Season with pepper and salt.
3. Put potatoes on the grill. Flip every 15 minutes till potatoes are tender.
4. Mash with butter, cream, salt, and pepper.
5. Enjoy.

10.6 Baked Breakfast Mini Quiches

(Ready in about: 30 minutes| **Serving:** 8| **Difficulty:** Medium)
Nutrition per serving: Kcal: 219| **Fat:** 10 g| **Net Carb** 9 g| **Protein:** 30 g

Ingredients:
- 1 tablespoon of olive oil
- 4 ounces of shredded cheddar
- 3 cups of fresh spinach
- 10 whole eggs
- 1/4 cup of fresh basil
- 1/2 teaspoon of black pepper:
- 1/2 diced yellow onion
- 1 teaspoon of kosher salt

Instructions
1. Take a 12-cup muffin tray and spray with oil.
2. In a skillet, sauté onion in oil for 7 minutes, until translucent.
3. Add spinach cook for 2 minutes.
4. Take out on a cutting board, chop it roughly.
5. Preheat the Traeger to 350°F.
6. In a bowl, whisk eggs until foamy add spinach mix, black pepper, salt, basil, and cheese. Mix well and pour into the muffin tray.
7. Place the tin on the grill and bake for 18-20 minutes.
8. Serve right away.

10.7 Roasted Butternut Squash Soup

(**Ready in about**: 1 hour and 20 minutes| **Serving**: 4| **Difficulty**: Medium)
Nutrition per serving: Kcal: 211| **Fat**: 9 g| **Net Carb** 10 g| **Protein**: 29 g

Ingredients:
- Olive oil
- 2 pounds of butternut squash
- Traeger Veggie rub
- 1/2 of diced onion
- 1/2 apple
- 4 sage leaves
- 1 teaspoon of salt
- 1 tablespoon of butter
- 1 cup of water
- 1/4 teaspoon of black pepper
- 1 and 1/2 cups of chicken broth
- 1 teaspoon of salt
- 1/3 cup of heavy cream
- 1/2 cup of pumpkin seeds
- 1/4 teaspoon of ground nutmeg
- 2 tablespoons of sour cream
- 2 tablespoons of Bacon Bits X

Instructions
1. Preheat the Traeger to high.
2. Cut the squash in half. Place each 1/2 in aluminum foil, season the cut side with veggie rub and olive oil.
3. Roast the squash for 40-50 minutes, until it is tender.
4. Dice the apple, onion. In a Dutch oven, add butter, sage, onion, apple, salt, and pepper. Cook for 7 minutes, until softened. Turn off the heat.
5. Take the flesh out of the squash and add it into the Dutch oven.
6. Add water, broth, season with salt and pepper, let it boil on medium flame.
7. Turn heat to low and let it simmer for 15 minutes.
8. Turn off the heat, take out sage leaves, add in the cream, nutmeg.
9. With an immersion blender, puree the soup.
10. Season with salt and pepper if needed.
11. Serve hot.

10.8 Grilled Veggie Burgers with Lentils and Walnuts

(**Ready in about**: 30 minutes| **Serving**: 4| **Difficulty**: Medium)
Nutrition per serving: Kcal: 183| **Fat**: 7 g| **Net Carb** 12 g| **Protein**: 25 g

Ingredients:
- 1 cup of toasted walnuts
- 3/4 cup of dried lentils
- 1 onion diced
- 2 tablespoon of extra-virgin olive oil
- 2 cloves of minced garlic
- 1 tablespoon of ground flaxseed
- 3/4 cup of breadcrumbs
- 6 burger buns
- 1 teaspoon of ground cumin
- 1 teaspoon of paprika
- Salt and black pepper, to taste

Instructions
1. In a pot, add water, let it boil, add lentils, and cook for 15 minutes. Drain and set it aside.
2. In a bowl, add flaxseed, 4 tablespoons of water. Let it sit for 5 minutes.
3. In a pan, add olive oil sauté onion for 4-6 minutes. Add garlic, salt, and pepper to cook for 30 seconds.
4. In a food processor, add garlic, onion mix, flaxseed, toasted walnuts, breadcrumbs, ¾ of lentils, paprika, and cumin.
5. Pulse until it becomes smooth. If it is too dry, add 1 tablespoon of water. Add in the rest of the lentils.
6. Make 5-6 patties from this mix and keep in the fridge for 1-24 hours.
7. Preheat the Traeger to 425°F.
8. Cook the patties directly on the grill for 8-10 minutes. Flip once.
9. Serve in a burger with condiments.

10.9 Smoked Hummus with Roasted Vegetables

(**Ready in about**: 55minutes| **Serving**: 4| **Difficulty**: Medium)
Nutrition per serving: Kcal: 192 | **Fat**: 9 g| **Net Carb** 9 g| **Protein**: 20 g

Ingredients:
- 1 and 1/2 cups of chickpeas
- 1/3 cup of tahini
- 6 tablespoons of olive oil
- 1 thinly sliced onion
- 1 tablespoon of garlic minced
- 1 teaspoon of salt
- 2 cups of cauliflower florets
- 4 tablespoons of lemon juice
- 2 cups of fresh Brussels sprouts
- 2 cups of butternut squash
- 2 Portobello mushrooms
- Salt and black pepper

Instructions
1. Preheat the Traeger to 180°F.
2. On a baking sheet, add chickpeas and smoke for 15-20 minutes.
3. In a bowl, add all other ingredients (except for vegetables) with chickpeas. Pulse until combined.
4. Preheat the grill to high.
5. Coat vegetables with oil and roast for 15-20 minutes on a baking sheet.
6. Serve roasted vegetables with smoked hummus.

10.10 Baked Creamed Spinach

(**Ready in about**: 45 minutes| **Serving**: 6| **Difficulty**: Easy)
Nutrition per serving: Kcal: 187 | **Fat**: 8 g| **Net Carb** 3 g| **Protein**: 12 g

Ingredients:
- 1 chopped shallot
- 1 and 1/2 cups of heavy cream
- 2 10-ounce packages of frozen spinach, thawed
- 1 teaspoon of red pepper flakes
- 2 tablespoons of butter
- 2 cloves of garlic
- 3/4 cup of sour cream
- 1 teaspoon of ground nutmeg
- Salt and black pepper, to taste
- 1/2 cup of parmesan cheese, panko breadcrumbs, and Romano cheese, each

Instructions
1. In a pan, sauté garlic, shallot in butter. Cook for 3 minutes, add chili flakes and cook for two more minutes.
2. Add nutmeg and cream let it boil. Add black pepper and salt.
3. Add sour cream, spinach, add more seasoning if required.
4. Take off from heat and add in cheese.
5. Remove from heat and stir in cheeses.
6. Transfer to a baking dish and sprinkle panko on top.
7. Pour mixture into a baking dish and top with panko.
8. Cook in Traeger at 375 °F, for 1/2 an hour, with the lid closed.

10.11 Butter Braised Green Beans

(**Ready in about**: 1 hour and 15 minutes| **Serving**: 6| **Difficulty**: Easy)
Nutrition per serving: Kcal: 131 | **Fat**: 9 g| **Net Carb** 6 g| **Protein**: 30 g

Ingredients:
- Traeger Veggie rub
- 24 ounces of trimmed green beans
- 8 tablespoons of butter, melted

Instructions
1. Preheat the Traeger to 325°F.
2. On a baking sheet, add beans, coat with melted butter.
3. Season with the veggie rub.
4. Roast for 60 minutes, keep stirring every 20 minutes, until light brown in places.

10.12 Traeger Stuffed Peppers

(**Ready in about**: 21 minutes| **Serving**: 6| **Difficulty**: Medium)
Nutrition per serving: Kcal: 422 | **Fat**: 22 g| **Net Carb** 24 g| **Protein**: 34 g

Ingredients:
- 3 bell peppers, cut in 1/2 and remove seeds
- 1 diced onion
- 1 15-ounce can of stewed tomatoes
- 1/4 teaspoon of pepper
- 1 pound of ground beef, lean
- 1/2 cup of white rice
- 1/2 teaspoon of onion powder
- 1/2 teaspoon of garlic powder
- 1/2 teaspoon of salt
- 1/2 teaspoon of red pepper flakes
- 1 cup of tomato sauce
- 2 cups of shredded cheddar cheese
- 1 and 1/2 cups of water
- 6 cups of shredded cabbage

Instructions
1. Preheat the Traeger to 325°F.
2. In a skillet, cook the onions with beef, salt, garlic powder, red pepper flakes, onion powder, salt, and pepper.
3. As the meat is no longer pink, add rice, water, shredded cabbage, stewed tomatoes, and tomato sauce. Cover it and let it simmer until cabbage is soft and rice is cooked.
4. Stuff the bell peppers halves with the beef mix, add cheese on top, and bake for 1/2 an hour.

10.13 Traeger Lasagna

(**Ready in about**: 2 hours and 25 minutes| **Serving**: 12| **Difficulty**: Medium)
Nutrition per serving: Kcal: 301 | **Fat**: 18 g| **Net Carb** 9 g| **Protein**: 25 g

Ingredients:
- 1 box of lasagna noodles
- 1 and 1/2 cups of ricotta cheese
- 8 cups of shredded mozzarella cheese
- 9 cups of spaghetti sauce
- 1/4 cup of shredded parmesan cheese
- 1/4 teaspoon of onion powder
- 1/2 teaspoon of basil
- 1/4 teaspoon of garlic powder
- 1/2 cup of cottage cheese
- 2 teaspoons of parsley
- 2 whole eggs
- 1/2 teaspoon of salt

Instructions
1. Cook noodles till al dente. Drain and rinse with hot water.
2. In a bowl, add all cheeses, eggs, parsley, mozzarella, milk, 1/2 Italian cheese, onion powder, salt, garlic powder. Mix well.
3. Spread a little bit of sauce at the bottom of the pan. Add noodles layer, 1/2 of the cheese the mix, add 3 cups of sauce.
4. Another layer of noodles, the rest of the cheese mix, and sauce on top.
5. As the meat is no longer pink, add rice, water, shredded cabbage, stewed tomatoes, and tomato sauce. Cover it and let it simmer until cabbage is soft and rice is cooked.
6. Stuff the bell peppers halves with the beef mix, add cheese on top, and bake for 1/2 an hour.

10.14 Twice Baked Potatoes

(**Ready in about**: 1 hour and 25 minutes| **Serving**: 8| **Difficulty**: Medium)
Nutrition per serving: Kcal: 312| **Fat**: 14 g| **Net Carb** 21 g| **Protein**: 9 g

Ingredients:
- 12 tablespoons of butter, melted
- 8 russet potatoes
- 6 strips of cooked crumbled bacon
- 2 tablespoons of chives
- 2 cups of hot milk
- 2 cup of shredded cheddar cheese
- Salt and pepper, to taste

Instructions
1. Preheat the Traeger to 450°F.
2. Pierce clean potatoes with a fork, all over.
3. Place potatoes on grill and cook for 1 hour and 15 minutes, until they are cooked completely.
4. Place potatoes in a baking pan and let them cook for 5-10 minutes.
5. Switch the grill's temperature to 375°F.
6. Slice the potatoes open, and scoop the flesh out, leave a 1/4inch skin and potato.
7. In a mixer, whip potatoes flesh for 30 seconds. Gradually add melted butter and milk.
8. Switch to medium-high speed whip for 1-2 minutes, until smooth and fluffy
9. Add in bacon, chives, salt, and pepper.
10. Stuff the hollow potatoes with whipped potatoes, add cheese on top.
11. Bake for 20 minutes at 375°F.
12. Serve right away.

10.15 Smoked Bean Salad

(**Ready in about**: 50 minutes| **Serving**: 6| **Difficulty**: Medium)
Nutrition per serving: Kcal: 171| **Fat**: 7 g| **Net Carb** 15 g| **Protein**: 24 g

Ingredients:
- 1/2 tablespoon of olive oil
- 1 15-ounce can of northern beans, drained
- 1 pound of fresh green beans
- 1 teaspoon of Dijon mustard
- 1 tablespoon of chopped flat-leaf parsley
- 1 clove of minced garlic
- 2 tablespoons of red wine vinegar
- Salt and pepper, to taste
- 1 thinly sliced shallot

Instructions
1. Preheat the Traeger to 180 °F or super smoke.
2. On a baking sheet, add drained beans and place them on the grill
3. Smoke for 15-20 minutes, and take them off the grill.
4. Switch the temperature to high.
5. Coat fresh beans with salt, pepper, and olive oil. Roast them for 10 minutes at 500°F.
6. Take off the grill, keep in the fridge to cool.
7. In a bowl, add vinegar, garlic, Dijon, shallots. Whisk and gradually add olive oil. Add salt, pepper, and parsley.
8. In a bowl, add all beans and pour overdressing.
9. Serve right away and enjoy.

10.16 Pasta Salad

(**Ready in about**: 50 minutes| **Serving**: 8| **Difficulty**: Medium)
Nutrition per serving: Kcal: 189| **Fat**: 10 g| **Net Carb** 14 g| **Protein**: 19 g

Ingredients:
- 1/2 cup of extra-virgin olive oil
- 1 pound of rotini pasta
- 1 pound of salami
- 1/2 cup of mozzarella cheese
- 3 cups of cherry tomatoes, cut into slices
- 3/4 cup of black olives
- 1 jar of roasted red peppers, cut into slices
- 1/2 cup of red wine vinegar
- 1 diced red onion
- 1 tablespoon of Italian seasoning
- 3 clove garlic, minced
- 1 tablespoon of honey
- 1/4 cup of chopped flat-leaf parsley
- Salt and black pepper

Instructions
1. Preheat the Traeger to 180°F. use Super Smoke if possible.
2. In a bowl, add olive oil, minced garlic, red wine vinegar, salt, pepper, honey, and Italian seasoning. Mix well.
3. Put all ingredients on a baking sheet except for pasta—smoke for 10 minutes.
4. Cook pasta as per instructions. Drain and rinse.
5. In a bowl, add pasta, all other roasted ingredients, salt, and pepper. Pour over vinaigrette, mix well.
6. Chill for 1/2 an hour, then serve.

10.17 Green Bean Casserole with Shallots

(**Ready in about**: 75 minutes| **Serving**: 10| **Difficulty**: Medium)
Nutrition per serving: Kcal: 322| **Fat**: 11 g| **Net Carb** 13 g| **Protein**: 14 g

Ingredients:
- 3 pounds of trimmed green beans
- 2 tablespoons of olive oil
- 1 tablespoon of kosher salt
- 2 tablespoons of unsalted butter
- 1/2 pound of sliced shitake
- 4 cups of vegetable oil
- 1/2 cup of sherry cooking wine
- 1 cup of parmesan cheese, grated
- 1 pinch of salt
- 1/4 cup of minced shallot
- 8 shallots, cut into rings
- 1/4 cup + 1/2 cup rice flour
- 2 cups chicken stock
- 1 cup of slivered almonds

Instructions
1. Preheat the Traeger to high.
2. In a large pot, add water and 1 tablespoon of salt to fill 2/3 on high flame. As water is boiling, add 1/2 of the green beans. Cook for 2 minutes until 1/2 cooked.
3. Take out and submerge in an ice bath.
4. Take out beans and pat dry with a paper towel.
5. Remove with a strainer and place the beans in the ice bath to cool. Remove the green beans from the water and place on paper towels to dry.
6. Cook 1/2 of the beans, repeat the process.
7. In a pan, add olive oil and butter. Add mushrooms, minced shallots, salt and cook for 5 minutes.
8. Add 1/4 cup of rice flour to this mix and cook for 2 minutes.
9. Add sherry, let it reduce, add in the stock, let it become thick.
10. Add in cheese, salt, pepper, and cream. Add beans to sauce.
11. Pour in a baking dish and top with almonds.
12. Bake for 1/2 an hour.
13. Mix 1/2 a cup of rice flour, salt in a bowl. Coat shallots' rings in rice flour, fry the shallots for 30-60 seconds in heated oil 350°F.
14. Serve the casserole with crispy shallots.

10.18 Herbs Infused Creamy Mashed Potatoes

(**Ready in about**: 1 hour and 20 minutes| **Serving**: 6| **Difficulty**: Medium)
Nutrition per serving: Kcal: 311| **Fat**: 12 g| **Net Carb** 17 g| **Protein**: 9 g

Ingredients:
- 2 sticks of unsalted butter, softened
- 1 pound of russet potatoes
- 2 cups of heavy cream
- 6 sage leaves
- 2 sprigs of fresh rosemary
- 1 and 1/2 cups of water
- 2 cloves of chopped garlic
- 3 sprigs of fresh thyme
- 6 black peppercorns
- Salt and black pepper

Instructions
1. Preheat the Traeger to 350°F.
2. Cut potatoes into one-inch cubes. Place in the baking dish, with water, and bake until fork-tender or for 60 minutes.
3. In a pan, add garlic, herbs, cream, and peppercorn. Put on the grill and let it cook for 15 minutes.
4. Strain herb cream mixture. Pour back in the pan and keep warm.
5. Drain and Rice the potatoes in a pot. Gradually add 1 stick of butter, 1 teaspoon of salt, 2/3 of the cream mix. Keep adding salt, butter, cream to get the desired consistency.
6. Serve right away

10.19 Squash Au Gratin

(**Ready in about**: 60 minutes| **Serving**: 8| **Difficulty**: Medium)
Nutrition per serving: Kcal: 299| **Fat**: 11 g| **Net Carb** 9.9 g| **Protein**: 24 g

Ingredients:
- 1 peeled butternut squash, cut into cubes
- 1 peeled acorn squash, cut into cubes
- 3 cup of Gruyere cheese, shredded
- 4 cloves of diced garlic
- 3 peeled potatoes, cut into cubes
- 2 tablespoons of Butter
- 2 cups of heavy cream
- Salt and pepper, to taste

Instructions
1. Preheat the Traeger to 375°F.
2. In a pan, add cream keep mixing until it starts to boil. Add cheese, garlic, salt, and pepper. Mix until cheese has melted.
3. Take a 9 by 13" baking dish coated with butter. In a bowl, add all squashes and potatoes. Add in cheese mix and pour in prepared baking dish.
4. Bake for 45 minutes, until vegetables are tender.
5. Let it rest for 10 minutes, then serve.

10.20 Baked Sweet Potato Hash

(**Ready in about**: 60 minutes| **Serving**: 4| **Difficulty**: Medium)
Nutrition per serving: Kcal: 288| **Fat**: 10 g| **Net Carb** 10 g| **Protein**: 21 g

Ingredients:
- 2 cloves of minced garlic
- 2 tablespoons of olive oil
- Salt and black pepper, to taste
- 1/2 cup of oyster mushrooms
- 1 pound of unpeeled sweet potatoes, cut into cubes
- 1/2 diced red onion
- 2 tablespoons of thyme leaves
- 1/4 cup of goat cheese
- 1 teaspoon of smoked paprika
- Black pepper, to taste
- Chopped herbs
- 5 whole eggs

Instructions
1. Preheat the Traeger to high with a cast-iron skillet.
2. Add oil to skillet with mushrooms, sweet potatoes, salt, and onion. Mix and bake for 20 minutes. Stir once.
3. Add in 1/2 tsp. of paprika, thyme leaves, black pepper, 1 clove of minced garlic. Cook with grill's lid closed. Cook for 10 minutes or until potatoes become browned and onion is tender.
4. Make space for 5 eggs and crack eggs in these spots—Cook for 10 minutes.
5. Serve with cheese, paprika, herbs.

10.21 Roasted Onion Bacon Salad

(**Ready in about**: 2 hours and 15 minutes| **Serving**: 6| **Difficulty**: Medium)
Nutrition per serving: Kcal: 234| **Fat**: 8 g| **Net Carb** 6 g| **Protein**: 20 g

Ingredients:
- 1/2 cup of olive oil
- 10 ounce of cherry tomatoes
- 4 yellow onion
- 2 tablespoons red wine vinegar
- 6 slices of bacon
- 2 cups lettuce
- Salt and pepper, to taste
- 1 cucumber

Instructions
1. Preheat the Traeger to 180 °F; use super smoke if possible.
2. Place onions on the grill, cook for 1/2 an hour, and then individually wrap each in foil and place back on the grill.
3. Switch the grill's temperature to 350 °F. Cook onions for 1 hour, take off the grill and let them cool down.
4. Put bacon on the grill and cook for 30-35 minutes. Take off the grill and crumble.
5. Chop up the roasted onions.
6. In a bowl, mix red wine vinegar, olive oil, salt, and pepper. Whisk well.
7. In a bowl, add tomatoes, lettuce, roasted onions, bacon, cucumber, pour over vinegar mix.
8. Mix well and serve.

10.22 Veggie Sandwich

(**Ready in about**: 60 minutes| **Serving**: 4| **Difficulty**: Medium)
Nutrition per serving: Kcal: 213| **Fat**: 9 g| **Net Carb** 15 g| **Protein**: 19 g

Ingredients:
- 4 buns
- 1 small zucchini, eggplant, yellow squash each cut into strips
- 1 and 1/2 cups of chickpeas
- 1 tablespoon garlic minced
- 1/3 cup of tahini
- 1 teaspoon of kosher salt
- 4 tablespoons of lemon juice
- 1/2 cup of ricotta cheese
- 2 tablespoons of olive oil
- 2 Portobello mushrooms
- Salt and pepper, to taste

Instructions
1. Preheat the Traeger to 180°F.
2. Add chickpeas to a baking sheet, bake for 15-20 minutes.
3. In a food processor, add baked chickpeas, tahini, 4 tablespoons of lemon juice, minced garlic, and salt. Pulse until combined, do not over mix.
4. Switch the grill's temperature to 400-500°F.
5. Coat all vegetables in salt, black pepper, lemon juice, olive oil to taste.
6. Place vegetables directly on grill and gill side up mushrooms.
7. Cook 10-15 minutes for vegetables and 20-25 minutes for mushrooms.
8. In a bowl, add ricotta, salt, pepper, ricotta, 1 clove of minced garlic, and lemon juice (as needed), mix well.
9. Slice buns open and serve grilled vegetables with the cheese mix and tahini mix.

10.23 Baked Corn Pudding

(**Ready in about**: 40 minutes| **Serving**: 6| **Difficulty**: Medium)
Nutrition per serving: Kcal: 312| **Fat**: 13 g| **Net Carb** 14 g| **Protein**: 7 g

Ingredients:
- 15 kernel corns
- 3 cloves of chopped garlic
- 3 tablespoons of butter
- 1/2 cup of cream cheese
- 1 cup parmesan cheese
- 1/2 cup of breadcrumbs
- 1 tablespoon of kosher salt
- 1 cup of cheddar cheese
- 1/2 tablespoon of black pepper
- 1 tablespoon of rosemary, chopped
- 1/2 cup of parmesan cheese
- 1 tablespoon of thyme, minced

Instructions
1. Preheat the Traeger to 350°F.
2. In a pan, add butter and garlic cook for 3-4 minutes. Add all cheese (except for parmesan), corn, cream cheese, salt, pepper.
3. Cook until cheese is melted and transfer to a baking dish.
4. In another bowl, add parmesan cheese, herbs, and bread crumbs.
5. Spread the herbs mix over the corn mix.
6. Bake for 25 minutes.
7. Serve right away.

10.24 Peach Salsa

(**Ready in about**: 30 minutes| **Serving**: 6| **Difficulty**: Medium)
Nutrition per serving: Kcal: 198| **Fat**: 8.8 g| **Net Carb** 2 g| **Protein**: 7 g

Ingredients:
- 4 tablespoons of olive oil
- 2 cloves of minced garlic
- 4 peaches, cut into halves
- 4 tomatoes
- 1 diced jalapeno
- Salt, to taste
- 1 Bunch of cilantro leaves, minced
- Juice from 2 limes

Instructions
1. Preheat the Traeger to 500°F.
2. Mix 2 tablespoons of olive oil and salt into the cut side of the peaches. Place on grill and cook for 20 minutes, until marks appear.
3. Dice the cooled down peaches. In a bowl, add all other ingredients with diced peaches.
4. Serve as a dip.

CHAPTER 11
Traeger Grill Bonus Recipe

Chapter 11: Traeger Grill Bonus Recipe

11.1 Traeger Banana Bread

(**Ready in about**: 1 hour and 10 minutes | **Serving**: 12| **Difficulty**: Medium)
Nutrition per serving: Kcal: 530| **Fat**: 22 g| **Net Carbs**: 77 g| **Protein**: 7 g

Ingredients:
- 1 cup of white sugar
- 4 bananas, extra ripe
- 1 and 1/2 tablespoons of vanilla
- 1 cup of canola oil
- 4 whole eggs
- 1 cup of sour cream
- 2 teaspoons of baking soda
- 1 cup of dark brown sugar
- 3 cups of flour
- Cinnamon Topping:
- 1 teaspoon of cinnamon
- 2/3 cup of white sugar

Instructions
1. Preheat the Traeger to 350°F.
2. In a bowl, add all ingredients, except for cinnamon toppings. Mix with a mixer for 2-3 minutes.
3. In an oiled bundt pan, add 1/2 of the batter.
4. Mix topping ingredients and sprinkle 1/2 on the batter. Pour the rest of the batter and sprinkle with 1/2 of the topping.
5. Place on the top rack—Cook for 1 hour. Hallway through rotates the pan.
6. Bake until a toothpick comes out a little moist.
7. Total time will vary.
8. Serve warm.

11.2 Smoked Baked Potato Soup

(**Ready in about**: 1 hour and 20 minutes | **Serving**: 8| **Difficulty**: Hard)
Nutrition per serving: Kcal: 387| **Fat**: 26 g| **Net Carbs**: 31 g| **Protein**: 9 g

Ingredients:
- 1 cup of beer
- 2 cups of chicken stock
- 3 pounds of russet potatoes
- 1/4 cup of flour
- 2 cups of milk
- 1 diced onion
- 1 cup of heavy cream
- 2 cups of shredded cheddar sharp cheese
- 1 pound of bacon, slice into 1" pieces
- Scallions
- 1 tablespoon of dried thyme
- Salt and pepper, to taste

Instructions
1. Preheat the Traeger to 225°F. Smoke potatoes for 60 minutes.
2. Raise the temperature of Traeger to 400 °F, cook until the internal temperature reaches 185°F.
3. Cook bacon in a Dutch oven until it starts to brown.
4. Add onions, cook until turn translucent. Take out ¼ cup of it.
5. Drain the fat and leave only ¼ cup of fat in the pot.
6. Smash two potatoes and fry them. Cut the rest of the potatoes into cubes and add in onion bacon mix.
7. Add beer and deglaze the oven.
8. Add flour cook for two minutes. Add mashed potatoes and stock.
9. Add milk, cream. and let it simmer. Do not boil.
10. Take off from stovetop, add in cheese until melts.
11. Turn heat on and add pepper, thyme, and salt.
12. Serve with scallions.

11.3 Traeger Eggnog Cheesecake

(**Ready in about**: 1 hour and 20 minutes | **Serving**: 8| **Difficulty**: Medium)
Nutrition per serving: Kcal: 439| **Fat**: 31 g| **Net Carbs**: 35 g| **Protein**: 7 g

Ingredients:
- 3 tablespoons of melted butter
- 7 graham crackers
- 3/4 cup of white sugar
- 1/2 cup of eggnog
- 2 whole eggs
- 2 tablespoons of dark rum
- 2 6-ounce packages of cream cheese, at room temperature
- 1 and 1/2 tablespoons of vanilla extract
- Cinnamon
- 2 tablespoons of flour

Instructions
1. Preheat the Traeger to 325°F.
2. In a bowl, mix crackers with melted butter. Press into 8" pie pan.
3. In a mixer, mix sugar and cream cheese on medium for 1 minute. Add in flour, eggnog, vanilla, and rum. Mix 1 minute. Stir in eggs and mix lightly with hands.
4. Pour batter on the crackers. Put on the grill on the top rack or on an inverted rack.
5. Bake for 60 to 75 minutes at 325 °F, until still jiggly.
6. Cool for 1 hour before serving.

11.4 Smoked Crumb Apple Pie

(**Ready in about**: 1 hour and 55 minutes | **Serving**: 8| **Difficulty**: Medium)
Nutrition per serving: Kcal: 482| **Fat**: 9 g| **Net Carbs**: 70 g| **Protein**: 5 g

Ingredients:
For Pie:
- 1/8 teaspoons of salt
- 1 pie crust
- 3 tablespoons of flour
- 5 and 1/2 cups of apple slices
- 1 teaspoon of Cinnamon
- 1/4 cup of sugar

Crumb Topping:
- 1/2 cup of butter
- 1/2 cup of flour
- 1/2 cup of quick oats
- 1/2 cup of brown sugar packed

Instructions
1. Preheat the Traeger to 300°F.
2. Place pie crust in a 9-inch pie pan.
3. In a bowl, add salt, sugar, cinnamon, and flour. Mix with apples.
4. Pour onto the pie crust.
5. Mix the topping ingredients. Sprinkle over apple mixture.
6. Bake for 1 and 1/2 hours.
7. Serve warm.

11.5 Smoked Strawberry Crisp

(**Ready in about**: 45 minutes | **Serving**: 8| **Difficulty**: Medium)
Nutrition per serving: Kcal: 471| **Fat**: 5 g| **Net Carbs**: 74 g| **Protein**: 9 g

Ingredients:
For Filling
- 1/4 cup of all-purpose flour
- 6 cups of strawberries, cut into halves
- 2 tablespoons of orange juice.
For Topping:
- 1/4 cup of flour
- 1/2 teaspoon of cinnamon
- 2 cups of classic granola
- 1/3 cup of brown sugar
- 4 tablespoons of softened butter

Instructions
1. Preheat the Traeger to 350°F.
2. In a bowl, add all the ingredients of filling—place in cast iron skillet.
3. In another bowl, mix the topping ingredients. Spread over the filling.
4. Place on grill and cook for 1/2 an hour with lid closed.
5. Serve warm.

11.6 Smoke S' mores Nachos

(**Ready in about**: 20 minutes | **Serving**: 6| **Difficulty**: Easy)
Nutrition per serving: Kcal: 211| **Fat**: 13 g| **Net Carbs**: 15 g| **Protein**: 3g

Ingredients:
- 1 chocolate bars
- 1 packet marshmallows
- Graham crackers

Instructions
1. Crush crackers and put them in a grill-safe pan.
2. Put broken pieces of chocolate bar on top of crackers.
3. Top with marshmallow.
4. Cook in Traeger for 10 minutes at 225°F.
5. Raise the temperature to 375 °F—Cook for 5 minutes.
6. Serve hot.

11.7 Hot Dog Burnt Ends

(**Ready in about**: 50 minutes | **Serving**: 5| **Difficulty**: Medium)
Nutrition per serving: Kcal: 143| **Fat**: 6 g| **Net Carbs**: 18 g| **Protein**: 6g

Ingredients:
- Mustard
- Poultry seasoning
- 12-15 hot dogs
- 1/4 cup of butter
- 1/4 cup of brown sugar
- 1/4 cup of BBQ sauce

Instructions
1. Preheat the Traeger to 225°F.
2. Mix poultry seasoning and mustard.
3. Coat hot dogs in the mustard mix.
4. Smoke for 60-90 minutes.
5. Raise the temperature to 350°F. Takes out the hot dogs. Slice into 2-inch lengths
7. Place in 9 by 13" pan.
8. In a bowl, add butter, BBQ sauce, and brown sugar. Mix well.
9. Pour over hot dogs and mix well.
10. Place in Traeger cook for 30-45 minutes.
11. Serve with toothpicks.

11.8 Baked Blueberry Brioche French Toast

(**Ready in about**: 55 minutes | **Serving**: 12| **Difficulty**: Medium)
Nutrition per serving: Kcal: 143| **Fat**: 6 g| **Net Carbs**: 18 g| **Protein**: 6g

Ingredients:
- 1/2 cup of brown sugar
- 1/2 loaf of brioche, cut into chunks
- 2 cups of milk
- 1 cup of blueberries
- 1 teaspoon of cinnamon
- 6 whole eggs
- 1 teaspoon of apple cinnamon blend

Instructions
1. Take a 10 by 13 pan and spray with oil.
2. Preheat the Traeger to 325°F.
3. Place the brioche in the pan at the bottom.
4. Mix cinnamon, milk, brown sugar, and eggs in a bowl and pour over the brioche.
5. Top with blueberries.
6. Put on grill cook for 30-40 minutes, until internal temperature reaches 160°F.
7. Serve with maple syrup..

11.9 Apple Cake

(**Ready in about**: 60 minutes | **Serving**: 12| **Difficulty**: Medium)
Nutrition per serving: Kcal: 452| **Fat**: 21 g| **Net Carbs**: 55 g| **Protein**: 5g

Ingredients:
For Cake:
- 2 and 1/2 cups of flour
- 1/2 cup of canola oil
- 1 and 1/2 cup of brown sugar, firmly packed
- 1 cup of sour cream
- 1 teaspoon of baking soda
- 1 whole egg
- 1/2 teaspoon of baking powder
- 2 finely diced apples
- 1 and 1/2 teaspoon of vanilla

For Streusel:
- 1/2 teaspoon of cinnamon
- 1/2 a cup of packed brown sugar
- 1/2 cup of flour
- 1 stick of softened butter, cubed
- 1/2 cup of oats

For Glaze:
- 3 tablespoons of milk
- 2 cups of powdered sugar

Instructions
1. Preheat the Traeger to 325°F.
2. In a mixer, add all ingredients of the cake mix. Mix until combined.
3. Fold in diced apples.
4. Pour batter in 9 by 13" buttered pan. Combine ingredients of streusel mix until crumbly. Put on top of the batter evenly.
5. Place the pan on the second rack on the grill, preferably. Or on an inverted pan.
6. Bake for 35-25 minutes.
7. Serve warm.

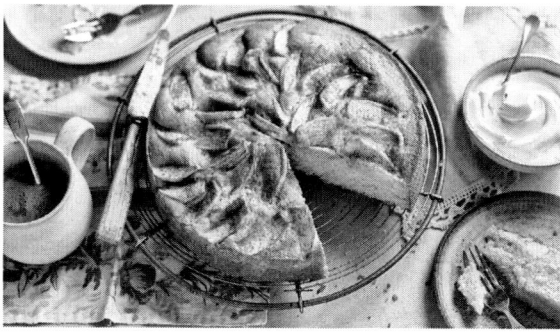

11.10 Bacon Cinnamon Rolls

(**Ready in about**: 35 minutes | **Serving**: 6| **Difficulty**: Medium)
Nutrition per serving: Kcal: 312| **Fat**: 13 g| **Net Carbs**: 21 g| **Protein**: 9g

Ingredients:
- 2 ounces of cream cheese
- 12 slices of bacon
- Cinnamon rolls, pre-made
- 1/3 cup of brown sugar

Instructions
1. Preheat the Traeger to 350°F.
2. Coat bacon slices in brown sugar.
3. Cook bacon on grill for 15-20 minutes.
4. Lower the temperature to 325 °F.
5. Open cinnamon rolls. Place cooked bacon slice in a cinnamon roll and roll it again.
6. Repeat with others.
7. Put rolls in an oiled baking dish. Cook for 10-15 minutes at 325°F.
8. Turn pan 90 degrees halfway.
9. Serve with cream cheese frosting.

11.11 Baked Deep Dish Supreme Pizza

(**Ready in about**: 40 minutes | **Serving**: 4| **Difficulty**: Medium)
Nutrition per serving: Kcal: 351| **Fat**: 21 g| **Net Carbs**: 22 g| **Protein**: 19g

Ingredients:
- 2 cup of mozzarella cheese
- Extra-virgin olive oil
- Pizza dough
- 1/2 cup of pizza sauce
- Parmesan cheese, as needed
- 1 teaspoon of fresh oregano
- 1 and 1/2 of red and green bell pepper
- 1 teaspoon of fresh basil
- 2 tablespoons of diced onion
- 1 pound of Italian sausage
- Pepperoni, mushrooms, and olives

Instructions
1. Preheat the grill to high.
2. Spray the cast iron skillet with olive oil: place and press dough on the skillet.
3. Add all other ingredients to pizza dough, with cheese on top and bottom.
1. Cook for 1/2 an hour, or until cheese is bubbly.
2. Slice and serve.

11.12 Smoked Apple Pie

(**Ready in about**: 55 minutes | **Serving**: 8| **Difficulty**: Hard)
Nutrition per serving: Kcal: 492| **Fat**: 25 g| **Net Carbs**: 51 g| **Protein**: 7g

Ingredients:

Pie Crust:
- 1 cup of cold butter, diced
- 2 and 1/2 cups of flour
- 4-6 tablespoons of cold water
- 1 teaspoon of kosher salt

Apple Pie Filling:
- 1/4 cup of flour
- 1 tablespoon of lemon juice
- 1/2 cup of brown sugar
- 1/2 teaspoon of ground cinnamon
- A pinch of ground nutmeg
- 2-3 granny smith, cut into slices
- Egg wash
- 2-3 honey crisp, cut into slices

Instructions

1. In a food processor, add pie crust ingredients except for water.
2. Pulse until dough is combined. Add water 1 tablespoon at a time. Add 1-2 tablespoons of more butter if too crumbly.
3. Form dough cut in half. Wrap separately in plastic wrap and keep in the fridge for 60 minutes.
4. Roll both pieces of dough into a 12" circle.
5. Place in 9" pie pan. Press into the bottom lightly.
6. Cook in Traeger on high for 20 minutes.
7. Meanwhile, mix all ingredients of apple pie filling.
8. Take the crust out and place the filling on top.
9. Place the second sheet of dough on top. Crimp and seal edges. Brush with egg wash.
10. Cook at 375 °F in Traeger for 1/2 1 hour.
11. Cover with foil and cook for another 1/2 an hour.
12. Let it rest before serving.

11.13 Cast Iron Pizza Lasagna

(**Ready in about**: 55 minutes | **Serving**: 10| **Difficulty**: Hard)
Nutrition per serving: Kcal: 550 | **Fat**: 17 g| **Net Carbs**: 31 g| **Protein**: 22 g

Ingredients:

- Homemade pizza dough

Pizza filling:
- 1 package of lasagna noodles, no-boil
- 1 pound of ground beef
- 3 cloves of garlic
- 1 28-ounce can of crushed tomatoes
- 1 pound of lightly ground Italian sausage
- 1/4 cup tomato paste
- 4 cups of mozzarella cheese, shredded
- 2/3 cup of water
- 3 tablespoons of parsley, minced.
- 2 tablespoons of sugar
- 1 and 1/2 cups of ricotta cheese
- 2 teaspoons of basil
- 3/4 teaspoons of salt

Instructions

1. In a pan, add ground sausage, beef, and diced onion. Cool completely and drain the juices.
2. Add tomatoes, sugar, tomato paste, salt, pepper, parsley, and garlic. Let it boil, then lower the heat to simmering.
3. Roll dough to cover the iron skillet. Place on the skillet.
4. Preheat the Traeger to 350°F.
5. Cook the dough for 15 minutes, or until the edges start to brown.
6. In a bowl, mix egg, ricotta cheese, parsley, and salt.
7. Place meat sauce on the cooked dough, egg mix, mozzarella, and lasagna noodles.
8. Place on grill and cook for 1/2 an hour, then cover with foil and cook until internal temperature reaches 165°F.
9. Serve hot.

11.14 Traeger Grilled French Toast

(**Ready in about**: 35 minutes | **Serving**: 6| **Difficulty**: Medium)
Nutrition per serving: Kcal: 323 | **Fat**: 16 g| **Net Carbs**: 30 g| **Protein**: 14 g

Ingredients:
- 1 and 1/2 teaspoons of cinnamon
- 8 whole eggs
- 1 teaspoon of vanilla extract
- 1/8 teaspoon of nutmeg
- 3 tablespoons of milk
- 1/4 teaspoon of salt
- 9-12 bread slices
- 1 tablespoon of sugar
- 4 tablespoons of butter, melted

Instructions

1. Preheat the Traeger to 350°F.
2. In a bowl, add all ingredients. Except for butter and bread. Mix well
3. In a 9 by 13" cake pan, add melted butter.
4. Soak bread slices in the egg mixture and place them into the cake pan.
5. Put the pan on the grill. Cook for 10 minutes, flip and cook for 5-10 minutes. Serve with maple syrup.

11.15 Greek Chicken Pizza

(**Ready in about**: 40 minutes | **Serving**: 6| **Difficulty**: Medium)
Nutrition per serving: Kcal: 213 | **Fat**: 11 g| **Net Carbs**: 25 g| **Protein**: 12 g

Ingredients:
- 3 tablespoons extra-virgin olive oil
- 3 chicken breasts
- Traeger Fin & Feather rub
- Fresh oregano
- 2 tomatoes, cut into slices
- 1 pizza dough
- 1/4 cup of feta cheese
- 1 cup of fresh spinach
- 2 ounces of Kalamata olives

Instructions

1. Coat chicken with olive oil and season with spice rub.
2. Preheat the Traeger to 375°F.
3. Put chicken directly on the grate, and cook for 18-20 minutes. Flip and cook until the internal temperature reaches 165°F.
4. Take chicken out and slice against the grain.
5. Raise Traeger temperature to 400°F.
6. Roll out pizza dough to your liking. Coat with olive oil and oregano.
7. Put dough directly on the grill. Cook for 3-5 minutes.
8. Take off the grill and add all toppings.
9. Serve hot.

11.16 Grilled Sweet Potatoes

(**Ready in about**: 60 minutes | **Serving**: 12| **Difficulty**: Medium)
Nutrition per serving: Kcal: 177 | **Fat**: 8 g| **Net Carbs**: 27 g| **Protein**: 8 g

Ingredients:
- 2 yams
- Maple syrup
- 2 sweet potatoes
- 1/2 cup of orange juice
- 1/4 cup of brown sugar bourbon
- 1/2 teaspoon of cinnamon
- 1/2 cup of butter
- 1 teaspoon of salt

Instructions

1. Preheat the grill to 325°F.
2. Peel yams, potatoes. Cut into rounds (1/4th thick).
3. In a 10 by 13" oiled baking dish, add layers of potatoes and yams.
4. In a pot, add orange juice, butter, maple syrup on medium flame. Mix until butter melts, for 5 minutes, let it simmer.
5. Turn off the heat.
6. Pour orange/butter sauce over layers of yams and potatoes.
7. Season with cinnamon and salt. Cover with foil.
8. Put on grill cook for 1/2 an hour. Uncover it and cook for 15-30 minutes.
9. Serve hot.

11.17 Grilled King Crab Legs

(**Ready in about**: 20 minutes | **Serving**: 4| **Difficulty**: Easy)
Nutrition per serving: Kcal: 441 | **Fat**: 7 g| **Net Carbs**: 0 g| **Protein**: 88 g

Ingredients:
- 1 batch of garlic butter, smoked
- 3-4 pounds of king crab legs

Instructions

1. Preheat the Traeger to 180-200°F.
2. Split the crab and coat with garlic butter, and place on grill.
3. Smoke for 5 minutes, raise the temperature to 350 to 375°F.
4. Cook for 5 more minutes, flip and cook for 5 minutes.
5. Serve with garlic butter.

11.18 Smoked Salmon Scrambled Eggs

(**Ready in about**: 16 minutes | **Serving**: 4| **Difficulty**: Medium)
Nutrition per serving: Kcal: 283 | **Fat**: 22 g| **Net Carbs**: 1 g| **Protein**: 19 g

Ingredients:
- 1/8 cup of whole milk
- 6 whole eggs
- 1 cup of hot smoked salmon
- 1/4 teaspoon of salt
- 1 tablespoon of salted butter
- A dash of white pepper
- 1 cup of shredded sharp cheddar

Instructions
1. In a bowl, whisk eggs, milk, white pepper, and salt. Mix well.
2. Preheat the Traeger to 350°F. Place skillet on the grill.
3. In the skillet, melt butter. Add in eggs, cook to set.
4. Add salmon chunks, cheese. Cook until cheese is melted.
5. Serve salmon eggs with the muffins.

11.19 Grilled Peaches with Yogurt and Granola

(**Ready in about**: 10 minutes | **Serving**: 4| **Difficulty**: Medium)
Nutrition per serving: Kcal: 209 | **Fat**: 3 g| **Net Carbs**: 43 g| **Protein**: 6 g

Ingredients:
- 1/4 cup of honey
- 4 peaches cut in 1/2
- 1/2 cup of super grains granola
- 1/2 cup of Greek yogurt

Instructions
1. Preheat the Traeger to high.
2. Put peach halves, remove the pit, pit side down, on the grill and cook for 5 minutes
3. Take off the grill and top with yogurt and drizzle honey over.
4. And serve on a bed of granola.

11.20 Smoked Buffalo Shrimp

(**Ready in about**: 15 minutes | **Serving**: 6| **Difficulty**: Easy)
Nutrition per serving: Kcal: 57| **Fat**: 1 g| **Net Carbs**: 1 g| **Protein**: 10 g

Ingredients:
- 1/4 teaspoon of onion powder
- 1-pound raw shrimp, with tails, peeled and deveined
- 1/4 teaspoon of garlic powder
- 1/2 cup of Buffalo sauce
- 1/2 teaspoon of salt

Instructions
1. Preheat the Traeger to 450°F.
2. Coat the shrimps with all spices.
3. Place directly on grill cook on each side for 2-3 minutes.
4. Take off the grill coat with buffalo sauce.
5. Serve hot.

11.21 Traeger Mini Meatloaf Burgers

(**Ready in about**: 30 minutes| **Serving**: 6| **Difficulty**: Medium)
Nutrition per serving: Kcal: 198| **Fat**: 8.8 g| **Net Carb** 2 g| **Protein**: 7 g

Ingredients:
- 3 pounds of ground beef
- 1 diced onion
- 2 egg yolks
- 1/4 cup of milk
- 1/2 teaspoon of dry mustard
- 3 whole eggs
- 1/2 teaspoon of salt
- 1/2 cup of ketchup
- 1/4 teaspoon of ground black pepper
- 1/2 teaspoon of onion powder
- 1 teaspoon of dried parsley
- 1 tablespoon of minced garlic
- 1 cup of saltine crackers, crushed
- 1/4 teaspoon of garlic powder:
- 1/2 cup of panko breadcrumbs

Instructions
1. Preheat the Traeger to 325°F.
2. In a bowl, mix all ingredients except for beef.
3. Now add ground beef, mix but do not over mix.
4. Shape into patties and set them aside.
5. Place directly on grates and cook for 10-15 minutes. Brush with BBQ sauce and cook for 5 more minutes until the internal temperature reaches 160°F.
6. Put cheese on top and melt.
7. Serve hot in buns.

11.22 The Best Grilled Pizza

(**Ready in about**: 30 minutes | **Serving**: 4| **Difficulty**: Easy)
Nutrition per serving: Kcal: 525| **Fat**: 34 g| **Net Carbs**: 17.2 g| **Protein**: 36.1 g

Ingredients:
- 1/2 onion, cut into slices
- 1 homemade pizza crust
- 1 cup of pizza sauce
- 2 tablespoons of olive oil
- 12-15 pepperoni slices
- 1/2 cup of cooked crumbled Italian sausage
- 1/2 cup of shredded mozzarella

Instructions
1. Preheat the Traeger to 450°F.
2. Roll out the dough on a floured surface.
3. With 1/2 of the oil, brush the dough. Cook on grill for 2 minutes until grill marks appear.
4. Flip the dough, brush with oil.
5. Add pizza sauce and all other toppings. Cook with the lid closed for 5 minutes until cheese melts.
6. Slice and serve.

11.23 BBQ Smoked Sausage Bites

(**Ready in about**: 50 minutes | **Serving**: 12| **Difficulty**: Medium)
Nutrition per serving: Kcal: 482| **Fat**: 34 g| **Net Carbs**: 30 g| **Protein**: 14 g

Ingredients:
- 3 cups of barbecue sauce
- 3 pounds of sliced smoked sausage
- 1 tablespoon of vegetable oil

Instructions
1. Preheat the pan and heat the sausage slices. Brush with oil.
2. Cook on each side for 3-5 minutes.
3. Preheat the Traeger temperature to 350°F.
4. Place slices in grill-safe pan and coat in BBQ sauce.
5. Put on grill, cook for 1/2 an hour uncovered.
6. Serve hot.

11.24 Spinach Dip Rollups

(**Ready in about**: 40 minutes | **Serving**: 12| **Difficulty**: Medium)
Nutrition per serving: Kcal: 403| **Fat**: 35 g| **Net Carbs**: 15 g| **Protein**: 9 g

Ingredients:
- 1 roll of crescent dough
- 2 teaspoons of butter
- 6-ounce of baby spinach
- 8-ounce of softened cream cheese
- 1 teaspoon minced garlic
- 2 cups of shredded mozzarella
- 1 cup of mayo
- 1 cup of sour cream
- 1/4 teaspoon of black pepper
- 1 cup of shredded parmesan
- 1/2 teaspoon of salt

Instructions
1. Sauté garlic in butter for 10 seconds, add baby spinach, cook for 2 minutes.
2. In a bowl, mix sour cream, mayo, cream cheese, salt, and pepper.
3. Add in the wilted spinach mix.
4. Add in cheeses, save 1/2 of a cup for later.
5. Roll the crescent dough; use flour so it will not become sticky.
6. Add in the spinach filling and roll the dough.
7. Place on a baking sheet. Top with cheese and bake for 20 to 25 minutes, at 325 °F in Traeger.
8. Slice into single servings and serve.

11.25 Pellet Grill Pasties

(**Ready in about**: 1 hour and 25 minutes | **Serving**: 6| **Difficulty**: Medium)
Nutrition per serving: Kcal: 648| **Fat**: 17 g| **Net Carbs**: 44 g| **Protein**: 14 g

Ingredients:
- For Crust:
- 3/4 to 1 cup of ice-cold water
- 1/2 cup of chilled salted butter
- 3 cups of flour
- 1/2 cup of chilled flavored shortening
- For Filling:
- 1/4 rutabaga
- 1/4 pound of ground beef
- 1 onion
- 1/4 pound of ground pork
- Salt and pepper, to taste
- 1 russet potato
- 1 carrot
- A handful of flat-leaf fresh parsley
- 1 egg whisked with 1/8 cup of milk
- 3 tablespoons of butter

Instructions
1. Preheat the Traeger to 350°F.
2. Place parchment paper on a pan.
3. Slice shortening and butter into dice.
4. Add flour to the butter and mix with hands. Add ¾ of water and mix. Add water if required to form a crumbly dough. In a plastic wrap, wrap the dough and keep it in the fridge for 1/2 an hour.
5. Chop up vegetables in pieces.
6. In a pan, add all vegetable pieces. Sauté in butter for 6-7 minutes. Let it cool.
7. Slice dough into 6 pieces. Roll each piece into a large sheet, bigger than hand.
8. Place meat and filling and seal and crimp the edges with drops of water.
9. Repeat with the rest of the filling and dough and put in the pan.
10. Coat lightly with egg wash.
11. Bake for 60 minutes at 350°F.
12. Serve with dip.

11.26 Broccoli Chicken Divan

(**Ready in about**: 1 hour and 15 minutes | **Serving**: 8| **Difficulty**: Hard)
Nutrition per serving: Kcal: 548| **Fat**: 34 g| **Net Carbs**: 31 g| **Protein**: 30 g

Ingredients:
- 4 cups of broccoli florets
- 1-pound of egg noodles
- 1 tablespoon of oil
- 2 chicken breasts, cut into cubes
- 1 can of cream chicken soup
- Salt and pepper, to taste
- 1/4 teaspoon Black pepper
- 1/2 teaspoon of onion powder
- 1/2 teaspoon of garlic powder
- 1 can of cream mushroom soup
- 1 cup of 1/2 and half
- 4 cups of shredded cheese
- 1 cup of chicken broth
- 1/4 cup of white wine
- Crushed Ritz crackers
- 1/2 cup of sour cream

Instructions
1. Preheat the Traeger to 325°F.
2. Cook 1/2 of the noodles in salted water.
3. Season meat with pepper and salt. In a pan, sauté until 1/2 cooked. Set it aside.
4. Steam broccoli to half-cooked. Set it aside.
5. In a large pot, mix soups, 1/2 and half, garlic powder, black pepper, chicken broth, white wine, sour cream, onion powder. Add in chicken juices.
6. In an oiled casserole pan, add noodles, broccoli, 1/2 cheese, sauce, chicken.
7. Top with Ritz and cheese.
8. Bake at 325-350 °F for 45-60 minutes until the chicken is completely cooked. If the top is becoming too brown, cover with aluminum foil.
9. Serve right away.

11.27 Grill Carnitas

(**Ready in about**: 10 hours and 10 minutes | **Serving**: 12| **Difficulty**: Medium)
Nutrition per serving: Kcal: 560| **Fat**: 41 g| **Net Carbs**: 2 g| **Protein**: 44 g

Ingredients:
- 5 pounds of roast pork shoulder
- Pork Rub:
- 1 teaspoon of chipotle chili powder
- 2 tablespoons of salt
- 1 and 1/2 teaspoons of granulated garlic
- 1 teaspoon of cumin
- 1 teaspoon of paprika
- 2 teaspoons of brown sugar
- 1 teaspoon of cayenne pepper
- 1 tablespoon of onion powder

Instructions
1. Mix all the ingredients of rub and set them aside.
2. Season the roast with spice rub.
3. Preheat the Traeger to 180-200°F.
4. Place coated roast in a foil pan, and place on grill.
5. Let it smoke for two hours, and raise the temperature to 325°F.
6. Cook for 8-9 hours until the internal temperature reaches 190-195°F.
7. Shred the roast. Fry and serve in tacos.

11.28 Traeger Bean Tostadas

(**Ready in about**: 20 minutes | **Serving**: 6| **Difficulty**: Medium)
Nutrition per serving: Kcal: 283| **Fat**: 17 g| **Net Carbs**: 26 g| **Protein**: 9 g

Ingredients:
- 1/4 cup of sauce
- 1 can of refried beans
- 6 shells corn tostada
- 1/4 cup of cheddar cheese, shredded
- 1 tablespoon of taco seasoning
- garnish
- 1/8 cup of chopped cilantro
- 1/4 cup of sour cream
- Tomato, avocado, lettuce
- Shredded cheese

Instructions
1. Preheat the Traeger to 350°F.
2. In a bowl, mix cheddar cheese, sauce, beans, and taco seasoning.
3. Fill the tostadas with bean mix.
4. Put tostadas on grill and grill for 6-7 minutes.
5. Take off and serve with toppings.

11.29 Spot Prawn Skewers

(**Ready in about**: 20 minutes | **Serving**: 6| **Difficulty**: Medium)
Nutrition per serving: Kcal: 221| **Fat**: 7 g| **Net Carbs**: 3 g| **Protein**: 34 g

Ingredients:
- 2 tablespoons of oil
- 2 pounds of clean spot prawns
- Salt and pepper

Instructions
1. Preheat the Traeger to 400°F.
2. Thread shrimp on skewers, coat with oil, and generously season with salt and pepper.
3. Grill with lid closed for 4 to 5 minutes.
4. Serve hot.

11.30 Bacon Sweet Potato Pie

(**Ready in about**: 75 minutes | **Serving**: 8| **Difficulty**: Medium)
Nutrition per serving: Kcal: 342| **Fat**: 29.7 g| **Net Carbs**: 38 g| **Protein**: 23 g

Ingredients:
- 5 egg yolks
- 1 pound of sweet potatoes, cut into cubes
- 3/4 cup of dark brown sugar
- 1/2 teaspoon of cinnamon
- 1 cup of chopped toasted pecans
- 1 and a 1/4 cup of plain yogurt
- 1 tablespoon of maple syrup
- 1/4 teaspoon of nutmeg
- 1/4 teaspoon of salt
- 4 cooked strips of bacon, diced
- 9" frozen pie shell

Instructions
1. Steam the sweet cubed potatoes, mash and set them aside.
2. Preheat the Traeger to 350°F.
3. In a stand mixer with a paddle, add nutmeg, yogurt, yolks, brown sugar, salt, and cinnamon. Mix until combined.
4. Pour batter in pie shell and put in a sheet pan.
5. Top with bacon, pecans, and maple syrup.
6. Bake for 45-60 minutes, until the internal temperature reaches 165-180°F.
7. Serve chilled

11.31 Grilled Apple Crisp

(**Ready in about**: 55 minutes | **Serving**: 6| **Difficulty**: Medium)
Nutrition per serving: Kcal: 298| **Fat**: 21 g| **Net Carbs**: 13 g| **Protein**: 13 g

Ingredients:
- 1 tablespoon of pumpkin pie spice
- 3 apples
- 1/2 cup of granola cereal
- 1 tablespoon of maple syrup
- Lemon juice
- Raisins
- 1 and 1/2 tablespoons of brown sugar
- 1/2 stick of butter
- 2 tablespoons of pecan chips

Instructions
1. Preheat the Traeger to 400°F.
2. Slice apples in 1/2 and remove the core, cut from the back to be flat on a baking sheet.
3. In a bowl, mix the rest of the ingredients.
4. Stuff mixture on apples.
5. Bakr for 1/2 an hour, until apples are soft.
6. Serve with vanilla ice cream.

11.32 Smoked Maple Cupcakes

(**Ready in about**: 75 minutes | **Serving**: 10| **Difficulty**: Medium)
Nutrition per serving: Kcal: 321| **Fat**: 28 g| **Net Carbs**: 33 g| **Protein**: 22 g

Ingredients:
- Yellow cupcake mix

  Buttercream:
- 1 pinch of salt
- 1 tablespoon of maple flavoring.
- 4 cups of sifted powdered sugar
- 4 tablespoons heavy cream
- 1 cup Softened butter

  Bacon:
- 1/2 cup of brown sugar
- 1/2 cup of BBQ rub

Instructions
1. Preheat the Traeger to 350°F.
2. Mix cupcake mix with milk, 1 cup melted butter, and 4 egg, lightly mix.
3. Pour in muffin tins and place on grill, cook for 20 minutes.
4. Take them out and lower the grill temperature to 300°F.

1. Coat bacon with BBQ brown sugar mix. Smoke bacon on the pan for 45 minutes. Take off the grill.
2. In a stand mixer, add butter, powdered sugar cream. Add maple flavoring with a pinch of salt. Add heavy cream.
3. Spread cream mix to cupcakes with bacon on top serve.

11.33 Chocolate Pecan Bacon Pie

(**Ready in about**: 75 minutes | **Serving**: 8| **Difficulty**: Medium)
Nutrition per serving: Kcal: 354| **Fat**: 30 g| **Net Carbs**: 28 g| **Protein**: 20 g

Ingredients:
- 4 whole eggs
- 3/4 cup of crumbled bacon
- 1 cup of chopped pecans
- 1/2 cup of chocolate chips, semi-sweet
- 1 tablespoon of vanilla extract
- 1/2 cup of dark corn syrup
- 3/4 cup of white sugar
- 1/2 cup of white sugar
- 1/2 cup of light corn syrup
- 1/4cup of Bourbon
- 4 tablespoons of butter
- 1 tablespoon of cornstarch
- 1/2 cup of brown sugar
- 1 package of pie dough, refrigerated

Instructions
1. Preheat the Traeger to 350°F.
2. In a bowl, mix brown sugar, butter, white sugar.
3. In another bowl, mix eggs with 1 tablespoon of cornstarch.
4. Add to the previous mix. Add corn syrups, chopped pecans, bacon, vanilla, bourbon to mix.
5. Take a 9" pie pan and place lightly floured dough inside.
6. Add 1/2 a cup of chocolate chips.
7. Pour mixture.
8. Bake for 40 minutes or until cooked through.
9. Serve with whipped cream..

11.34 Pear Cobbler

(**Ready in about**: 75 minutes | **Serving**: 8| **Difficulty**: Medium)
Nutrition per serving: Kcal: 322| **Fat**: 27 g| **Net Carbs**: 25 g| **Protein**: 19.3 g

Ingredients:
- Cranberries
- 2 large cans of pear in syrup cut in halves
- 1 cup of whole milk
- Brown sugar
- 1 cup of sugar
- 1 cup of flour
- 1/2 teaspoon of vanilla extract
- 1 stick of butter

Instructions
1. Preheat the Traeger to 400°F.
2. In a bowl, mix sugar, flour, vanilla extract, and milk.
3. Take a baking dish and spray generously with oil spray.
4. Place stick of butter in pan and place on grill. Take excess butter out and pour the batter into it.
5. Add cranberries on top and raw sugar on top.
6. Bake for 40 minutes, until the top, is lightly golden.

11.35 Baked Deep Dish Apple Pie

(**Ready in about**: 75 minutes | **Serving**: 8| **Difficulty**: Medium)
Nutrition per serving: Kcal: 321| **Fat**: 24 g| **Net Carbs**: 27 g| **Protein**: 20 g

Ingredients:
- 10 apples, cut into slices
- 2 tablespoons of butter
- 2 and 1/2 cups + 1/3 cup of flour
- 1 cup of butter
- 7 tablespoons of ice water
- 1 teaspoon of salt
- 1 tablespoon of sugar
- 1 tablespoon of cinnamon
- 1/3 cup of fresh cranberries
- Juice of 1/2 lemon
- 1 tablespoon of raw sugar
- 1/3 cup of brown sugar
- Zest from the whole orange
- 1 egg whisked
- 1 teaspoon of ginger

Instructions
1. In a food processor, add salt, two and a half cups of flour, 1 tablespoon of sugar. Pulse to mix.
2. As the blender is running, add small pieces of cold butter (1 cup) until it looks like rough cornmeal. Add 1 tablespoon of cold water at a time, use as much less or more water you need until it becomes a dough.
3. Put dough on a floured clean surface and make into two rounds to cover the pie dish. Place in a pie dish and pierce with a fork
4. Preheat the Traeger to 350°F.
5. In a bowl, add sliced apples, butter, flour, ginger, lemon juice, cinnamon, brown sugar, and orange zest. Mix well, and place on a baking sheet.
6. Put the baking sheet on the grill and let it cook for 10-15 minutes until apples become juicy.
7. Take apples out, mix with cranberries pour in a prepared pan, without juices.
8. Place another round of dough on top, seal the edges, brush with egg, and add raw sugar on top.
9. Place on grill and bake for 40 minutes, until dough is light golden
10. Serve with vanilla ice cream.

11.36 Maple Bacon Pull-Apart

(**Ready in about**: 55 minutes | **Serving**: 8| **Difficulty**: Medium)
Nutrition per serving: Kcal: 315| **Fat**: 21 g| **Net Carbs**: 25 g| **Protein**: 16 g

Ingredients:
- 1 cup of maple syrup
- 12 slices of bacon
- 1 cup of brown sugar
- 1 cup of butter
- 2 teaspoon of ground cinnamon
- 2 cans of biscuits
- 1/2 cup of water

Instructions
1. Preheat the Traeger to high, and keep the lid closed for 16 minutes.
2. Cook bacon on each side for 5-8 minutes, crumble it.
3. Cut every biscuit into 4 pieces, and split in half.
4. In a pan, mix brown sugar, water, syrup, and butter. Let it boil, lower the heat and let it simmer for 60 seconds. Mix in cinnamon.
5. To biscuits, quarters add syrup and crumbled bacon, coat well, and put in the Bundt pan.
6. Set the Traeger to 350 °F, place the Bundt pan on the grill and cook for 1/2 an hour with the lid closed.
7. Flip on a serving pan and serve.

11.37 Cast Iron Berry Cobbler

(**Ready in about**: 50 minutes | **Serving**: 6| **Difficulty**: Medium)
Nutrition per serving: Kcal: 345| **Fat**: 25 g| **Net Carbs**: 21 g| **Protein**: 15 g

Ingredients:
- 1/2 cup of butter
- 4 cup of berries
- 1/3 cup of orange juice
- 4 tablespoons + 1/2 cup of sugar
- 2/3 cup of flour
- 1 pinch of salt
- 3/4 teaspoon of baking powder

Instructions
1. Preheat the Traeger to 350 °F with the lid closed for 15 minutes.
2. In a small cast iron pan, mix orange juice, 4 tablespoons of sugar with berries.
3. In a bowl, mix flour, salt, and baking powder.
4. In a bowl, cream the sugar and butter. Add vanilla extract and egg. Fold with flour mix.
5. Spread batter on berries and sprinkle raw sugar.
6. Bake for 35-45 minutes. Serve with cream.

11.38 Smoked Cocktail

(**Ready in about**: 50 minutes | **Serving**: 1| **Difficulty**: Easy)
Nutrition per serving: Kcal: 72| **Fat**: 1 g| **Net Carbs**: 0 g| **Protein**: 2 g

Ingredients:
- 1 and a half-ounce of dry Vermouth
- 1 Jar of soaked cocktail onions
- 1 and a half-ounce of Vodka

Instructions
1. Preheat the Traeger to 500 °F, with the lid, closed.
2. In a baking dish, add lemonade and put it on the grill. Cook for 20-30 minutes, until internal temperature reaches 200 °F
3. Pour smoked lemonade into a glass. Add all tea bags in lemonade for 2-4 minutes, take them out, and add whiskey.
4. Serve with a cinnamon stick and lemon slice.

11.40 Garden Gimlet Cocktail

(**Ready in about**: 50 minutes | **Serving**: 1| **Difficulty**: Easy)
Nutrition per serving: Kcal: 56| **Fat**: 0.9 g| **Net Carbs**: 2 g| **Protein**: 3 g

Ingredients:
- 1-and-a-half-ounce Vodka
- 1 cup of honey
- 2 sprig of rosemary
- Zest of 2 lemons
- 2 slices of cucumber
- 1/4 cup of water
- 3/4 ounce of lime juice

Instructions
1. Preheat the Traeger to 180 °F, use super smoke.
2. In a pan, add honey with water, lemon zest, and rosemary.
3. Put the pan on the grill and smoke for 45-60 minutes. Strain and let it cool
4. In a cup, muddle cucumber with lime juice, 1 ounce of rosemary lemon syrup
5. Add ice transfer to a clean glass after straining.

11.41 Gin & Tonic

(**Ready in about**: 55 minutes | **Serving**: 1| **Difficulty**: Easy)
Nutrition per serving: Kcal: 77| **Fat**: 1 g| **Net Carbs**: 2 g| **Protein**: 3 g

Ingredients:
- 2 tablespoons of granulated sugar
- 1/4 cup of berries
- 1 sprig of fresh mint
- 1 and a half-ounce of gin
- 1/2 cup of tonic water
- 1 orange, cut into slices

Instructions
1. Preheat the Traeger to 180 °F with the lid closed; use super smoke if possible.
2. Place berries on baking pan and place on grill. Let it smoke for 1/2 an hour at 180°F.
3. Raise the Traeger temperature to 450 °F with the lid closed.
4. Coat orange slices with sugar and put them directly on the grill—Cook for 5 minutes, or till grill marks appear.
5. In a glass, add berries, ice, gin, and fill with tonic water.
6. Serve with fresh thyme and grilled orange.

CHAPTER 12
Dressings and Sauces

Chapter 12: Dressings and Sauces

12.1 Traeger Smoked Salsa Verde

(**Ready in about:** 50 minutes | **Serving:** 6| **Difficulty:** Easy)
Nutrition per serving: Kcal: 25| **Fat:** 1 g| **Net Carbs:** 2g| **Protein:** 1 g

Ingredients:
- 3 seeded Anaheim peppers
- 1 tablespoon of canola oil
- 2 seeded Pasilla peppers
- 1 seeded jalapeno
- 1/2 diced medium onion
- 6 medium Mexican husk tomato
- 3 cloves of minced garlic
- 1 cup of chopped cilantro
- Juice of 1 lime
- 1 teaspoon of salt
- 1/2 cup of chicken stock

Instructions
1. On a silicone baking sheet, place garlic, husk tomatoes, onion, and seeded peppers.
2. Let the Traeger preheat to 225°F. Place the tray of vegetables in Traeger and let it cook for 1/2 an hour.
3. Take out from the grill and let it cool. Put all of these in a blender and pulse on high until pureed.
4. In a pan, add canola oil over medium flame. Add in the puree. Let it simmer over low heat for 10-15 minutes.

12.2 Traeger Thanksgiving Dressing

(**Ready in about:** 85 minutes | **Serving:** 12| **Difficulty:** Easy)
Nutrition per serving: Kcal: 241| **Fat:** 8 g| **Net Carbs:** 21 g| **Protein:** 4 g

Ingredients:
- 1 13-ounce bag of dried crouton mix dressing
- 1/2 cup of salted butter
- 4 stalks of celery, cleaned and chopped
- Seasoning packet from dressing mix
- 2 and 1/2 cups of chicken broth
- 1 diced onion

Instructions
1. In a pan, add onion, butter, and celery, on medium flame. Cook for 10-15 minutes, until vegetables are tender.
2. Stir in chicken broth and seasoning packet, and let it simmer.
3. Combine the croutons with the broth mix—place in a grill pan.
4. Cover with foil place into a preheated Traeger at 350 °F grill.
5. Cook for 35-40 minutes. Remove the foil and cook for 10-15 minutes.
6. Serve hot.

12.3 Smoked Caramelized Onion Dip

(**Ready in about:** 50 minutes | **Serving:** 6| **Difficulty:** Easy)
Nutrition per serving: Kcal: 242| **Fat:** 7 g| **Net Carbs:** 25 g| **Protein:** 3 g

Ingredients:
- 1 tablespoon of brown sugar
- 1/2 cup of salted butter
- 1/2 teaspoon of salt
- 6 cups of sliced onion

Instructions
1. In a cast-iron skillet, add all ingredients
2. Preheat the Traeger to 325°F.
3. Put the skillet on the grill, close the lid, and cook for 15 minutes.
4. Mix the ingredients well and cook for 10 more minutes with the lid closed.
5. Continue the cycle until onions become browned and shrinks.

12.4 Sherri Mushroom Sauce

(**Ready in about:** 20 minutes | **Serving:** 12| **Difficulty:** Easy)
Nutrition per serving: Kcal: 33| **Fat:** 1 g| **Net Carbs:** 4 g| **Protein:** 2 g

Ingredients:
- 1 teaspoon of sherry
- 2 cups of milk
- 1 onion, chopped
- 1 and 1/2 cups of sliced fresh mushrooms
- 2 teaspoons of olive oil
- 2 tablespoons of All-purpose flour, plain
- 1 tablespoon of chopped chives
- Salt and black pepper, to taste

Instructions
1. In a pan, heat the milk.
2. In a skillet, sauté onions for 3 minutes in olive oil.
3. Add mushrooms slices and cook for another 3 minutes. Add in the flour and cook for 2-3 minutes.
4. Add in the warmed milk.
5. Continue to stir until it becomes thick, for 3 minutes.
6. Add the rest of the ingredients.
7. Smoke in Traeger for 10 minutes at smoke mode.
8. Serve.

12.5 Savory Vegetable Dip

(**Ready in about:** 20 minutes | **Serving:** 8| **Difficulty:** Easy)
Nutrition per serving: Kcal: 57| **Fat:** 1.5 g| **Net Carbs:** 7 g| **Protein:** 4 g

Ingredients:
- 1 cup of fat-free cottage cheese
- 3 cloves of garlic, chopped
- 1/3 cup of plain fat-free yogurt
- 3/4 cup of chopped and sun-dried tomatoes, oil-packed drained
- 1/3 cup of fat-free mayonnaise

Instructions
1. Place all ingredients in the food processor. Pulse until smooth.
2. Smoke in Traeger for 10 minutes at smoke mode.
3. Chill in the refrigerator for 3 hours and serve.

12.6 Hot Pepper Sauce

(**Ready in about:** 50 minutes | **Serving:** 10| **Difficulty:** Easy)
Nutrition per serving: Kcal: 67| **Fat:** 2.1 g| **Net Carbs:** 6 g| **Protein:** 0.5 g

Ingredients:
- 1/4 cup of olive oil
- 1 ancho chili pepper, dried
- 1 jalapeno chili pepper, fresh
- 1 chipotle chili pepper, dried
- 1/2 cup of water
- 1 cup of white wine vinegar
- 1 New Mexico chili pepper, dried

Instructions
1. Remove stems, seeds from all chilies.
2. In a bowl, mix vinegar and water soak the dried chilies.
3. In a saucepan, add chilies and liquid, add fresh chili.
4. Let it cook for 1/2 an hour. Turn off the heat and let it cool.
5. Blend in a blender until smooth.
6. Smoke in Traeger for 10 minutes at smoke mode.
7. Store in refrigerator.

12.7 Nut Butter Hummus

(**Ready in about:** 15 minutes | **Serving:** 16| **Difficulty:** Easy)
Nutrition per serving: Kcal: 131| **Fat:** 4 g| **Net Carbs:** 18 g| **Protein:** 7 g

Ingredients:
- 2 cups of garbanzo beans
- 1 cup of water
- 1/2 cup of powdered peanut butter
- 1/4 cup of peanut butter
- 2 tablespoons of honey
- 1 teaspoon of vanilla extract

Instructions
1. In a blender, add all ingredients.
2. Blend until smooth.
3. Smoke in Traeger for 10 minutes at smoke mode.
4. Refrigerate for 1 week.

12.8 Honey Peachy Spread

(**Ready in about**: 15 minutes | **Serving**: 4| **Difficulty**: Easy)
Nutrition per serving: Kcal: 56| **Fat**: 3 g| **Net Carbs**: 14 g| **Protein**: 1 g

Ingredients:
- 1/2 teaspoon of cinnamon
- 1 15-ounce can of peach unsweetened, drained, cut in half
- 2 tablespoons of honey

Instructions
1. In a bowl, add all ingredients, mash up with a fork until desired consistency.
2. Smoke in Traeger for 10 minutes at smoke mode.

12.9 Orange Basil Vinaigrette

(**Ready in about**: 20 minutes | **Serving**: 8 | **Difficulty**: Easy)
Nutrition per serving: Kcal: 49| **Fat**: 2 g| **Net Carbs**: 8 g| **Protein**: 0.3 g

Ingredients:
- 2 teaspoons of Dijon mustard
- 2 cups of unsweetened orange juice
- 1/3 cup of white wine vinegar
- 1 tablespoon of fresh basil
- 2 teaspoons of extra-virgin olive oil
- 2 tablespoons of cornstarch

Instructions
1. In a pan, mix cornstarch and orange juice. Let it boil for one-minute keep mixing.
2. Pour in a bowl, chill, in refrigerate. After chilled, add the basil, vinegar, olive oil, and mustard. Mix until well combined.
3. Smoke in Traeger for 10 minutes at smoke mode.
4. Serve.

12.10 Citrus Vinaigrette

(**Ready in about**: 20 minutes | **Serving**: 8 | **Difficulty**: level: Easy)
Nutrition per serving: Kcal: 143| **Protein**: 4 g| **Net Carbs**: 7 g| **Fat**: 3 g

Ingredients:
- 1/2 cup of olive oil
- 1/4 cup of rice wine vinegar
- 1 cup of water
- 2 tablespoons of honey
- 1/2 cup of orange juice
- 1 tablespoon of fresh thyme
- Dash of ground black pepper
- 1/4 teaspoon of salt

Instructions
1. Add all ingredients to a blender.
2. Pulse until smooth.
3. Smoke in Traeger for 10 minutes at smoke mode.
4. Keep in the refrigerator for 2 weeks.

12.11 Cilantro Lime Dressing

(**Ready in about**: 15 minutes | **Serving**: 6 | **Difficulty**: level: Easy)
Nutrition per serving: Kcal: 54| **Protein**: 4 g| **Net Carbs**: 2 g| **Fat**: 2 g

Ingredients:
- Lime juice of two limes
- 1/4 cup of olive oil
- 2 cups of 1% cottage cheese
- 1/4 teaspoon of black pepper
- 1 clove of garlic
- 1/2 cup of cilantro
- 1/2 teaspoon of honey
- 1/2 teaspoon of salt

Instructions
1. Add all ingredients to a blender.
2. Pulse on high until smooth.
3. Smoke in Traeger for 10 minutes at smoke mode.

12.12 Italian Salad Dressing

(**Ready in about**: 15 minutes | **Serving**: 8 | **Difficulty**: level: Easy)
Nutrition per serving: Kcal: 50| **Protein**: 0.1 g| **Net Carbs**: 0.2 g| **Fat**: 5 g

Ingredients:
- 2 teaspoons of Dijon mustard
- 3 tablespoons of olive oil
- 1 tablespoon of lemon juice
- 1 clove of minced garlic
- 1 teaspoon of dried parsley
- 2 tablespoons of red wine vinegar
- 1/8 teaspoon of dried oregano
- 1/8 teaspoon of red pepper flakes
- 1 teaspoon of dried basil, crumbled

Instructions
1. In a jar, mix all ingredients.
2. Smoke in Traeger for 10 minutes at smoke mode.
3. Shake well before use.

12.13 Special Vinaigrette

(**Ready in about**: 20 minutes | **Serving**: 16 | **Difficulty**: level: Easy)
Nutrition per serving: Kcal: 38| **Protein**: 0.1 g| **Net Carbs**: 9 g| **Fat**: 2 g

Ingredients:
- 6 tablespoons of fresh orange juice
- 1 garlic clove, minced
- 5 tablespoons of extra-virgin olive oil
- 1/4 cup of white wine vinegar
- 1/4 teaspoon of salt
- 1 tablespoon of Dijon mustard

Instructions
1. In a bowl, mix oil, minced garlic, mustard, salt, and vinegar. Whisk well.
2. Add 4 tablespoons of juice, taste, and add more.
3. Smoke in Traeger for 10 minutes at Smoke mode.

12.14 Grilled Mango Chutney

(**Ready in about**: 20 minutes | **Serving**: 6 | **Difficulty**: level: Easy)
Nutrition per serving: Kcal: 58| **Protein**: 6g|**Net Carbs**: 15 g| **Fat**: 4 g|

Ingredients:
- 1 mango
- 1/4 tablespoon of fresh rosemary chopped
- 1/4 cup of honey
- 2 tablespoons of cider vinegar
- 2 tablespoons of finely chopped green bell pepper
- 1/4 cup of chopped red onion
- 1 tablespoon of grated fresh ginger
- 1/2 teaspoon of ground ginger
- 1/8 teaspoon of ground cloves

Instructions
1. Preheat the Pellet grill, place the oiled rack 4-6 inches away from the heat source.
2. Grill the mango on medium heat for 3 minutes on every side.
3. Let the mango cool, cut into bite-size pieces.
4. Add the rest of the ingredients and mix.
5. Chill for 1 hour and serve.

12.15 Lemon-Garlic Dressing

(**Ready in about**: 5 minutes | **Serving**: 8-10 | **Difficulty**: level: easy)
Nutrition per serving: Kcal: 81|**Fat**: 4 g| **Protein**: 6g|**Net Carbs**: 2 g

Ingredients:
- 8 cloves of garlic
- Juice of 1 lemon
- 1/8 teaspoon of red pepper flakes
- 1 dash of salt
- 1/4 teaspoon of sea salt
- 1/2 cup of olive oil

Instructions
1. Put all the ingredients in a blender, pulse till combine.
2. Smoke in Traeger for 10 minutes at smoke mode.
3. Let them infuse overnight for better taste.
4. Serve and enjoy.

12.16 Sweet Potato Caramel

(**Ready in about**: 15 minutes | **Serving**: 8-10 | **Difficulty**: level: Easy)
Nutrition per serving: Kcal: 150|**Proteins**: 25 g |**Net Carbs**: 10 g |**Fat**: 8g

Ingredients:
- 1 cup of water
- 3 pounds of sweet potatoes, cubed

Instructions
1. Let the oven preheat 425°F. In a baking dish, put diced potatoes and 1/2 cup of water sealed with foil.
2. Bake for 1 hour, then uncover for 15 minutes. And bake takes out the dish from the oven and uses the 1/2 cup of water to break up some pieces in the dish.
3. Put all the liquids, solids into a cheesecloth-lined strainer. Let it drain and cool in a pan for 1/2 an hour.
4. Squeeze out the juice as much as possible You could end up with a 1-1/2 cup of liquid.
5. Put the sweet potato liquid to a boil in a saucepan, then lower heat for a slow simmer.
6. Let the liquid decrease for almost 20 minutes before it thickens and develops a caramel color.
7. Smoke in Traeger for 20 minutes at smoke mode. Store it in a container in the refrigerator.

12.17 Creamy Avocado Lime Dressing

(**Ready in about**: 10 minutes | **Serving**: 8-10 | **Difficulty**: level: Easy)
Nutrition per serving: Kcal: 123 |**Fat**: 12.3g |**Net Carbs**: 4g | **Protein**: 0.8g

Ingredients:
- 1/4 cup of olive oil
- 1/4 cup of water
- 1 and 1/2 avocado
- 1/8 teaspoon of pepper
- 1/4 cup of lime juice
- 1/4 cup of cilantro
- 1/4 teaspoon of salt
- 1/8 teaspoons of cumin
- 1/2 teaspoon of crushed garlic

Instructions
1. Put all ingredients in the blender.
2. Pulse till well combined.
3. Smoke in Traeger for 10 minutes at smoke mode.
4. Store or serve right away.

12.18 Ranch Coconut Milk Dressing

(Ready in about: 10 minutes | Serving: 8-10 | Difficulty: level: Easy)
Nutrition per serving: Kcal: 232|Proteins 25 g |Carbs 15 g |Fat: 10g

Ingredients:
- 1 can of full-fat coconut milk
- 3 tablespoons of chives
- 1 tablespoon of dill
- 1 and 1/2 tablespoons of basil
- 2 tablespoons of apple cider vinegar
- 2 tablespoons of chopped shallots
- 1 clove of chopped garlic
- 1 teaspoon of sea salt
- Black pepper
- 1 and 1/2 tablespoons of parsley

Instructions
1. Put the coconut cream in a bowl, leave the coconut water behind.
2. Add 4 tablespoons of coconut water to coconut cream, mix until creamy.
3. Add Garlic, shallots, apple cider vinegar, parsley, chives, dill basil, salt, and black pepper. Mix it and at least left in the fridge for 1/2 an hour for flavoring-infusing.
4. Smoke in Traeger for 10 minutes at smoke mode.
5. Enjoy this sauce over favorite foods.

12.19 Shallot Lemon Dressing

(Ready in about: 10 minutes | Serving: 8-10 | Difficulty: level: Easy)
Nutrition per serving: Kcal: 140 |Proteins 11.7g |Net Carbs: 12g |Fat: 6g

Ingredients:
- 1/2 cup of olive oil
- 1/2 teaspoon of freshly ground pepper
- 1 tablespoon of minced shallot
- 1 garlic clove
- 1 teaspoon of kosher salt
- 1/4 cup of lemon juice

Instructions
1. Put all ingredients in a shaker and mix well.
2. Smoke in Traeger for 20 minutes at smoke mode.
3. Cool it before serving.

12.20 Mango Guacamole

(Ready in about: 15 minutes | Serving: 8-10 | Difficulty: level: Easy)
Nutrition per Serving: Kcal: 137 |Total Fat: 11g| Net Carbs: 12g |Protein: 2g

Ingredients:
- 1 mango, diced
- 1 cup of cilantro
- 1/2 teaspoon of kosher salt
- 1/2 red onion, chopped
- Juice from 1 lemon
- 3 avocados, ripe

Instructions
1. Roughly chop the avocados and put the rest of the ingredients in the mix well.
2. Smoke in Traeger for 15 minutes at smoke mode.
3. Enjoy with any salad.

12.21 Blueberry Salsa

(**Ready in about**: 15 minutes | **Serving**: 2| **Difficulty**: level: Easy)
Nutrition per serving: Kcal: 140|**Proteins**: 10 g |**Carbs** 9 g |**Fat**: 3 g

Ingredients:
- 1 small jalapeño, roughly minced
- 3 cups and 1/2 of blueberries, chopped roughly
- 1/4 teaspoon of kosher salt
- 1/2 teaspoon of ginger
- 1 onion, diced
- Basil leaves
- Juice and zest of 1 lemon

Instructions
1. Combine all ingredients mix them well. Let them infuse overnight in the refrigerator.
2. Smoke in Traeger for 20 minutes at smoke mode.
3. Serve with your favorite food.

12.22 Texas Barbeque Rub

(**Ready in about**: 20 minutes | **Serving**: 1 | **Difficulty**: Easy)
Nutrition per serving: Kcal: 22| **Fat**: 0.5 g| **Net Carbs**: 2 g| **Protein**: 0.6 g

Ingredients:
- 5 ounces of onion
- 10 garlic cloves
- 2 tablespoons of sugar
- 1 tablespoons of salt
- 1 tablespoons of black pepper
- 150 ml soy sauce

Instructions
1. Put all the ingredients, except onions and garlic, in a bowl and mix.
2. Grill at 200°F during 20 minutes.
3. In the meantime, chop the onions and garlic thinly.
4. Withdraw the sauce from the oven and let it cool for 5 minutes.
5. While still warm, add onion and garlic.
6. Keep stored in a jar under refrigeration. It is ready to use.

12.23 Varied Grilled Vegetables

(**Ready in about**: 50 minutes | **Serving**: 4| **Difficulty**: Easy)
Nutrition per serving: Kcal: 160| **Fat**: 7 g| **Net Carbs**: 20 g| **Protein**: 4 g

Ingredients:
- 1 onion, cut in cubes
- 2 red bell peppers, cut in cubes
- 2 potatoes, cut in cubes
- 1 tablespoon fresh rosemary, finely chopped
- 1 tablespoon fresh thyme, finely chopped
- 1 cup broccoli, finely chopped
- 1 tablespoon ground black pepper
- 1 tablespoons vinegar
- 2 tablespoons olive oil
- 1 tablespoon salt

Instructions
1. Put potatoes, onion, broccoli, and peppers, in a recipient.
2. Mix in a container olive oil, vinegar, thyme, rosemary,
3. salt, and pepper.
4. Add the marinade to vegetables. Let it rest for 30 minutes.
5. Preheat your grill to 425°F.
6. Place marinated vegetables in a grill basket, and grill for about 40 minutes.
7. Let it to cool for 5 minutes.
8. You have now delicious-grilled veggies to accompany your meal.

Conclusion

The Traeger is a multifunction grill that uses hardwood pellets. In the grill, pellets are guided into a centralized burn chamber by an auger through a side-mounted hopper and ignited by a heated metal rod. All the functions need electricity, so you have to plug it in. Integrated with meat thermometers, it provides digital, reliable temperature monitoring. All one has to do is fill the hopper with specifically made flavored wood pellets, turn it on, and dial in at any temperature you choose, everything from "smoke" to 500°F.

You do not need to use charcoal or gas grill anymore; cooking with wood pellets simply tastes better. Traeger established the first wood-pellet grill as the perfect way to achieve the wood-fired taste. The Interactive Pro Controller has specialized grilling logic to hold temps under +/-15 °F for assured precise grilling. The series supports reliable temperature regulation.

The Traeger grill Pro Series 22 grill pellet provides 6-in-1 flexibility to BBQ, grill, bake, smoke, roast, and braise, to flavorful perfection. It offers flexible barbecue cooking: hot and quick, or low and steady. Given the Traeger grill's sophistication, especially on Timberline, sometimes, it always requires a human touch. Wood Pellets may get attached to the walls of the pellet hopper after long smoking hours. This issue can cause the fire on the Traeger to sputter. In exchange, this can allow the Timberline to bring into its burner a surplus of unburned pellets.

That may contribute to a risky condition called "over-firing" by the Traeger. Over-firing is a house fire possibility or ignition of too many pellets of wood-burning at once. This is the only issue, even after naming all the good things of the Traeger Timberline 850. This grill serves a completely fabulous barbecue. After one cooking session, you can turn into a Traeger fan. For seconds, people still returned to Traeger. Yes, a lot of it will be because of various recipes for killer pork rib and brisket, as all of these are provided in this recipe and guide book.

If you want to grill meat consistently to excellence with minimal work, you would wish to use the Traeger. Every single time it delivers continuous, efficient, great results. Although utilizing wood as a fuel source, it gives digital power, simplifying the method of grilling and rendering it positively feasible.

For the very first time on the Traeger with almost a 100 percent expectation of efficiency, you can cook a smoked brisket-a traditionally challenging item to barbecue, and a costly hunk of beef to perfection.

Recipe Index

A

Alabama Chicken Leg Quarters....50

Apple..........................76, 77, 78, 80, 81

Apple Cake..77

Avocado..85

B

Bacon Cinnamon Rolls 77

Bacon Sweet Potato Pie 80

Baked Blueberry Brioche French Toast. 77

Baked Breakfast Mini Quiches 71

Baked Chicken Pot Pie....................53

Baked Corn Pudding 46

Baked Corned Beef Au Gratin.......46

Baked Creamed Spinach 72

Baked Deep Dish Apple Pie 81

Baked Deep Dish Supreme Pizza .81

Baked Potato Skins with Pulled Pork.. 30

Baked Sweet Potato Hash 74

BBQ Pulled Pork Cubano Sandwich.38

BBQ Pulled Pork With Paleo Vinegar Sauce 36

BBQ Salmon with Bourbon Glaze.60

BBQ Smoked Sausage Bites 60

BBQ Spare Ribs with Spicy Mandarin Glaze 40

Beef Birria Tacos.............................45

Beef Sirloin and Tomato Vinaigrette.48

Beer Can Chicken............................56

Blackened Catfish Tacos.................58

Blueberry Salsa...............................85

Braised Brunswick Stew.................53

Braised Irish Lamb Stew 68

Braised Lamb Shank 66

Braised Pork Chile Verde...............40

Brined Smoked Turkey 50

Brisket Chili......................................47

Broccoli Chicken Divan..................47

Butter Braised Green Beans 72

C

Carne Asada 47

Cast Iron Berry Cobbler 81

Cast Iron Pizza Lasagna 81

Cheese Trinity with Grilled Potatoes and Chives 34

Cheesy Traeger Broccoli Au Gratin .29

Cherry Coke Ribs 39

Chicken Lollipops 51

Chicken Sausage Rolls 51

Chicken Wings 52

Chipotle Lamb 69

Chipotle Rubbed Tri-Tip 44

Chocolate Pecan Bacon Pie 81

Cider Brined Pork Chops with Apple Pear Compote 83

Cider Brined Pulled Pork 38

Cilantro Lime Dressing 84

Citrus Brined Pork Roast with Fig Mostarda 75

Citrus Turkey 52

Citrus Vinaigrette 84

Crab-Stuffed Lingcod 63

Creamy Avocado Lime Dressing .85

Crispy Pork Belly 36

Cuban Pork Sandwich 36

E

Easy Grilled Curry Chicken 55

Easy Lamb Chops 69

Easy Shrimp Diablo 59

Easy Smoked Pork Butt 37

Easy Smoked Pork Loin 37

Exquisite Ribs 35

F

Foil Packet Salmon 59

G

Garden Gimlet Cocktail 63

Garlic Dill Smoked Salmon 63

Garlic Herb Grilled Pork Chops ...41

Gin & Tonic 82

Gold BBQ Grilled Chicken 55

Greek Chicken Marinade 55

Greek Chicken Pizza 78

Greek Style Roast Leg of Lamb 68

Green Bean Casserole with Shallots ..73

Grill Carnitas 80

Grilled Apple Crisp 80

Grilled Bacon-Wrapped Pork Chops with Rosemary................................ 40

Grilled BBQ Orange Chicken 51

Grilled Beef Bulgogi....................... 47

Grilled Beef Short Rib Lollipop..... 47

Grilled Butterflied Leg of Lamb.... 68

Grilled Caesar Pasta Salad............. 32

Grilled Chicken Salad..................... 53

Grilled Crab Cakes......................... 62

Grilled Curried Flank Steak........... 48

Grilled Curried Sardines................ 64

Grilled Dinner Rolls....................... 29

Grilled Filet Mignon 47

Grilled Garlic Rosemary Smashed Potatoes.. 33

Grilled King Crab Legs 78

Grilled Lamb Burger....................... 67

Grilled Lamb Chops with Rosemary Sauce 68

Grilled Lamb Lollipops with Mango Chutney 67

Grilled Lingcod 62

Grilled Mango Chutney 84

Grilled Marinated Chicken............ 56

Grilled Mexican Street Corn.......... 32

Grilled Mexican Style Surf & Turf1..46

Grilled Nashville Hot Chicken Mac & Cheese... 54

Grilled New York Strip 47

Grilled Onions 29

Grilled Peaches With Yogurt & Granola 79

Grilled Pork Chops with Pineapple-Mango Salsa 38

Grilled Rack of Lamb...................... 69

Grilled Salmon in Onion Sauce..... 64

Grilled Salmon Sandwich 60

Grilled Shrimp in Chives 64

Grilled Steak Fajitas 46

Grilled Sweet Cajun Wings............ 54

Grilled Sweet Potatoes 34, 78

Grilled Teriyaki Salmon................. 61

Grilled Veggie Burgers with Lentils & Walnuts.. 72

Ground Meat Kebabs..................... 66

H

Herb Buttered Chicken................... 52

Herbs Infused Creamy Mashed Potatoes 72

Honey Lime Chicken Adobo Skewers.53

Honey Peachy Spread 84

Hot & Seasoned Grilled Corn........34

Hot Dog Burnt Ends 77

Hot Pepper Sauce...........................83

I

Italian Salad Dressing....................84

L

Lamb Burgers with Pickled Onions.67

Lamb Sausage Smoked..................69

Lamb Stew......................................68

Lamb Wraps BBQ Style 66

Leg of Lamb Gyros 66

Lemon Garlic Grilled Asparagus in Foil 33

Lemon Pepper Traeger Grilled Salmon 61

Loaded Smoked Mashed Potatoes.32

M

Mango Guacamole........................85

Marinated Smoked Flank Steak 45

Mashed Red Potatoes 71

Mayo & Herb Roasted Turkey 53

Meatball Stuffed Shells..................43

Mexican Carne Asada....................46

Mini Smoked Meatloaf 45

Molasses Glazed Salmon..............62

N

Nut Butter Hummus......................83

O

Orange Basil Vinaigrette 84

P

Pan Seared Lingcod 62

Pasta Salad 73

Peach Salsa 74

Pear Cobbler 81

Pellet Grill Jerk Chicken Thighs....56

Pellet Grill Pasties 79

Pellet Grill Picanha 44

Philly Cheese Steak Sandwich 45

Pigs in Blanket 41

Pineapple-Glazed Smoked Ham...39

Pistachio Crusted Roasted Lamb..69

Pork Butt Burnt Ends 87

Pork Shoulder 39

Pork Tenderloin Wrapped in Fresh Rosemary 35

Pretzel Mustard Chicken 54

Prime Rib Sandwich Pinwheel 46

Pulled Pork Enchiladas with Smoke-Roasted Red Sauce 35

R

Red Snapper Recipe 60

Reverse-Seared Flat Iron Steak 43

Roasted Broccoli Cheese Soup 71

Roasted Butternut Squash Soup ... 72

Roasted Carrots with Pistachio & Pomegranate Relish 71

Roasted Elk Jalapeno Poppers 33

Roasted Onion Bacon Salad 34

Roasted Rack of Lamb 68

Rosemary Citrus Grilled Lamb Chops 69

Rosemary Lamb 69

S

Salmon Miso Poke Bowl 60

Salmon Orzo Pasta Salad 60

Sausage Stuffed Mushrooms 39

Savory Grilled Chicken 55

Savory Vegetable Dip 83

Sesame Crusted Halibut With Tahini Mayonnaise 61

Shake & Bake Pork Chops 41

Sherri Mushroom Sauce 83

Shrimp Ceviche 63

Slow Roasted BBQ Lamb Shoulder. 67

Slow Smoked Pulled Pork 35

Smoke S'mores Nachos 77

Smoked & Braised Duck Legs 54

Smoked & Seared Strip Steak 54

Smoked Apple Pie 78

Smoked Bacon Wrapped Meatballs. 40

Smoked Baked Potato Soup 76

Smoked Bean Salad 73

Smoked Beef Ribs 47

Smoked Brisket 47

Smoked Buffalo Shrimp 79

Smoked Buttermilk Fried Chicken. 56

Smoked Caramelized Onion Dip. 83

Smoked Chicken Breasts 51

Smoked Chicken Thighs 51

Smoked Cocktail 82

Smoked Crumb Apple Pie 76

Smoked Eggs..............................34

Smoked Garlic Butter 30

Smoked Hassel back Pesto Chicken.52

Smoked Herb Butter Turkey 52

Smoked Hummus with Roasted Vegetables 72

Smoked Lobster Tails 59

Smoked Maple Cupcakes...............80

Smoked Moink Burger 39

Smoked Pork Chops with Ale-Balsamic Glaze 38

Smoked Pork Loin Tacos 36

Smoked Pork Tenderloin 39

Smoked Prime Rib 45

Smoked Pulled Pork Enchiladas ...38

Smoked Pumpkin Soup..................71

Smoked Ribs 37

Smoked Salmon Chowder 64

Smoked Salmon Dip 33

Smoked Salmon Eggs Benedict 63

Smoked Salmon Scrambled Eggs .79

Smoked Scalloped Potatoes...........63

Smoked Spicy Asian Pork Ribs 40

Smoked Spiral Ham with Honey Glaze 37

Smoked Strawberry Crisp..............76

Smoked Teriyaki Beef Jerky...........43

Smoked Tri-Tip..............................43

Smoked Trout 60

Smoked Whole Chicken.................50

Smokey Wings...............................51

Special Vinaigrette 84

Spicy Tenderloin Steaks 48

Spinach Dip Rollups 79

Spot Prawn Skewers 80

Squash Au Gratin...........................73

Sriracha Salmon Stuffed Mushrooms.53

Sticky Teriyaki BBQ Pork & Pineapple Skewers..39

Sweet Chili Chicken Leg Quarters.55

Sweet Potato Caramel....................84

Sweet Tea BBQ Chicken Thighs....55

T

T-Bone Grilled Steak 43

Tequila Lime Beef Tacos 44

Texas Barbeque Rub 85

The Best Grilled Pizza 79

Traeger Bacon-Wrapped Scallops. 33

Traeger Banana Bread 76

Traeger Bean Tostadas 80

Traeger Blackened Pork Chops 41

Traeger Chicken Teriyaki 51

Traeger Chicken Wings with Spicy Miso 56

Traeger Chimichurri Shrimp 59

Traeger Cioppino 58

Traeger Corn on the Cob 31

Traeger Eggnog Cheesecake 76

Traeger Funeral Potatoes 29

Traeger Grilled Brussels Sprouts .. 29

Traeger Grilled Butternut Squash. 31

Traeger Grilled Carrots 29

Traeger Grilled Cheddar Bay Biscuits 31

Traeger Grilled Chicken Breast 51

Traeger Grilled Crab Legs 59

Traeger Grilled French Toast 78

Traeger Grilled Homemade Croutons 30

Traeger Grilled Lemon Dill Salmon. 61

Traeger Grilled Nashville Hot Chicken 54

Traeger Grilled Prosciutto Asparagus 31

Traeger Grilled Rockfish 62

Traeger Grilled Salmon with Togarashi 61

Traeger Grilled Shrimp Scampi 60

Traeger Grilled Spaghetti Squash. 31

Traeger Grilled Spinach 30

Traeger Grilled Tomahawk 46

Traeger Grilled Vegetables 71

Traeger Grilled Zucchini & Yellow Squash 57

Traeger Halibut with Parmesan 58

Traeger Honey Garlic Salmon 58

Traeger Lasagna 72

Traeger Lobster Rolls 58

Traeger Mini Meatloaf Burgers 79

Traeger Pork Tenderloin with Mustard Sauce 40

Traeger Pot Roast 45

Traeger Smoked Baked Potato 32

Traeger Smoked Cornish Hens 55

Traeger Smoked Mac & Cheese 41

Traeger Smoked Meatloaf.............46

Traeger Smoked Mississippi Pot Roast 48

Traeger Smoked Salmon 61

Traeger Smoked Salsa Verde.........83

Traeger Smoked Smashed Potatoes.30

Traeger Smoked Stuffed Pork Tenderloin 41

Traeger Smoked Turkey.................50

Traeger Smoked Turkey Legs 55

Traeger Spicy Fried Shrimp...........59

Traeger Stuffed Peppers.................72

Traeger Teriyaki Smoked Shrimp.83

Traeger Thanksgiving Dressing....83

Traeger Tuna Melt Flatbread.........59

Traeger Turkey Breast 56

Twice Baked Potatoes.....................73

V

Varied Grilled Vegetables..............85

Veggie Sandwich............................74

W

Whole BBQ Chicken 52

Index by Ingredients

A

Alabama Chicken Leg Quarters....50

Apple........................76, 77, 78, 80, 81

Apple Cake......................................77

Avocado..85

B

Bacon Cinnamon Rolls 77

Bacon Sweet Potato Pie 80

Baked Blueberry Brioche French Toast. 77

Baked Breakfast Mini Quiches 71

Baked Chicken Pot Pie....................53

Baked Corn Pudding 46

Baked Corned Beef Au Gratin.......46

Baked Creamed Spinach 72

Baked Deep Dish Apple Pie 81

Baked Deep Dish Supreme Pizza .81

Baked Potato Skins with Pulled Pork..30

Baked Sweet Potato Hash 74

BBQ Pulled Pork Cubano Sandwich.38

BBQ Pulled Pork With Paleo Vinegar Sauce 36

BBQ Salmon with Bourbon Glaze.60

BBQ Smoked Sausage Bites 60

BBQ Spare Ribs with Spicy Mandarin Glaze 40

Beef Birria Tacos..............................45

Beef Sirloin and Tomato Vinaigrette.48

Beer Can Chicken............................56

Blackened Catfish Tacos.................58

Blueberry Salsa...............................85

Braised Brunswick Stew.................53

Braised Irish Lamb Stew 68

Braised Lamb Shank 66

Braised Pork Chile Verde...............40

Brined Smoked Turkey 50

Brisket Chili......................................47

Broccoli Chicken Divan..................47

Butter Braised Green Beans 72

C

Carne Asada 47

Cast Iron Berry Cobbler 81

Cast Iron Pizza Lasagna 81

Cheese Trinity with Grilled Potatoes and Chives 34

Cheesy Traeger Broccoli Au Gratin. 29

Cherry Coke Ribs 39

Chicken Lollipops 51

Chicken Sausage Rolls 51

Chicken Wings 52

Chipotle Lamb 69

Chipotle Rubbed Tri-Tip 44

Chocolate Pecan Bacon Pie 81

Cider Brined Pork Chops with Apple Pear Compote 83

Cider Brined Pulled Pork 38

Cilantro Lime Dressing 84

Citrus Brined Pork Roast with Fig Mostarda 75

Citrus Turkey 52

Citrus Vinaigrette 84

Crab-Stuffed Lingcod 63

Creamy Avocado Lime Dressing .85

Crispy Pork Belly 36

Cuban Pork Sandwich 36

E

Easy Grilled Curry Chicken 55

Easy Lamb Chops 69

Easy Shrimp Diablo 59

Easy Smoked Pork Butt 37

Easy Smoked Pork Loin 37

Exquisite Ribs 35

F

Foil Packet Salmon 59

G

Garden Gimlet Cocktail 63

Garlic Dill Smoked Salmon 63

Garlic Herb Grilled Pork Chops ... 41

Gin & Tonic 82

Gold BBQ Grilled Chicken 55

Greek Chicken Marinade 55

Greek Chicken Pizza 78

Greek Style Roast Leg of Lamb 68

Green Bean Casserole with Shallots..73

Grill Carnitas 80

Grilled Apple Crisp 80

Grilled Bacon-Wrapped Pork Chops with Rosemary..............................40

Grilled BBQ Orange Chicken 51

Grilled Beef Bulgogi......................47

Grilled Beef Short Rib Lollipop.....47

Grilled Butterflied Leg of Lamb....68

Grilled Caesar Pasta Salad.............32

Grilled Chicken Salad....................53

Grilled Crab Cakes........................62

Grilled Curried Flank Steak...........48

Grilled Curried Sardines................64

Grilled Dinner Rolls......................29

Grilled Filet Mignon 47

Grilled Garlic Rosemary Smashed Potatoes......................................33

Grilled King Crab Legs 78

Grilled Lamb Burger......................67

Grilled Lamb Chops with Rosemary Sauce 68

Grilled Lamb Lollipops with Mango Chutney 67

Grilled Lingcod 62

Grilled Mango Chutney 84

Grilled Marinated Chicken............56

Grilled Mexican Street Corn..........32

Grilled Mexican Style Surf & Turf1..46

Grilled Nashville Hot Chicken Mac & Cheese..54

Grilled New York Strip 47

Grilled Onions 29

Grilled Peaches With Yogurt & Granola 79

Grilled Pork Chops with Pineapple-Mango Salsa 38

Grilled Rack of Lamb.....................69

Grilled Salmon in Onion Sauce.....64

Grilled Salmon Sandwich 60

Grilled Shrimp in Chives 64

Grilled Steak Fajitas 46

Grilled Sweet Cajun Wings............54

Grilled Sweet Potatoes 34, 78

Grilled Teriyaki Salmon.................61

Grilled Veggie Burgers with Lentils & Walnuts......................................72

Ground Meat Kebabs....................66

H

Herb Buttered Chicken 52

Herbs Infused Creamy Mashed Potatoes 72

Honey Lime Chicken Adobo Skewers.53

Honey Peachy Spread 84

Hot & Seasoned Grilled Corn 34

Hot Dog Burnt Ends 77

Hot Pepper Sauce 83

I

Italian Salad Dressing 84

L

Lamb Burgers with Pickled Onions.67

Lamb Sausage Smoked 69

Lamb Stew 68

Lamb Wraps BBQ Style 66

Leg of Lamb Gyros 66

Lemon Garlic Grilled Asparagus in Foil 33

Lemon Pepper Traeger Grilled Salmon 61

Loaded Smoked Mashed Potatoes.32

M

Mango Guacamole 85

Marinated Smoked Flank Steak 45

Mashed Red Potatoes 71

Mayo & Herb Roasted Turkey 53

Meatball Stuffed Shells 43

Mexican Carne Asada 46

Mini Smoked Meatloaf 45

Molasses Glazed Salmon 62

N

Nut Butter Hummus 83

O

Orange Basil Vinaigrette 84

P

Pan Seared Lingcod 62

Pasta Salad 73

Peach Salsa 74

Pear Cobbler 81

Pellet Grill Jerk Chicken Thighs 56

Pellet Grill Pasties 79

Pellet Grill Picanha 44

Philly Cheese Steak Sandwich 45

Pigs in Blanket 41

Pineapple-Glazed Smoked Ham ... 39

Pistachio Crusted Roasted Lamb .. 69

Pork Butt Burnt Ends 87

Pork Shoulder 39

Pork Tenderloin Wrapped in Fresh Rosemary 35

Pretzel Mustard Chicken 54

Prime Rib Sandwich Pinwheel 46

Pulled Pork Enchiladas with Smoke-Roasted Red Sauce 35

R

Red Snapper Recipe 60

Reverse-Seared Flat Iron Steak 43

Roasted Broccoli Cheese Soup 71

Roasted Butternut Squash Soup ... 72

Roasted Carrots with Pistachio & Pomegranate Relish 71

Roasted Elk Jalapeno Poppers 33

Roasted Onion Bacon Salad 34

Roasted Rack of Lamb 68

Rosemary Citrus Grilled Lamb Chops 69

Rosemary Lamb 69

S

Salmon Miso Poke Bowl 60

Salmon Orzo Pasta Salad 60

Sausage Stuffed Mushrooms 39

Savory Grilled Chicken 55

Savory Vegetable Dip 83

Sesame Crusted Halibut With Tahini Mayonnaise 61

Shake & Bake Pork Chops 41

Sherri Mushroom Sauce 83

Shrimp Ceviche 63

Slow Roasted BBQ Lamb Shoulder. 67

Slow Smoked Pulled Pork 35

Smoke S'mores Nachos 77

Smoked & Braised Duck Legs 54

Smoked & Seared Strip Steak 54

Smoked Apple Pie 78

Smoked Bacon Wrapped Meatballs. 40

Smoked Baked Potato Soup 76

Smoked Bean Salad 73

Smoked Beef Ribs 47

Smoked Brisket 47

Smoked Buffalo Shrimp 79

Smoked Buttermilk Fried Chicken.56

Smoked Caramelized Onion Dip. 83

Smoked Chicken Breasts 51

Smoked Chicken Thighs 51

Smoked Cocktail 82

Smoked Crumb Apple Pie 76

Smoked Eggs..................................34

Smoked Garlic Butter 30

Smoked Hassel back Pesto Chicken.52

Smoked Herb Butter Turkey 52

Smoked Hummus with Roasted Vegetables 72

Smoked Lobster Tails 59

Smoked Maple Cupcakes...............80

Smoked Moink Burger 39

Smoked Pork Chops with Ale-Balsamic Glaze 38

Smoked Pork Loin Tacos 36

Smoked Pork Tenderloin 39

Smoked Prime Rib 45

Smoked Pulled Pork Enchiladas...38

Smoked Pumpkin Soup..................71

Smoked Ribs 37

Smoked Salmon Chowder 64

Smoked Salmon Dip 33

Smoked Salmon Eggs Benedict.....63

Smoked Salmon Scrambled Eggs .79

Smoked Scalloped Potatoes...........63

Smoked Spicy Asian Pork Ribs.....40

Smoked Spiral Ham with Honey Glaze 37

Smoked Strawberry Crisp..............76

Smoked Teriyaki Beef Jerky..........43

Smoked Tri-Tip..............................43

Smoked Trout 60

Smoked Whole Chicken................50

Smokey Wings...............................51

Special Vinaigrette 84

Spicy Tenderloin Steaks 48

Spinach Dip Rollups 79

Spot Prawn Skewers 80

Squash Au Gratin...........................73

Sriracha Salmon Stuffed Mushrooms.53

Sticky Teriyaki BBQ Pork & Pineapple Skewers...39

Sweet Chili Chicken Leg Quarters.55

Sweet Potato Caramel……………84

Sweet Tea BBQ Chicken Thighs….55

T

T-Bone Grilled Steak………………43

Tequila Lime Beef Tacos ……………44

Texas Barbeque Rub ………………85

The Best Grilled Pizza ………………79

Traeger Bacon-Wrapped Scallops. 33

Traeger Banana Bread ……………76

Traeger Bean Tostadas ……………80

Traeger Blackened Pork Chops……41

Traeger Chicken Teriyaki……………51

Traeger Chicken Wings with Spicy Miso
……………………………………………56

Traeger Chimichurri Shrimp…………59

Traeger Cioppino …………………58

Traeger Corn on the Cob……………31

Traeger Eggnog Cheesecake…………76

Traeger Funeral Potatoes ……………29

Traeger Grilled Brussels Sprouts ..29

Traeger Grilled Butternut Squash.31

Traeger Grilled Carrots ……………29

Traeger Grilled Cheddar Bay Biscuits 31

Traeger Grilled Chicken Breast…..51

Traeger Grilled Crab Legs …………59

Traeger Grilled French Toast………78

Traeger Grilled Homemade Croutons 30

Traeger Grilled Lemon Dill Salmon.61

Traeger Grilled Nashville Hot Chicken
……………………………………………54

Traeger Grilled Prosciutto Asparagus 31

Traeger Grilled Rockfish……………62

Traeger Grilled Salmon with Togarashi
……………………………………………61

Traeger Grilled Shrimp Scampi ….60

Traeger Grilled Spaghetti Squash.31

Traeger Grilled Spinach ……………30

Traeger Grilled Tomahawk …………46

Traeger Grilled Vegetables …………71

Traeger Grilled Zucchini & Yellow Squash……………………………………57

Traeger Halibut with Parmesan…..58

Traeger Honey Garlic Salmon………58

Traeger Lasagna ……………………72

Traeger Lobster Rolls………………58

Traeger Mini Meatloaf Burgers……79

Traeger Pork Tenderloin with Mustard Sauce 40

Traeger Pot Roast 45

Traeger Smoked Baked Potato 32

Traeger Smoked Cornish Hens 55

Traeger Smoked Mac & Cheese 41

Traeger Smoked Meatloaf 46

Traeger Smoked Mississippi Pot Roast 48

Traeger Smoked Salmon 61

Traeger Smoked Salsa Verde 83

Traeger Smoked Smashed Potatoes. 30

Traeger Smoked Stuffed Pork Tenderloin 41

Traeger Smoked Turkey 50

Traeger Smoked Turkey Legs 55

Traeger Spicy Fried Shrimp 59

Traeger Stuffed Peppers 72

Traeger Teriyaki Smoked Shrimp. 83

Traeger Thanksgiving Dressing 83

Traeger Tuna Melt Flatbread 59

Traeger Turkey Breast 56

Twice Baked Potatoes 73

V

Varied Grilled Vegetables 85

Veggie Sandwich 74

W

Whole BBQ Chicken 52

Made in United States
North Haven, CT
11 January 2022